Gathered around Jesus

MATRIX
The Bible in Mediterranean Context

EDITORIAL BOARD

John H. Elliott   John S. Kloppenborg
Anselm Hagedorn   Douglas E. Oakman
K. C. Hanson   Gary Stansell

•

Richard L. Rohrbaugh
The New Testament in Cross-Cultural Perspective

Markus Cromhout
*Jesus and Identity:
Reconstructing Judean Ethnicity in Q*

Pieter F. Craffert
*The Life of a Galilean Shaman:
Jesus of Nazareth in Anthropological-Historical Perspective*

Douglas E. Oakman
Jesus and the Peasants

Stuart L. Love
*Jesus and the Marginal Women:
Healing in Matthew's Gospel*

Gathered around Jesus

An Alternative Spatial Practice in the Gospel of Mark

ERIC C. STEWART

CASCADE *Books* • Eugene, Oregon

GATHERED AROUND JESUS
An Alternative Spatial Practice in the Gospel of Mark

Matrix: The Bible in Mediterranean Context 6

Copyright © 2009 Eric C. Stewart. All rights reserved. Except for brief quotations in critical publications or reviews, no part of this book may be reproduced in any manner without prior written permission from the publisher. Write: Permissions, Wipf & Stock, 199 W. 8th Ave., Suite 3, Eugene, OR 97401.

Cascade Books
A Division of Wipf and Stock Publishers
199 W. 8th Ave., Suite 3
Eugene, OR 97401

www.wipfandstock.com

ISBN 13: 978-1-60608-084-9

Cataloging in Publication data:

Stewart, Eric C.
    Gathered around Jesus : an alternative spatial practice in the gospel of Mark / Eric C. Stewart.

    Matrix: The Bible in Mediterranean Context 6

    xiv + 238 p. ; 23 cm.

    ISBN 13: 978-1-60608-084-9

    1. Bible. N.T. Mark—Criticism, interpretation, etc. 2. Bible. N.T. Mark—Social scientific criticism. 3. Geography—Social aspects. 4. Human geography—Mediterranean Region. I. Title. II. Series.

BS2585.2 S72 2009

Manufactured in the U.S.A.

To Aron and Jordan,
for the joy you have brought into my life

Contents

Acknowledgments ix

Abbreviations xi

1 Mark and Space in Recent Discussion 1
2 Critical Spatial Theory 30
3 Space in Ancient Texts 62
4 Categories for Understanding Ancient Space 128
5 The Spatial Presentation of Mark's Gospel 179
6 Conclusion 220

Bibliography 227

Acknowledgments

A PROJECT OF THIS magnitude is never undertaken easily. From the onset of my undergraduate education, I have been especially blessed with gifted friends and mentors. The faculty of the Religion Department at Pacific Lutheran University set me on this course some sixteen years ago. Paul Ingram, Lyman Lundeen, and Nancy Howell were treasured teachers and allowed me room to stumble over myself in the path of following my bliss. Douglas E. Oakman was and is a cherished friend, mentor, and advisor. His knowledge of social theory and the New Testament continue to challenge and inspire me to this day. At the Claremont School of Theology, I was privileged to work with Burton L. Mack in his last year as active faculty. Though he inspires no small amount of controversy, his classes were stimulating, rigorous, and fun. His energy has stimulated me often over the years and is a major reason this book is completed. The members of the Context Group, as well, have been especially treasured colleagues and conversation partners. The fellowship of the group has reinvigorated me each time I am with them. I offer thanks especially to K. C. Hanson for his encouragement of this project and willingness to see it through to publication.

The members of my dissertation committee, of which this book is a substantially revised edition, deserve special thanks for their generosity of time and concern for the project. Brian E. Daley agreed to become part of the committee at a late hour in order to facilitate my graduation from Notre Dame. For his participation and keen insight, I am grateful. John P. Meier was a friend and mentor from his arrival at Notre Dame, and his careful reading of many of my papers and of these chapters over the years is much appreciated. David E. Aune also arrived at Notre Dame after me, but his breadth and depth of knowledge, his encouragement, his sense of humor, and his willingness to deal with endless inane questions from his students make him an excellent teacher and role model. Finally, Jerome H. Neyrey has been a mentor to me in every conceivable way. Perhaps it is an irony that the book is finished the week that he has left the University of Notre Dame and settled into "retirement" in his home state of Louisiana. Jerry is everything a person could want in a mentor and *Doktorvater*. He is a most decent, kind, and thoughtful man, and a Southern gentleman in the best sense of the word. He presided not only over the dissertation, but my many moments of self-doubt and fatigue, as well as my entry into fatherhood. To him I will be eternally grateful.

Finally to my parents, Tom and Judi, who always knew that I could accomplish whatever I set my mind to and frequently told me so, I offer my deepest love. Their support over these many years of graduate education is much appreciated. To my wife Rikka and my children, Aron and Jordan, I offer thanks for all of those late nights and weekends they would have preferred to have me around rather than off in the library or office. It is my hope that I can someday make it up to them.

Abbreviations

Ancient

1QM	War Scroll (*Milḥamah*)
1QS	Rule of the Community (*Serek ha-Yaḥad*)
3 Bar.	*3 Baruch*
Aen.	Virgil, *Aeneid*
Agr.	Cicero, *De Lege agraria*
Anab.	Arrian, *Anabasis*
Ant.	Josephus, *Antiquities of the Judeans*
Ant. rom.	Dionysius of Halicarnassus, *Antiquitates romanae*
Apoc. Zeph.	*Apocalypse of Zephaniah*
Arch.	Vitruvius, *Architecture*
Astr.	Manilius, *Astronomicon*
Bell. gall.	Caesar, *Bellum gallicum*
B.J.	Josephus, *Judean War*
Cael.	Aristotle, *De caelo*
Caes.	Plutarch, *Caesar*
Cat.	Cicero, *In Catalinam*
Civ.	Augustine, *De civitate Dei*
Def. Orac.	Plutarch, *De defectu oraculorum*
Demon.	Lucian, *Demonax*
Descr.	Pausanias, *Graeciae description*
DSS	Dead Sea Scrolls
Ep.	Pliny the Younger, *Epistles*
Fast.	Ovid, *Fasti*
Gen. Socr.	Plutarch, *De genio Socratis*
Geogr.	Strabo, *Geographica*

Heir	Philo, *Who Is the Heir?*
Hist.	Herodotus, *Historiae*
Hist. Rech.	*History of the Rechabites*
Hypoth.	Philo, *Hypothetica*
Icar.	Lucian, *Icaromenippus*
Il.	Homer, *Iliad*
Jub.	*Jubilees*
Jul.	Suetonius, *Divus Julius*
Leg.	Plato, *Leges*
Legat.	Philo, *Legatio ad Gaium*
Lev. Rab.	*Leviticus Rabbah*
LXX	Septuagint
Men.	*Menippus*
Metam.	Apuleius, *Metamorphoses*
Metam.	Ovid, *Metamorphoses*
Mete.	Aristotle, *Meteorologica*
Nat.	Pliny the Elder, *Naturalis hisoria*
Nat.	Seneca, *Naturales quaestiones*
Nat. d.	Cicero, *De natura deorum*
Nub.	Aristophanes, *Nubes*
Od.	Homer, *Odyssey*
Or.	Aelius Aristides, *Orationes*
Or.	Dio Chrysostom, *Orationes*
Or.	Isocrates, *Orationes*
Or.	Libanius, *Orationes*
Or.	Maximus of Tyre, *Orationes*
Or.	Menander Rhetor, *Orationes*
Pan.	Pliny the Younger, *Panegyricus*
Pol.	Aristotle, *Politica*
Pyth.	Pindar, *Pythian Ode*
Ran.	Aristophanes, *Ranae*
Rep.	Cicero, *Republica*
Resp.	Plato, *Respublica*
Rhet.	Dionysus of Halicarnassus, *Ars rhetorica*
Rom. Hist.	Dio, *Roman History*
Scaur.	Cicero, *Pro Scauro*
Sib. Or.	*Sibylline Oracles*
Spec. Leg.	Philo, *De specialibus legibus*

Tan.	*Tanḥuma*
Theog.	Hesiod, *Theogonia*
Tim.	Plato, *Timaeus*
Tusc.	Cicero, *Tusculanae disputationes*
T. Mos.	*Testament of Moses*
T. Zeb.	*Testament of Zebulon*
Ver. Hist.	Lucian, *Vera historia*
Vit. Apoll.	Philostratus, *Vita Apollonii*
Vit. Mos.	Philo, *De vita Mosis*

Modern

ANE	ancient Near East
ARA	*Annual Review of Anthropology*
BTB	*Biblical Theology Bulletin*
CBQ	*Catholic Biblical Quarterly*
CQ	*Classical Quarterly*
CW	*Classical World*
JAAR	*Journal of the American Academy of Religion*
JBL	*Journal of Biblical Literature*
JHS	*Journal of Hellenic Studies*
JRS	*Journal of Roman Studies*
JSJ	*Journal for the Study of Judaism*
JSJSup	Journal for the Study of Judaism Supplements
JSNT	*Journal for the Study of the New Testament*
JSOT	*Journal for the Study of the Old Testament*
JSOTSup	Journal for the Study of the Old Testament Supplement Series
LCL	Loeb Classical Library
NovTSup	Novum Testamentum Supplements
NTS	*New Testament Studies*
OTP	*Old Testament Pseudepigrapha*, 2 vols. Edited by James H. Charlesworth
SAC	Studies in Antiquity and Christianity
WUNT	Wissenschaftliche Untersuchungen zum Neuen Testament

CHAPTER 1

Mark and Space in Recent Discussion

Overview of the Study

THE STUDY OF FIRST-CENTURY Jesus movements has long focused largely on temporal questions.[1] This is seen most clearly, perhaps, in the debate regarding the historical Jesus and the coming of the kingdom of God. *When* Jesus expected the kingdom has been a crucial question to biblical scholars for more than a century.[2] This focus on temporal matters has been matched by a substantial lack of focus on issues of spatiality in first-century Jesus movements. Critical social theory has also focused on history (that is, temporality) to the exclusion of geography (that is, spatiality).[3] It is not surprising, therefore, to find that biblical scholarship also lacks concern for critical spatial theory. There have been, to be sure, recent attempts to redress this problem both in social theory and in biblical studies.[4] The present study is an attempt to bring a critical social theory of spatiality to bear on one early text from the Jesus movement, the Gospel of Mark.

---

1. On avoiding the terminology of "Christian/Christianity" for the first-century Jesus movement, see Elliott, "Jesus was Neither a 'Jew' nor a 'Christian.'"
2. See Malina, "Exegetical Eschatology," 49–59.
3. See the incisive comments in Soja, *Postmodern Geographies*.
4. The list of new works on theory in "human geography," "narrative geography" and "landscape theory" is too long to detail here. Several of these works are discussed in detail in chapter two of the present work. Recent works in biblical studies that have taken spatiality into account are also numerous. Among those more directly relevant to the present work are Malbon, *Narrative Space and Mythic Meaning in Mark*; Van Eck, *Galilee and Jerusalem*; Riches, *Conflicting Mythologies*; Malina, "Apocalyptic and Territoriality"; MacDonald, *Acts of Andrew*; Leyerle, "Landscape as Cartography"; and Moxnes, *Putting Jesus in His Place*.

Mark's geographical difficulties have long captured the attention of scholars. Numerous attempts have been made to explain them, and there have been three major solutions posited. The first of these solutions is simply that Mark is ignorant of the geographical layout of Galilee and Judea since he had never been to these places himself. The second proposed solution is that Mark, rather than presenting a straightforward cartographic understanding of Galilee and Judea, crafts a specific image of both places in his selection of materials and in his composition of the Gospel. The final solution, one that has been largely rejected, is that Mark does not really demonstrate any difficulties at all in relation to geography since he presents geographic detail in a manner consistent to the peasantry of his time. The following study attempts to address elements of the second solution (that Mark exerts editorial and/or compositional control over the geographic presentation of Jesus' ministry), and in doing so, substantially modifies the third solution to suggest that Mark presents the world spatially in a manner widely consistent with geographic traditions found in Greek and Roman texts.

Galilee and Jerusalem in Mark's Gospel

Hedrick suggests that geography may be the one organizing principle in the gospel genre. He describes Mark 1–13 in the following way: "the geographic and spatial locations . . . provide the only clear structural unity to *all* the individual episodes in Mark 1–13, as well as to the sub-groupings of material that Mark has organized."[5] Mark's spatial presentation, then, provides the reader with an important element to the overall understanding of his Gospel.

Historical Approaches

The earliest studies to focus significantly on space in Mark are Lohmeyer's *Galiläa und Jerusalem* and Lightfoot's *Locality and Doctrine in the Gospels*.[6] Their basic argument runs as follows. Mark's Gospel originally ended at 16:8 and contained no appearances of the resurrected Jesus.[7] For this rea-

---

5. Hedrick, "What is a Gospel?" 259–60.

6. Lohmeyer, *Galiläa und Jerusalem*; and Robert Henry Lightfoot, *Locality and Doctrine in the Gospels*. See also the summary article of Malbon, 'Galilee and Jerusalem."

7. Though there is not universal agreement on this question even today, the position

son, the words of the young man (νεανίσκος) at the tomb take on an additional significance. In Mark 16:7, he tells the women at the tomb that the resurrected Jesus will appear to his disciples only once they have returned to Galilee, "just as he told you" (καθὼς εἶπεν ὑμῖν).[8] Rather than having Jesus appear in Jerusalem after his death, Mark "preserves" the tradition that Jesus would appear in Galilee. Lohmeyer and Lightfoot argue that the reason for such a tradition is that the Gospel preserves a portrait of Galilee as the place of Jesus' acceptance and Jerusalem as the place of his rejection and death. Not only does Jesus' death occur in Jerusalem, but his public ministry does not begin until he returns to Galilee from the Jordan River after his baptism. It is in Galilee (and its surrounding territories) that his public ministry largely takes place.[9]

Lightfoot highlights several instances of this pattern in Mark's Gospel. He notes that Jesus' true identity, revealed at the Transfiguration (Mark 9), occurs "not in the hallowed city of Jerusalem, but in the remote north of Galilee."[10] All of the exorcisms and miraculous healings, except for one, occur in the land of Galilee.[11] There is no "proclamation of the gospel, and also, we may add, no summons or invitation to repentance"

---

taken by Lohmeyer and Lightfoot is less controversial today than it was in the 1930s.

8. This phrase, spoken by the νεανίσκος, or young man, at the tomb recalls to the reader's mind Mark 14:28, where Jesus had told the disciples that he would go before them to Galilee after his resurrection.

9. Lightfoot, *Locality and Doctrine*, 124–25, "Galilee and Jerusalem therefore stand in opposition to each other, as the story of the gospels runs in St. Mark. The despised and more or less outlawed Galilee is shewn (sic) to have been chosen by God as the seat of the gospel and of the revelation of the Son of man, while the sacred city of Jerusalem, the home of jewish (sic) piety and patriotism, has become the centre of hostility and sin. Galilee is the sphere of revelation, Jerusalem the scene only of rejection. Galilee is the scene of the beginning and middle of the Lord's ministry; Jerusalem only of its end . . . . But the dark passage through which he is led has an end, and this is given in the words, 'After I am raised up I will go before you into Galilee,' the land where the divine fulfillment began and the land where it will receive its consummation."

10. Ibid., 122. Lightfoot treats the geographic areas surrounding Galilee as part of one larger "greater Galilee."

11. The exception is the healing of blind Bartimaeus which occurs while Jesus and his disciples are leaving Jericho (Mark 10:46–52). There is one other "act of power" located in Jerusalem. The withering of the fig tree, though, "owes its position in the narrative to its symbolic importance" according to Lohmeyer (ibid., 123). Lohmeyer and Lightfoot both accept the Gentile territories that surround Galilee as part of a *terra Christiana* that is encompassed with the environs of Galilee. Miraculous events, therefore, that happen in Gentile territory outside of Galilee are considered within this greater Galilee.

in Jerusalem.[12] Perhaps more telling are the "traces of a longer or a more frequent residence of the Lord at Jerusalem than is apparent from the book itself."[13] These traces includes the fact that Jesus "has friends at Bethany," "the willingness of a resident [of Jerusalem] to set apart a room in his house for the last supper," and the idea that Jesus "was daily . . . in the temple teaching," a fact that makes little sense in Mark's Gospel since Jesus has only been in the city for a few days.[14] According to Lightfoot, these traces of a longer residence in Jerusalem are de-emphasized by Mark in an attempt to highlight the positive nature of Galilee while eliminating any positive portrayal of Jerusalem in his received sources.

Lohmeyer and Lightfoot argue that the reason that Mark portrayed Galilee in a positive light over against Jerusalem is that Galilee represented an alternative center of early Christianity that emphasized the eschatological return of the Son of Man and rejected the Jerusalem cult.[15] Lohmeyer believes that this type of Christianity existed very early after the resurrection based on Mark's presentation of the eschatological return of the Son of man there.[16] He attributes the attachment of this type of significance to Galilee to Jesus himself: "he makes Galilee the home of his Gospel and of his community."[17] Lohmeyer compares *T. Zeb.* 9:8 with Mark 16:7. *Testament of Zebulon* 9:8 reads "the Lord, the light of righteousness, will visit in your land and you will see him in Jerusalem on account of his name."[18] Both Mark and the *Testament of Zebulon* contain the future tense

12. Ibid., 123.
13. Ibid., 125.
14. Ibid., 125–26.
15. See the discussion of Lohmeyer's position with regard to the eschatological manifestation of the Son of Man in ibid., 73–77. Lightfoot asserts that Mark is not privy to some traditions of resurrection appearances in Galilee, but rather that the appearance of Jesus (as the Son of Man) in Galilee will be the consummation of the ages (ibid., 65). "It may be, to judge from the plan and statements of his book, especially if, as is possible, it ends and was meant to end at 16:8, that St. Mark should be regarded as a witness to an expectation of one appearance or manifestation of the crucified and risen Lord in Galilee; and that this appearance or manifestation was to be the consummation itself."
16. In addition to the works of Lohmeyer and Lightfoot, see Grant, *The Earliest Gospel*, 125–47.
17. Lohmeyer, *Galiläa und Jerusalem*, 30. Translation is my own.
18. Translation is my own based on the text quoted in Lohmeyer, *Galiläa und Jerusalem*, 12. The Greek text, as quoted by Lohmeyer, reads, καὶ μετὰ ταῦτα ἀνατελεῖ ἐν ὑμῖν ὁ Κύριος, τὸ φῶς τῆς δικαιοσύνης καὶ ἐπιστρέψετε εἰς τὴν γῆν ὑμῶν καὶ ὑμεῖς ὄψεσθε αὐτὸν ἐν Ἰερουσαλὴμ διὰ τοῦ ὀνόματος αὐτοῦ.

of ὁράω and the coming advent of God in the one case and the Son of Man in the other. Lohmeyer concludes that the type of tradition found in the *Testament of Zebulon* is exactly what Mark has in mind "only it is not the Parousia of God, but rather of Jesus, and it happens not in Jerusalem, but rather in Galilee. This is, therefore, the holy land of his eschatological coming."[19] Galilee, then, represents an alternative eschatological center for Jesus' return.[20] Lohmeyer especially understands the contrast between Galilee and Jerusalem to have begun during the ministry of the historical Jesus.

Redactional Approaches

In contrast to Lohmeyer and Lightfoot, Marxsen focuses on Mark's redactional elements. Though he denies the role of author in the modern sense to Mark, Marxsen suggests that by examining the framework material of the Gospel one can "get a clearer grasp of what is typically Markan on the basis of later formulation."[21] Marxsen sees two basic ways to explain the geographic framework of Mark's Gospel. "One is that he constructs it for historical purposes" while the "other explanation is that with his outline Mark has in mind a purpose other than the historical and uses the geographical data to express it."[22] Marxsen rejects the first possibility, claiming that "due to his ignorance of the territory or to the incompleteness of his materials" Mark would not have been able to accomplish such a task.[23] He opts for the second possibility, that is, that Mark shaped his geographical material with a specific purpose in mind.

Marxsen, however, modifies the position of Lohmeyer. He is not content to conclude that a "Son of man eschatology" predominated in Galilee, providing the reason for Mark's presentation of Galilee and Jerusalem in his Gospel. He wishes to "distinguish, perhaps even more sharply than Lohmeyer, the traditional material from the work of the evangelist him-

---

19. Ibid., 12. Translation is my own.

20. Ibid., 10–15.

21. Marxsen, *Mark the Evangelist*, 29. Marxsen relies heavily on form criticism and the work of Bultmann and Schmidt, particularly in his attempt to separate tradition from redaction.

22. Ibid., 54–55.

23. Ibid.

self."[24] Marxsen distinguishes three stages of development of the early Christian traditions. The first stage occurs during the period of the ministry of Jesus. Marxsen believes that the historical Jesus "worked in Galilean (and neighboring) regions."[25] At this stage of the tradition, certain places became attached to certain stories, but this occurred in something of a haphazard fashion. There was no overall logic to the locations (except insofar as they might have recorded genuine historical reminiscences).[26] The second stage occurs within the primitive community at which point the church "in all probability attached itself to Jerusalem"; but Marxsen sees a shift toward a Galilean location because it "is natural to suppose the Second Coming was awaited where the first coming occurred."[27] It is at this second stage that Marxsen sees Galilee becoming a new center for the early church. The third stage occurs with the penning of Mark. Mark "stands in the midst" of this new "orientation to Galilee."[28] Rather than a "historical-geographical" interest, Mark demonstrates an "eschatological-geographical" interest.[29] Marxsen moves past the historical questions of Lohmeyer into the redactional framework of Mark's Gospel. The spatial elements of the Gospel reflect the concerns of the late first century CE rather than the concerns of the earlier part of that century.

Werner Kelber argues that the Gospel of Mark was written after 70 CE in order to respond to the crisis generated by the destruction of the temple.[30] The Gospel's aim is to bring Jesus into the author's present. Since Jesus' initial preaching occurs in Galilee (Mark 1:14), this is where the kingdom of God "accomplished its realization."[31] Kelber prefers to focus on this realization of the kingdom of God in Galilee during Jesus' (narrated) lifetime as the "gist of the gospel program" rather than on its future realization with the coming of the Son of man.[32] In doing so, he

---

24. Ibid., 56. Marxsen notes in footnote 7 on the same page that Lightfoot's distinction between tradition and redaction is also lacking.

25. Ibid., 92.

26. Marxsen himself is unconcerned whether the data of these received traditions preserves accurate historical information or not.

27. Ibid., 93.

28. Ibid.

29. Ibid.

30. Kelber, *The Kingdom in Mark*.

31. Ibid., 11.

32. Ibid.

departs from Marxsen's focus on the risen Christ as the centerpiece of Mark's Gospel.³³

Kelber adopts the views of Lohmeyer, Lightfoot, and Marxsen regarding the opposition between Galilee and Jerusalem in the Gospel. He argues that the Gospel divides the sayings of Jesus into two major clusters, one in Galilee (4:1–34) and the other in Jerusalem (13:5–37).³⁴ Kelber, however, differs from Lohmeyer, Lightfoot, and Marxsen on the reason for an anti-Jerusalem bias in the Gospel. He understands Mark to reject the Davidic kingdom and focus instead on God's kingdom. Kelber reads the disagreement over the status of the Messiah as David's son as a refutation of the Davidic kingdom (Mark 12:35–37). Since Jesus argues that the Christ must be the lord of David rather than his son, Kelber says that "Jesus rejects the Davidic sonship in favor of the sonship of God."³⁵

As a result of his anti-Jerusalem, anti-David bias, Mark presents a "break with the center of Jerusalem and an orientation toward a new goal."³⁶ Mark presents the temple, therefore, as "the nerve center of the city . . . the seat of Davidic promises which Jesus is about to disclaim, as well as the core of hostility and opposition."³⁷ Kelber notes that in combination with the plot to murder Jesus (Mark 11:18), the late hour (11:19), and the withered fig tree (11:20–21), Mark has in mind the destruction of the temple rather than a cleansing.³⁸ "Far from being 'cleansed' in order to serve in a new and purified fashion, the temple is condemned and ruined beyond all hope of recovery."³⁹ All is not lost, however, since Mark's Jesus inaugurates a rival place of eschatological authority. To that end, Kelber argues that Jesus' activity on the Mount of Olives is intended "to divest the temple mount of its eschatological authority."⁴⁰ Through the exorcisms introduced in Mark 1:21–28, 5:1–20 and 7:24–30, "Galilee was cleansed

33. Ibid. Kelber argued that, absent further proof, one should not assume Pauline influence on the Gospel of Mark. Without this influence, Kelber believed, the idea of the risen Christ could no longer be taken to be the focal point of the work.

34. Ibid., 25.

35. Ibid., 95.

36. Ibid., 97.

37. Ibid., 100.

38. Ibid., 101–2. It is significant to note that Kelber is arguing for Mark's status as a post-70 gospel in distinction from the majority of scholars before him (1). The destruction of the temple for Mark, then, is a *fait accompli*.

39. Ibid., 102.

40. Ibid., 104.

and created because it is to become the New Jerusalem for those caught in the crisis of the old Jerusalem."[41]

Kelber further sees the Gospel divided into two "designations"—one Jewish and one Gentile.[42] According to Kelber, "the idea of the lake as the boundary line of Galilee is broken down" in Mark 4:35—8:21.[43] This section of the Gospel serves to bridge the gap between Jews and Gentiles in Mark's story world. Kelber notes that just as Jesus' public activity in Galilee began with an exorcism (Mark 1:21–28), so does his activity in the region of the Decapolis (5:1–20).[44] Kelber treats Mark 6:1–6 as a rejection of family ties and 7:1–23 as a rejection of the authority of Jerusalem.[45] He sees the rejection of the "southern capital" as an "emancipation" that "engenders new freedom of movement."[46] This new freedom of movement provides the opportunity for the kingdom to expand northward into the region of Tyre and Sidon. Here again, when Jesus enters a new region, an exorcism is the first act performed (Mark 7:24–30).[47] The conclusion drawn from Mark's first eight chapters is that Jews and Gentiles alike are invited into the kingdom. The Lake of Galilee, rather than serving as a barrier, "is transposed into a symbol of unity, bridging the gulf between Jewish and Gentile Christians."[48]

Kelber differs from Lohmeyer, Lightfoot, and Marxsen by arguing that Mark was written after the destruction of the temple in Rome for Jerusalem-based Christians who had survived the destruction and violent takeover of the city by Roman troops. In order to provide them new hope, Mark showed that "more than forty years ago Galilee had been designated

---

41. Ibid., 107.

42. Scholars are becoming increasingly sensitive to the use of "Jew" or "Jewish" to translate Ἰουδαῖος. Elliott, "Jesus the Israelite," makes a convincing case that Ἰουδαῖος is best understood as an outsider term for resident of Judea, while those who descended from the twelve tribes of Israel referred to themselves as Israelites. This distinction holds up in most cases. While sensitive to these sociolinguistic issues, I have retained the more common modern usage of "Jew" or "Jewish" to refer to the people and texts of the post-exilic period of Israel/Judah. In so doing, I have tried to represent faithfully the problems and concerns of the modern authors' whose work I am treating throughout this book. See also Hanson and Oakman, *Palestine in the Time of Jesus*, 11.

43. Ibid., 46. Kelber largely accepts Lightfoot's notion of a "greater Galilee."

44. Ibid., 51.

45. Ibid., 53–59.

46. Ibid., 59.

47. Ibid., 59.

48. Ibid., 62–63.

by Jesus to be the center of life."⁴⁹ It is not, however, a political kingdom that involves violent overthrow of Rome. It is rather a "new place," instituted by Jesus during his lifetime, for the Jesus movement of Mark's time that had been forced from Jerusalem.

Summary

The works of Lohmeyer and Lightfoot continue to exercise a tremendous influence among modern scholars. Their thesis, however, is not without problems. Though it is true that more miracles occur in the Galilean ministry of Jesus than the ministry in Jerusalem, there are clear occurrences of problems performing miracles in Galilee. Mark 6:1–6 is the clearest example of this problem. "And he could do no deed of power there, except that he laid his hands on a few sick people and cured them" (Mark 6:5). In this instance, albeit in a limited sense inasmuch as Jesus did cure some sick people, Jesus is unable to perform a deed of power (ποιῆσαι οὐδεμίαν δύναμιν) because it is his hometown. There is nothing in the narratives in Jerusalem that suggest that Jesus is unable to perform miracles there. Jesus does not encounter sick and possessed people in Jerusalem.⁵⁰

A further difficulty with the proposal of Lohmeyer and Lightfoot, and exacerbated by the studies by Marxsen and Kelber, is that there is no evidence for Galilee as a rival center to Jerusalem in early Christianity. Though it is clear that some Jesus group members (notably Paul) did have difficulty with the leadership of the Jerusalem community over certain issues, there are no existing traditions that indicate that there was tension between Galilee and Jerusalem during the period proposed by Marxsen and Kelber for Mark's composition. This point, as will be shown below, is the centerpiece of the criticism that has been leveled at the conclusions of Lohmeyer, Lightfoot, and Marxsen.

REACTIONS TO LOHMEYER AND LIGHTFOOT

Several scholars question the polarity of Galilee and Jerusalem in Mark, denying that Mark could have envisioned an eschatology in which Jerusalem was not central. There are two main responses to the positions

---

49. Ibid., 139.
50. The exception, of course, is blind Bartimaeus. This is the only person Jesus encounters in Judea in need of healing, and he is healed (Mark 10:46–52).

of Lohmeyer and Lightfoot. The first response rejects the idea that Mark contains geographical errors and argues that it is only according to modern standards of cartography that such errors are obvious. The second position reaffirms the centrality of Jerusalem in the Gospel of Mark. Those who argue for Jerusalem's centrality note that the "new centrality" of Galilee in the Gospel should be questioned since Jesus does encounter resistance within Galilee in the Gospel. These studies, like those against which they react, are largely interested in "centrality" in an eschatological setting.

"Problems" in Mark's Geography Due to Peasant Perception

Chapman argues that scholars who contend that Mark records geographical "mistakes" because of his ignorance of the sites in which the events recorded took place fail to appreciate the cartographic skills of pre-literate peasants.[51] His basic argument runs as follows. 1) To ask for cartographic exactness in the modern sense of critical mapping is to ask too much of Mark. If one judges by these standards, the Markan geographical "mistakes" stand out readily.[52] 2) Counter to the idea that Mark is unfamiliar with the sites of ancient Palestine is "the sheer number of place names, including several . . . which were not available to the author from the Hebrew Bible, the Greek Septuagint, or the foremost geographic writing of his time, Strabo's *Geography*."[53] Chapman notes two other factors that suggest that Mark had some firsthand knowledge concerning ancient Palestine: "Mark's accurate placement of references" and his "accurate sequences of geographical references."[54] 3) Because of this direct knowledge of Palestine, Chapman contests, any study that focuses on the geographical errors in Mark's Gospel misses the larger point that a narrow focus on the mistakes does not explain how Mark produces some (Chapman would contend many) correct details about the geography of ancient Palestine.[55]

Chapman aims to resolve the issue by recourse to perception theory, using the work of Piaget regarding the perception of space by children. Briefly, Chapman argues that perception and mental representation of space in the Euclidean, projective sense, common to modern cartography,

51. Chapman, "Locating the Gospel of Mark."
52. See the list of geographical errors listed in ibid., 24.
53. Ibid.
54. Ibid.
55. Ibid.

is the final stage in the representation of space. Peasant societies, according to the studies cited by Chapman, represent space in a colloidal manner that is characterized by "egocentrism," "lack of scale," "limits defined by personal experience," "topological characteristics," "plasticity," and "three-dimensionality."[56] This representation of space is most concerned with proximity. Chapman draws two conclusions about ancient Palestinian peasants from these studies of space.

> First, I do not believe anything like a true map was ever consciously represented in its totality in the mind of a Palestinian peasant. Such a representation would require greater familiarity with Euclidean and projective space. Second, since colloidal geography must retain its three-dimensional realism, a resident of Jerusalem would have thought of "map," if at all, rather as a constellation of actual places, than as a constellation of symbols.[57]

Such an understanding, Chapman concludes, explains Mark's geographical "errors." The more remote the place was from the author, the more likely the "scale" of places might become distorted. Chapman argues that the author of Mark, given the amount of geographic detail in the Passion narrative, resided in Jerusalem.[58] The "correct" geographic references in Galilee are likely due to "Mark's repeated contact with residents from that area."[59] For Chapman, then, Mark presents space fairly straightforwardly, only lacking the spatial perception of a modern cartographer.

Eschatological Centrality of Jerusalem

Davies represents a second critique of Lohmeyer, Lightfoot and Marxsen.[60] He rejects the view that Galilee is the "favored" geographical setting in the Gospel of Mark, offering three arguments against this position. The first, and perhaps most telling, criticism is the fact that there is "no convincing evidence for the existence of a distinct Galilean Christianity" that "could have imposed itself on the tradition" in such a way as to create a

---

56. Ibid., 30–31.
57. Ibid., 31.
58. Ibid., 34.
59. Ibid., 35.
60. Davies, *Gospel and the Land*. In footnotes on 221 and 409, Davies lists a number of scholars who disagree with Lohmeyer, Lightfoot and Marxsen.

gospel that favored Galilee over Jerusalem.⁶¹ The second critique is that the scheme "acceptance at Galilee/rejection at Jerusalem" does not work out neatly with the text of Mark's Gospel.⁶² Davies' final critique is that there is no evidence for an eschatological tradition locating the coming of the Messiah in Galilee. He contends that because "there is no connection made between the Messiah and Galilee . . . any marked eschatological or theological significance ascribed to Galilee by a primitive Christian community would be extremely difficult to understand."⁶³

In summarizing his opposition to Lohmeyer and Lightfoot, Davies concludes:

> Not for him [Matthew] nor for Mark was Galilee *terra Christiana*; it was not Messianic holy land in either Gospel. Failure as well as success marked the Galilean ministry from the start. That failure knew no geographic boundaries. There is no Galilean idyll for Jesus in Mark or Matthew. For them both, Galilee found much to object to in Jesus, as he found much to condemn in it. Lohmeyer and Lightfoot too easily overlooked the fact that even when the Galileans 'understood' Jesus they misunderstood him: for this reason, at the very height of his popularity there, Jesus found that he had to escape from Galilee.⁶⁴

After rejecting the position of Lohmeyer and Lightfoot, Davies attempts to discuss Mark's presentation of Galilee "as objectively as possible, that is, without any attempt to ascribe a theological dimension to it."⁶⁵ He notes four factors that he argues should be interpreted to mean that Galilean Jews never set up a rival center to Jerusalem: (1) pilgrims constantly moved from Galilee to Jerusalem, (2) Galilean revolutionaries focused on Jerusalem rather than Galilee (indeed Galileans were "among the most audacious Zealots in Jerusalem"), (3) they were ready "to accept the

---

61. Ibid., 222.

62. Indeed, Davies points to the inclusion of an entire chapter in Lightfoot's earlier book, *History and Interpretation in the Gospels*, titled "The Rejection in the Patris," and notes that there is simply no mention of the significance of this text in his later book. Davies argues that the rejection at Nazareth comes immediately after three works of power, culminating with Jesus raising Jairus' daughter from the dead (Mark 5:35–43). He compares this scene, followed by Jesus' rejection at Nazareth, to the Gospel of John's account of Jesus' raising of Lazarus and the plot to kill him that ensues.

63. Davies, *Gospel and the Land*, 222.

64. Ibid., 241.

65. Ibid., 239.

leadership of a priest," and (4) they had "conviction . . . that they 'could never fear captivity since the city was God's' (*Jewish Wars*, VI. 2.1)."[66] Davies, then, rejects the idea that Galilee had attained a status as holy land over and against Jerusalem either in early Judaism or in early Christianity. He asserts, instead, that "Jerusalem was the 'inevitable' Messianic centre" in Mark.[67]

In *Galilee, Jesus and the Gospels*, Freyne argues that the traditional way that biblical scholars, including form and redaction critics, read Gospels is inadequate in several ways.[68] He prefers a literary approach that takes the Gospels as whole narratives and opposes paring away redactional material from original material in the Gospels.[69] Attempts to pare away later elements of the Gospel frequently involve removing the references to geographic and spatial locations for Jesus' activity.

Freyne's major concern in *Galilee, Jesus and the Gospels* is that studies of the historical Jesus have not taken seriously his Galilean provenance. Freyne, while noting the significance of Galilee as "the main theatre for the action to follow" in the first few chapters of Mark, rejects Lohmeyer's distinction between Galilee and Jerusalem in Mark, particularly his assertion that Galilee is not "Jewish."[70] Several factors attest to the "Jewishness" of Mark's Galilee: (1) synagogues are community centers to which all people in their various locales gather, (2) the inhabitants of Capernaum show respect for the Sabbath (Mark 1:32) and (3) Jesus "also is careful to show respect for Pentateuchal law, by telling the cured leper to show himself to the priest before rejoining the community."[71] Jesus' freedom to travel between Gentile territory and Galilee and the fact that Gentile and Jewish territories are listed together in summarizing statements in the Gospel (i.e. Mark 3:7), however, show that Galilee "is not a Jewish world that is turned

66. Ibid., 235.
67. Ibid., 241.
68. Freyne, *Galilee, Jesus and the Gospels*, 10–13.

69. Freyne bemoans the fact that this process leaves out the editorial seams of the Gospel as "worthless in terms of historical reconstruction, for anything but the final level of redaction" (ibid., 12). Indeed among these "editorial seams" one finds the most information relevant to the geographical and spatial settings of the Gospels.

70. Ibid., 33–35. Following Malbon, he believes that Lohmeyer relies too heavily on extra-textual materials for his overall presentation and, for this reason, Freyne finds it unconvincing.

71. Ibid., 35.

in on itself in any exclusive fashion."[72] Freyne also notes that we see no instances of "grinding poverty in Galilee,"[73] and that the overall portrait of Galilee presented by Mark is that of a rural territory.[74]

In a recent article, Freyne addresses the relationship of Galilee and Jerusalem in historical Jesus scholarship under the rubric "geography of restoration"—by which he means "the significance and role of territory within the various idealisations of Jewish restoration in the Hellenistic and Roman periods."[75] The Gospel of Mark, Freyne notes, contains several items that link Galilee and Jerusalem together in the scheme of restoration. First, he notes that a synchronic reading shows that "the Galilee-Jerusalem relations of the gospel . . . point to a deliberate reversal of expectations at the deeper level of meaning with regard to the significance of these places."[76] These two territories are mediated, however, "at the eschatological level . . . that is inspired by the Jerusalem temple and what is stands for."[77] Mark 14:58, Freyne concludes, shows that the Gospel envisions a "new centre of divine presence" of which "the Jerusalem temple offers the proper symbolic field of reference in order to understand its deeper significance."[78] Ultimately Freyne sees the possibility of two models of restoration at work in the Gospel of Mark. On the one hand, Jesus' journeys into Gentile territories suggest a friendly relation with outsiders that does not require the strict maintenance of ethnic boundaries. On the other hand, "the journey to Jerusalem takes on the character of a ritual pilgrimage to the centre of Israel in order to renew it also at the divinely appointed time

---

72. Ibid., 35.

73. Ibid., 38.

74. Ibid., 38–41.

75. Freyne, "Geography of Restoration," 291. Freyne distinguishes two types of restoration in the article. The first, found in texts like 1 Enoch, offer "a symbolic counterpole to Jerusalem" that "functioned as a critique of the existing Jerusalem." These texts do not, however present a true geographic alternative to Jerusalem, but "rather, a different Israel is envisaged, whose centre would still be in Jerusalem and its temple, but whose personnel would be of a different calibre to those presently functioning there" (296). The other type of restoration, found in texts like Ezekiel and the Genesis Apocryphon, understand restoration to involve the gradual expansion of the limits of the territories inhabited by the tribes of Israel.

76. Ibid., 305.

77. Ibid., 307.

78. Ibid.

of Passover."⁷⁹ In this sense, the ultimate aim of restoration still lies at Jerusalem for Mark's Gospel.

Freyne also discusses the contrasts between house and synagogue and between the deserted place (Mark 1:35) and the synagogue as places of prayer.⁸⁰ He notes especially how these contrasts serve to reinforce the idea that Jesus' authority represents the new teaching of the kingdom of God while the scribes' teaching represents a now outdated order. The scribes, with their ties to Jerusalem, represent "the real source of opposition to Jesus, whose deeds of power gave his teaching an authoritative quality as being from God in a way that the scribes could never match."⁸¹ These scribes have Jerusalem as their base of authority and operation, but are able to operate independently of the city in coming to Galilee to confront Jesus.⁸²

Mark's Galilee, in contrast to Jerusalem, is presented as a land that lends itself to a disregard for boundaries. Easy access to Gentile territories makes Galilee a place with naturally porous boundaries.⁸³ In Galilee, Jesus is constantly moving, whereas in Jerusalem he is located almost exclusively in the temple during his visits to the city: he taught there daily (Mark 14:49). Jerusalem is a place with a localized holy center (the temple) while "Galilee is exploited to the full as the proper setting for portraying this new mode of divine presence which is no longer to be localised, and hence knows no boundaries."⁸⁴

Summary

These studies that reject or modify the positions of Lohmeyer, Lightfoot, Marxsen and Kelber are not without their own difficulties. Merely because Jesus encountered difficulty in Galilee does not mean that Jerusalem is necessarily positively valued by Mark. Jesus does not go to Jerusalem on pilgrimage.⁸⁵ Davies' link between Galilean rebels and zealots is not readily

---

79. Ibid.
80. Freyne, *Galilee, Jesus and the Gospels*, 43.
81. Ibid., 46. See his discussion of the scribes on 43–50.
82. For more on these points see chapter 5 below.
83. Freyne, *Galilee, Jesus and the Gospels*, 54–59.
84. Ibid., 63.

85. Contrary to Freyne's and Davies's readings, nothing in Mark 1–13 suggests that Jesus goes to Jerusalem for any reason but to die. It is not until the Passion narrative that

applicable to Jesus, and certainly not to Mark's report of Jesus since Mark definitely does not view Jesus as a military revolutionary. Finally, whether or not the Galileans accepted the leadership of the priesthood, Mark's Jesus seems ultimately to reject it.

Davies responds to Lohmeyer, Lightfoot and Marxsen mostly on their own terms, denying that the interpretation of Galilee as a *terra Christiana* is legitimate for either the early or mid-first century CE. He does not, however, clearly explain why Mark presents Galilee and Jerusalem as he does.[86] Davies and Freyne, focused as they are on the localities of Jerusalem and Galilee, are still primarily concerned with questions of eschatology. The timing of the future kingdom animates the discussion in all four of these works. While each of these authors treats space in some way, none of them goes beyond the "theological" value of the categories of "Jerusalem" and "Galilee."[87]

Chapman's study is somewhat more problematic. There are three major difficulties associated with it. His argument for the author's location based on geographic detail could easily be flip-flopped. In other words, instead of arguing that Mark lived in Jerusalem and had contact with Galilean followers of Jesus, one could easily argue that Mark resided in Capernaum and knew residents of Jerusalem. There is no compelling reason to favor Jerusalem over Capernaum as the location for the writing of the Gospel in Chapman's argument. The second difficulty is related to the first. One could easily take his argument a bit further and suggest that Mark had sources from residents of both of these places and had never been to either one. The third major difficulty with the study is Chapman's hesitance to accept that Mark had sources. He rejects Marxsen's idea that geographic references come primarily from Mark's sources because it limits the control Mark has of the information presented in his Gospel.[88] In combination with his argument that Mark lived in first century Jerusalem, however, this

---

the reader discovers that it happens to be the time of the Passover.

86. In fairness to Davies, he is largely responding to Lohmeyer, whose work, though it is concerned with Mark's Gospel, is primarily devoted to the traditions concerning Galilee and Jerusalem in the eschatology of the early church.

87. It is unclear why Davies rejects understanding Galilee in a theological way but is comfortable understanding Jerusalem in that way.

88. See Chapman, "Locating the Gospel," 25. Chapman's reading of Marxsen on this point seems somewhat disingenuous. Marxsen argues that, in many instances, Mark added a reference to "Galilee," but not necessarily references to locations within Galilee. See Marxsen, *Mark the Evangelist*, 94.

smacks of a historical argument veiled in geographic disguise. Chapman wants to locate Mark geographically and temporally closer to Jesus as "a member of the early Christian church in Jerusalem!"[89] This conclusion stretches the data too far. Furthermore, it does not address at all the major distinctions highlighted by Marxsen (and Lightfoot and Lohmeyer before him).[90]

Beyond Galilee and Jerusalem: Other Spaces in Mark's Gospel

The studies summarized above treat Markan space only as it relates to the territorial units of Galilee and Jerusalem (Judea). They make little attempt to treat other types of spaces in the Gospel.[91] Several more recent studies have undertaken to understand Mark's space more broadly. While these studies do include discussions of Galilee and Jerusalem in the Gospel, they treat the other spaces of Mark's narrative as well—households, synagogues, mountains, the sea of Galilee, the temple and other spaces are analyzed in an attempt to gain an appreciation of Mark's overall representation of space. These studies are primarily concerned with the story world of Mark and its space rather than the geography of the eschaton.

Narrative based Readings

Malbon discusses Mark's presentation of space by means of a structural exegesis of the Gospel.[92] She divides Markan space into three suborders: geopolitical, topographical, and architectural. The geopolitical suborder, which consists of "those relations designating events reported or projected in the Gospel of Mark in spatial relation to a specific, named village, city, country, region, area, mountain, sea, or river,"[93] is divided into three major relational oppositions—Jewish homeland vs. foreign lands, Galilee vs.

---

89. Chapman, "Locating the Gospel," 35.

90. Despite its problems, Chapman's study does make important points about "scale" and "egocentrism" in ancient production of maps and spatial imagery. See the discussion in chapter three below.

91. An exception to this statement is Freyne, *Galilee, Jesus, and the Gospels*.

92. Malbon, *Narrative Space and Mythic Meaning*. Her analysis is based on the work of Claude Lévi-Strauss. See also Malbon, "Galilee and Jerusalem."

93. Malbon, *Narrative Space*, 17.

Jerusalem and the Jerusalem environs vs. Jerusalem proper.[94] Each of these pairs represents a "familiar" space and a "strange" space.[95] In the first pair, the Jewish homeland represents the familiar space while the foreign lands represent the strange space. The Gospel portrays mediation between these places when people come to Jesus from both the Jewish homeland and the foreign lands, and in Jesus' frequent travels between them.[96] Galilee itself, as Jesus' homeland, and specifically the Sea of Galilee, become the spaces of mediation. In the second opposing pair Mark inverts the normal expectation of the readers by making Galilee the "familiar" pole and Jerusalem, the symbolic center of Judaism, the "strange" pole.[97] These two spaces are mediated by the journeys of Jesus (and his disciples) between them, both at the beginning of the Gospel for the baptism and at the end for the Passover. These journeys are spatially represented by the road to Jerusalem.[98] The final geopolitical pair, which consists of Jerusalem proper and its environs, also reverses expectations.[99] Ordinarily one would expect the city itself to represent the "familiar" pole in this group, but it is the environs of Jerusalem that represent the "familiar" pole in this pair, while the city itself represents the "strange" pole.[100] This reversal is true because "Jerusalem is the power base of the religious establishment that opposes Jesus."[101] For this last oppositional pair, there is no clear mediation. There is movement toward mediation within each of these three pairs, but "no final mediator is presented with the geopolitical schema."[102]

The topographical suborder in Mark begins with the unmediated and irreconcilable pair "promise" and "threat." This pair is eventually replaced by the three mediating pairs, "heaven vs. earth," "land vs. sea," and "isolated

---

94. Ibid., 38–49.

95. Ibid., 38–40. See especially Figure 4 on p. 40. The "familiar" and "strange" opposition represents the irreconcilable opposition which is replaced by the other three pairs in an attempt to mediate between them.

96. Ibid., 43–44.

97. Ibid., 44–46. In this discussion she follows Lightfoot, noting that Mark characterizes "Galilee not only as the familiar home from which Jesus and the disciples have come but as the final home to which they will return" (45).

98. Ibid., 45–46.

99. The "environs of Jeruslaem," according to Malbon, consist of "Bethphage, Bethany, the Mount of Olives, Gethsemane, and Golgotha" (ibid., 46).

100. Ibid., 46–49.

101. Ibid., 46.

102. Ibid., 47.

areas" vs. "inhabited areas." These three pairs are, in the end, mediated by the "way."[103] The first two opposing pairs in this suborder, heaven vs. earth and land vs. sea, reinforce normal expectations inasmuch as heaven and land represent promise while earth and sea represent threat. The final pair contained within the topographical suborder, however, "isolated areas" vs. "inhabited areas," again inverts the reader's normal expectation because in Mark's Gospel isolated areas represent the "promise" while inhabited areas represent "threat."[104] This pair is mediated through the fact that Jesus always returns to inhabited areas after a retreat to isolated areas. The topographical suborder as a whole is mediated by the concept of the way. "The mediation of promise and threat is a dynamic process, not a static state; it is known in the experience of being on the way."[105] Malbon highlights the fact that at the end of the Gospel, Jesus is on the way to Galilee.

The final spatial suborder in Mark, architectural space, treats the unmediated mythic pair "sacred" and "profane," represented by the oppositions "house vs. synagogue and temple, room vs. courtyard, and tomb vs. temple."[106] The latter element in each of these pairs represents the "sacred," whereas the former elements, house, room and tomb, are profane spaces in Mark. Malbon notes that in the Gospel of Mark, "contrary to what one might expect of 'religious literature,' the positively valued pole of this Markan schema, the pole manifested by the architectural spaces most closely associated with Jesus, is the profane pole."[107] In the pair house vs. synagogue and temple, Malbon suggests that, with the temple destroyed and the synagogue abandoned by Jesus' movement, Mark presents the household as the locus of Jesus' teaching activity (from chapter 6 onward) because that is the locus of the emerging Markan community.[108] While there are no clear spaces of mediation between these oppositional pairs in the Gospel, the overall effect of Mark's presentation of these pairs is that they are "witnesses to the breakdown of the opposition of the sacred and the profane and the breakthrough into a new reality."[109]

103. Ibid., 95–105.
104. Ibid., 103.
105. Ibid., 104.
106. Ibid., 131–40.
107. Ibid., 140.
108. Ibid., 135–36.
109. Ibid., 140.

Malbon concludes her study by arguing that the overarching scheme of Mark's spatial presentation is the topographical suborder because "the topographical schema, in isolation, presents two mediators, whereas neither the geopolitical schema nor the architectural schema presents a final mediator."[110] The fact that the topographical schema entails cosmic space that is larger in scale than either geopolitical or architectural space may account for this presentation. The way, especially the way to Galilee, which is the "center of order" for this Gospel, is the final place of mediation between the fundamental opposition of order and chaos.[111] The spatial presentation of the Gospel of Mark presents the beginning of the overcoming of chaos by order. This "conflict between the chaos and order of life is overcome not in arriving, but in being on the way."[112]

The treatment of Markan space in Rhoads', Michie's and Dewey's *Mark as Story* is similar to Malbon's in that it deals with cosmic, topographical and political-cultural elements of Mark's space.[113] Markan cosmic space "includes social boundaries meant to keep some people holy before God by separating the Israelites from the impure Gentiles and by separating the leaders of Israel from Judeans considered to be defiled."[114] The Markan cosmos views the earth as a flat disk, of which Jerusalem is the center, in the center of the cosmos in which God, angels, demons, Satan, people and animals all live together. Creation, for Mark, however, is not as God intended it to be. Instead of humans having dominion over creation they oppress each other, "are possessed by demons, wracked by illnesses, and threatened by storms at sea."[115] The Gospel, however, presents a cosmos that is about to be changed. "The arrival of God's rule changes cosmic

---

110. Ibid., 155. Besides the "way," which Malbon sees as the final mediator of the topographical schema, the mountain functions as mediator between heaven and earth.

111. Ibid., 158.

112. Ibid., 168. The study of Van Eck, *Galilee and Jerusalem*, is very similar to Malbon's in many ways. Van Eck attempts to read the Gospel through the prism of social-scientific and narratological methods, but he largely condenses these two methodologies into one. His conclusions basically endorse the views of Lightfoot, Lohmeyer, Marxsen and Malbon. The major conclusion of his study can be summarized in his own words: "Galilee, and not Jerusalem, is portrayed by the narrator as the place where access to the Patron is available. And in Galilee, there is no temple, only the house" (295). In his focus on the house as the locus of the kingdom movement, he diverges somewhat from Malbon's focus on the "way" as the space of final mediation in Mark.

113. Rhoads et al., *Mark as Story*, 63–72.

114. Ibid., 64.

115. Ibid.

space, because the power of God from above is now available on earth for healing and exorcism. The power of God's rule breaks out of local, national, and natural boundaries to make all space into God's space."[116] The story of the Gospel of Mark, then, begins, according to Rhoads, Michie and Dewey, with the idea that creation is about to be set right for its intended purpose.

The social, or political cultural world, of Mark's Gospel is composed of a small group of elites (comprised of "high priests, the elders, and other aristocratic landowners" as well as the Roman rulers) and retainers (Pharisees and scribes in Mark) and the rest of the population ("common folk who live at the subsistence level").[117] The land of Israel is separate from the rest of the world, which "is comprised of the Gentile nation—the Roman Empire and the nations under its domination."[118] In the narrative world of Mark, it is the role of the disciples to bring the gospel to these other nations in the same manner that Jesus brought it to Israel.

Rhoads, Michie and Dewey read Mark largely as a travel story. These authors see the "journey of Jesus" as that element that "structures the narrative as a whole."[119] The journey motif consists of two major parts: travels in Galilee and the surrounding regions, and the pilgrimage to Jerusalem. The trip to Jerusalem is further divided into three parts: "first the pilgrimage to Jerusalem, then Jesus' actions and teachings in Jerusalem, and finally the story of the crucifixion and empty grave."[120] During Jesus' journeying, many of the places to which he comes recall Israel's past. The Jordan River is the sight at which the Israelites initially entered the land after the Exodus. The desert reminds the reader of the "place where God had prepared the Israelites to enter the land of Israel."[121] The Israelites again crossed the desert in returning to Judea after the Babylonian exile. Like the Israelites in the desert, Jesus was also tested in the desert. The sea

---

116. Ibid., 65.
117. Ibid., 65.
118. Ibid., 66.
119. Ibid.
120. Ibid. Following the earlier studies on Galilee and Jerusalem in Mark, Rhoads et al., note that Galilee is the first place to which Jesus brings his message of good news, and it is there that it is first received. They note that the Galilean ministry, however, is not without complications. Their position on this issue is similar to Malbon's.
121. Ibid., 69.

and the mountains of the Gospel also recall the parting of the Reed Sea and the time the Israelites spent on Mount Sinai.[122]

The final spaces that Rhoads, Michie and Dewey discuss are public and private spaces. The public spaces are those in which Jesus encounters crowds and his opponents. They are marked by Jesus' miracles, teaching and conflicts with his opponents. The private spaces are marked by encounters with the disciples. Jesus teaches and corrects his disciples in these private settings. These places "contribute to the secrecy motif of the story, because those characters who are present, the insiders (as well as the readers), have access to what goes on there, while the other characters, the outsiders, do not."[123]

Rhoads, Michie and Dewey understand the space of the Gospel of Mark in two distinct ways. The first way is from the perspective of the earth, in which the distinction between Israel and Gentile nations is of extreme significance. The second perspective, however, is from the heavens in which God dwells. Seen from this perspective the spatial divisions of the political and geographical kind prevent the earth from realizing the purpose of God's cosmos. For Mark, according to this reading, creation has gone awry and is about to be set right through the way of the Lord on which Jesus embarks.

Sacred Space in Mark

Riches' work is concerned with the roles of kinship and sacred space in the Gospels of Mark and Matthew.[124] Drawing upon the work of the anthropologist Clifford Geertz, Riches is especially interested in the cosmology of the texts of Matthew and Mark.[125] His project thus attempts "to take two of these common concepts, descent and attachment to the Land, and to use them to lead us into a discussion of the world-view and ethos of the first two Gospels."[126] Riches makes several insightful and important contributions to the idea of cosmic and terrestrial space in Mark. The first of these points is that Mark offers a worldview in which the ethnic divisions between Israel and the nations fall away since the true followers of Jesus

---

122. Ibid., 69–70.
123. Ibid., 71.
124. Riches, *Conflicting Mythologies*.
125. Ibid., 10–13.
126. Ibid., 14.

are gathered from the ends of the earth (Mark 13:27). Rather than draw an ethnic mental map of the world, Mark's space "is divided into those who think the things of God and those who think the things of men."[127] "Ethnic divisions are subordinated to the new—voluntarist—criteria for membership of the group, even if the new group takes its rationale from the history of a nation defined by just such markers."[128]

Mark's presentation of space, however, is more complicated than this notion of the eradication of ethnic markers. Through Jesus' numerous exorcisms, Riches notes that in Mark Galilee "represents in some sense a world purged of evil and suffering."[129] The place of the final resolution of this conflict between the demonic forces and God's anointed agent, however, is not specified in the Gospel. "Mark 13 displays a clear tendency to move away from direct and explicit reference to specific locations and to prefer a setting which is unspecified and cosmic."[130] Such a reading distances Riches from Lohmeyer and Lightfoot.

In discussing the "way of the Lord" in Mark, Riches suggests that Jesus' glory, revealed on the cross to the Roman centurion, is contrasted to the rending of the temple veil, which signifies the departure of the *Shekinah* from the temple.[131] The Isaian motif of the way in Mark points to "a salvation historical view which sees God as enabling his people to overcome sin by teaching and leading them."[132] Through the metaphor of the way, Mark creates a new kind of sacred space, one "which locates God's presence not in particular cultic sites" but "chooses instead to see the presence of God as disembedded, not limited but irrupting wherever the Gospel is preached and heard."[133] Mark's Gospel redraws the map of the world inasmuch as it draws the "boundaries of Gentile territory and the Land, of Galilee and Jerusalem," but these boundaries are "variously subverted" in the Gospel.[134] This subversion comes as a result of Mark's

---

127. Ibid., 111.

128. Ibid., 112. Here Riches argues that Mark 3:31–35 signals the rejection of biological family ties in favor of fictive kinship.

129. Ibid., 133.

130. Ibid., 134. Riches does not endorse the viewpoint of Lohmeyer, Lightfoot, and Marxsen that the eschaton will begin in Galilee with Jesus' return.

131. Ibid., 137–39.

132. Ibid., 140.

133. Ibid., 142.

134. Ibid., 147.

attempt to mediate between a cosmology interested in the restoration of Israel and another interested in an end time revolution in which the old order and its distinctions pass away.[135]

Summary

These studies of Markan space highlight previously neglected elements of Mark's spatial understanding. They treat space more holistically in some ways than did the other studies examined above. Each of these studies treats cosmic space and argues that when seen from a cosmic perspective, geopolitical distinctions lose some of their significance. The idea of the way of the Lord also figures prominently in these discussions. Markan space is seen as unfinished, "on the way" by Malbon; Rhoads, Michie, and Dewey; and Riches. The significance of the way is highlighted by Malbon and Rhoads, Michie and Dewey to suggest that Mark's text is essentially a travel narrative, while Riches prefers a more metaphorical and ethical understanding of the way. Each of these studies also suggests a rejection of and redefinition of sacred space. Jerusalem's temple is no longer the center for Mark's Gospel.[136]

Despite some advances, there are problematic elements in these studies as well. Malbon, for example, begins her study by suggesting that she will interpret Mark from within the text itself. In certain instances, however (most notably in the discussion of house vs. synagogue and temple), Malbon is forced to go outside of the text for explanations for her analysis. Secondly, and perhaps more importantly, the idea that "myth operates to mediate irreconcilable opposites by successively replacing them by opposites that do permit mediation" is not borne out in the geopolitical or architectural suborders since the original oppositional pairs (strange vs. familiar and profane vs. sacred) are not ultimately mediated.[137] The whole structural interpretation of the text is jeopardized by the fact that only one of the three suborders permits the type of mediation that structural analysis of mythic texts provides. It is also particularly noteworthy that the architectural suborder, in which the temple is located, does not assume the central position in Malbon's understanding of the Gospel. It is a difficulty

---

135. Ibid., 145–79.

136. It should be noted that the fact that Riches argues that the return in chapter 13 is not specifically located leaves open the possibility for Jerusalem's eschatological centrality.

137. Malbon, *Narrative Space*, 2–3.

with Malbon's study as well as that of Riches that there is an element of negativity in the portrayal of Jerusalem in the Gospel that is difficult to ignore. Especially with Riches' understanding that Mark creates a new sacred space "which locates God's presence not in particular cultic sites," it is difficult to assume this can be anything but a challenge to and/or rejection of the Jerusalem temple. Since Riches' work concentrates on the idea of restoration, it is difficult to understand why Mark would ultimately decide on a presentation of sacred space that rejected the temple to which he hoped the entire Israelite people would be restored.

CRITICAL SPATIALITY AND EARLY CHRISTIANITY

In a series of articles, Moxnes has evaluated the recent work of biblical scholars on Galilee and the role reconstructions of ancient Galilee have played in scholarly portrayals of the historical Jesus.[138] Moxnes notes that it is within nineteenth-century German scholarship, expanded later by Nazi ideologues, that a picture of Galilee as a place of open-mindedness, of mixed ethnicity and race and a lack of concern for purity first developed.[139] In response to this understanding of Galilee, Klausner argued for a thoroughly Torah-observant, temple-loyal Galilee.[140] Later, Geza Vermes, following this line of scholarship, introduced a picture of Galilean religion centered around the idea of Jesus (and others) as charismatic healers "in contrast to halakhic Judaism that became the corner stone of rabbinic Judaism."[141] Sanders's work, on the contrary, shows a more unified picture of Judea and Galilee under the rubric of Jewish religion. Galilee as a place bears no special significance in his reconstruction of Jesus.[142]

In the third quest of the historical Jesus, Galilee again has come to the fore. Moxnes credits this development to two things. The first is "a general trend in historical and religious studies toward social and local contexts," while the second is the greater number of archaeological excavations conducted in Galilee.[143] Moxnes asserts that two assumptions,

---

138. Moxnes, *Putting Jesus in His Place*; "The Construction of Galilee—Parts 1 and 2"; "Kingdom Takes Place"; and "Placing Jesus of Nazareth."
139. Moxnes, "Construction of Galilee—Part 1," 30–32.
140. Ibid., 33–34.
141. Ibid., 35.
142. Ibid., 36.
143. Moxnes, "Construction of Galilee—Part 2," 64.

common to the nineteenth-century depictions of Galilee, have continued to hold sway over various depictions of ancient Galilee. The first is that "one should strive to produce as accurate a representation of the world as possible, and indeed that such a mimetic representation was possible . . . without unnecessary theorizing."[144] The second assumption is that places shape people rather than the reverse. In other words, place is an actor that defines what people can be and what they are.[145]

Newer ideas from the study of space, however, are beginning to make their way into the study of Galilee.[146] The discussion of the race and ethnicity of the ancient Galileans has largely been replaced by an interest in the "cultural mix" of the Galileans.[147] In some recent works (such as those by Mack and Crossan), Galilee is seen as culturally "open" allowing for easy contact between Jews and non-Jews.[148] Meyers, however, argues for a less substantial influence of Hellenization on Galilee. Instead Galilee is a place of "negotiated Jewishness."[149] Indeed, "even with the influence of Hellenism there seems to be a basic unity to Judaism in Palestine."[150] In addition to this interest in cultural elements in Galilee, there is also a burgeoning interest in the social and political elements of Galilee.[151] This approach stresses things like power over space and peoples in ancient Galilee.[152] Whether ancient urban centers operated cooperatively or exploitatively in relation to villages is also a key question.[153]

Moxnes concludes his study by outlining four areas that need broader discussion. The first is the areas around Galilee. While many of the studies of ancient Galilee have focused on the relationship between that territory and Jerusalem, they "have overlooked the much closer areas to the North, East, and South, that are all within easy walking distance from any area in

144. Ibid., 67.

145. Ibid. See the discussion in chapter 3 below.

146. Ibid., 67–68. Moxnes uses the developments found in Sean Freyne's work as an example of how emphases are shifting in the study of Galilee.

147. Ibid., 68.

148. Ibid., 68–69.

149. Ibid., 69–70. The phrase is that of Moxnes. On Meyers's reading there is little difference between Galilee and Jerusalem.

150. Ibid., 70.

151. Ibid., 70–72.

152. Ibid., 70–71. Moxnes cites Horsley's work as a major example here.

153. Ibid., 71–72.

Galilee."[154] A second element that deserves more attention is the role of the interpreter of ancient Galilee. As Moxnes stresses, "the essentialism implied in earlier presuppositions of a mimetic representation of landscape is no longer a viable option."[155] Space encodes power relationships, patterns of behavior and cultural definitions that are not always immediately evident. The role of the interpreter in viewing space needs to be made explicit. A third element that needs attention is how spaces are created through resistance to dominating powers.[156] The final element that Moxnes wishes to stress is the role of Jesus in shaping Galilee.[157] By this he means that Jesus' way of speaking about and imagining space "as a landscape with an alternative spatial management of power" suggests, on the part of Jesus and his movement, "a give and take between their experience of landscape and their own attempts to recreate landscape in a different fashion."[158]

Moxnes brought the information from his studies of Galilee together in his book *Putting Jesus in His Place*. Since Moxnes's book is largely concerned with the historical Jesus, much of his information is drawn from Q, but there are several insightful comments about Mark as well. One of these insights, in particular, is significant for understanding space in Mark. Whereas in Q, Moxnes contends, Jesus invites his followers into "queer space" that involves homelessness (see Q 9:58),[159] in Mark the household serves as the metaphoric space for the new community. It is not, however, the household as normally configured in Galilean antiquity. Mark retains the radical nature of Jesus' call to leave everything (Mark 1:16–20), "but it is modified by the stories he tells."[160] Instead of locating Jesus in the no-man's land of "queer space" as the sayings in Q seem to do, "Mark provides a social and spatial location for the new, fictive kinship group. Jesus has a house (2:15; 3:20, 31–35), and that becomes a center for him and the group of disciples, and metaphorically, for the Markan commu-

---

154. Ibid., 74.
155. Ibid., 74.
156. Ibid., 75.
157. Ibid.
158. Ibid.
159. Queer space was a space characterized by "transgression, asceticism, and liminality" and "does not represent a new identity or a fixed position in place," Moxnes, *Putting Jesus in His Place*, 105.
160. Ibid., 57.

nity."[161] This house, however, is not like the ones the disciples left; "there is no father figure in the new household . . . and life in this household includes persecution, probably in the form of social exclusion from their old household and village."[162] Mark's alternative to the household that the disciples are called to leave, then, is a new household. This shows a truism in critique of space: "a criticism of existing structures is often, paradoxically, presented in similar structures."[163] Mark 10:30 suggests that those who have left their households to follow Jesus will become part of this new family and new household "in this time." Mark, in his critique of existing familial relationships within existing household structures, envisions a new type of familial life in a new type of household.[164]

Moxnes treats the exorcisms of Jesus in relation to the space of the kingdom of God as well.[165] Moxnes, following the work of Jonathan Z. Smith, treats demonic as a "locative category."[166] People who are demon-possessed are out of place. Exorcism, then, restores them to their rightful place in society. More than that, however, "exorcisms appeared to be a way to speak of control and domination of space. In exorcism it became visible that control over the world was contested."[167] Exorcisms are visible confirmations of the power of God's kingdom over the land. "In this way the kingdom was not just an 'imagined place,' but an experienced place."[168] Moxnes' understanding of how space encodes power relationships and how these power relationships can be challenged through alternative spatial configurations is a major advance in the study of space in the Gospel of Mark.

Conclusion

The study of Mark's spatial presentation began in earnest in the 1930s with the work of Lohmeyer and Lightfoot. Much of the early work on Mark's

161. Ibid., 69.
162. Ibid., 70. Moxnes cites Mark 3:31–35 and 10:29–30 as evidence of the idea of the new household of Jesus in Mark.
163. Ibid., 62.
164. More will be said on this point in chapter 5 below.
165. Moxnes, *Putting Jesus*, 125–41.
166. Ibid., 128.
167. Ibid., 139.
168. Ibid., 141.

space focused on the presentation of Galilee and Jerusalem. More recent studies have broadened the focus to include topographical features of the landscape as well as architectural spaces. With the exception of Moxnes, however, none of these authors address the critical study of space at all. They focus, rather, on theological and historical issues pertaining to space. These issues, while certainly not irrelevant to the understanding of space in an ancient text, do not tell the complete story. Ancient people did not understand geography in the same manner as modern people.[169] None of these studies have addressed the question of ancient perceptions of space. Theirs was a world spatially perceived in a much different manner from that in which geographers and cartographers today perceive space. None of the studies surveyed use comparative information from ancient authors. There is no consultation of Strabo, Pausanias, or any other ancient geographer or historiographer.

This study is an inquiry into ancient perceptions of space and place and how they underlie much of Mark's gospel. Rather than apply theological, psychological or structural readings to space in Mark, the present study will attempt to understand the social nature of space in antiquity, addressing questions related to power and its dissemination in space as well as to how Mark understands, accepts and subverts claims made by others to the space in which Jesus lived. Chapter two focuses on a discussion of modern theories concerning the use and organization of space. Chapter 3 details ancient understandings of place and how these are related to social definitions in antiquity. This chapter is followed by a chapter addressing various spaces in antiquity, analyzed using information highlighted in chapters two and three. Finally, all of this information will be used to understand more fully Mark's perspective on and understanding of the spaces of ancient Galilee and Judea.

---

169. Chapman, "Locating the Gospel," attempted to address this issue, but even he does not use information from ancient Greek, Roman, and Jewish authors about space and geography.

CHAPTER 2

Critical Spatial Theory

Social Theory, History, and Social-Scientific Models

UNDERSTANDING A CULTURE FUNDAMENTALLY different from one's own is an enormously difficult undertaking even under the best of circumstances. It involves understanding a different set of symboled communications, including speech, gestures, movements, mannerisms and many other aspects of interpersonal behavior. Ethnographers often spend much of their lives attempting to understand, as fully as possible, one other modern culture. They are able to immerse themselves in other cultural contexts through field studies, living among the people that they study. Historians, including biblical scholars, who seek to understand ancient cultures, are unable to do this direct fieldwork. They must reconstruct, through the use of textual and archaeological information, much of the world about which they speak. The daily life of a person in ancient Palestine (whether an elite or not) is in most respects now completely lost to those who would seek to understand that person. It is no longer possible to access this world except through limited written and material remains.

Problems arise in the interpretation of the data that remain from the ancient world in several ways. The first of these is that human perception is limited and highly selective. Human beings interpret as they perceive.[1] John Foster makes the case for a "representative theory" of perception that makes two major claims. The first of these is "that the physical world is something whose existence is logically independent of the human mind, and something which is, in its basic character, metaphysically fundamen-

---

1. See Foster, *The Nature of Perception*.

tal."² This concrete and independent physical reality, however, "is, in all cases, psychologically mediated."³ According to this theory of perception, there is no "unmediated" access to the physical world through the senses. Humans are conditioned both physically (insofar as they have five senses) and socially (insofar as they are trained to understand that certain phenomena bear certain meanings in certain contexts) to perceive "important" details. This means that one is more likely to note details that are "significant" to the "meaning" of an event (or text), while ignoring or giving less weight to other elements of that same event. One implicitly makes these judgments (whether consciously or unconsciously) all the time. Gould and White have demonstrated that such judgments affect how people perceive places and spaces.⁴ They argue that people have mental images of places that may or may not correspond clearly to any physical reality, and that these mental images are formed on the basis of filtered flows of information. People understand places according to these notions whether or not they correspond to the actual physical place.

A second problem that arises in the interpretation of information from the ancient world is that of anachronism. Without understanding the cultural distance between the interpreter and the text (or culture) that one interprets, it is difficult to recognize fully one's own biases in approaching a text. Scholars must necessarily fill in information in order to make sense of a text. "Interpretation is in fact supplying what is lacking in a text so that the text might mean something."⁵ Authors do not clearly spell out all of the agreed upon social conventions of their societies in their writings. They "rely upon the commonsense, socially maintained understandings that they share with their audiences."⁶ These commonsense elements, however, are known to audiences in the same social or cultural environment and not immediately available to those outside that specific social or cultural environment. Anachronism can result from the fact that the text, removed from its "full set of signifieds that constituted the social system of the first audiences" is now "free to be attached to whatever a reader seeks to attach them to."⁷ Without a proper understanding of the text's

2. Ibid., 196.
3. Ibid.
4. Gould and White, *Mental Maps*.
5. Malina, "Interpretation," 254.
6. Ibid.
7. Ibid., 255.

original social context, then, readers are inclined to apply "commonsense" notions from their own culture to information from another culture. This approach constitutes a problem if one aims to understand the significance of an ancient text (its meaning) to its original audience that would not share the modern interpreter's "commonsense" understandings.[8]

Social Systems and the Use of Models

Social theory calls attention to the both the temporal and cultural gap between modern and ancient cultures. While historians have sometimes been reluctant to make use of the work of social theorists, the aims and methods of historical study and the social sciences are not necessarily contradictory.[9] Social theory focuses on the generic elements of a human society and examines its organization and development, while history focuses on multiple societies "placing the emphasis on the differences between them and also on the changes which have taken place in each one over time."[10] In other words, social scientists focus on patterns of social activity and their relations to the structure of society, while historians focus on individual peoples, movements and structures to understand the unique elements of a given society. This fact leads social scientists generally to look for continuous elements in a society while historians generally look for that which is discontinuous.

No society can be examined in complete isolation. Burke calls attention to a number of procedures by which one might analyze a historical society.[11] The first and most basic of these procedures is simple comparison. Comparison involves taking elements from different areas and/or historical periods and analyzing them to see what is common and what is different. Comparison allows one to see what is part of a given society (or element of society) and "what is not there, in other words to understand the significance of particular absences."[12] The use of comparison, however, contains several pitfalls that one must avoid. Three major problems involve

---

8. On this point, see Geertz, *Interpretation of Cultures*.

9. On the relationship between social theory and history see Burke, *History and Social Theory*, 1–21.

10. Ibid., 2.

11. Ibid., 22–43; Burke discusses comparison, models (and types), quantitative analysis and microhistorical studies.

12. Ibid., 23.

the acceptance of the "evolutionary model" of social development, ethnocentric assumptions about other societies and the more basic problem of what elements of one society to compare with what elements of another society.[13] The "evolutionary model" of social development assumes that societies always evolve from less complex to more complex structures. This idea does not always hold true. Societies may, in fact, devolve, as was the case in the fall of the Roman Empire.

The second problem is related to the first in some ways. Ethnocentrism sees "the West as a norm from which other cultures diverge."[14] This ethnocentric perspective leads scholars to judge ancient or less "advanced" societies as inferior to modern European and North American societies. The third problem, determining which elements to compare, can lead to superficial comparisons. Some have tried to overcome this problem by seeking functional equivalents. This process involves comparing two social institutions that function in the same manner in different societies. To designate one society's institutions as functionally equivalent to another society's institutions "leads toward the comparisons between whole societies,"[15] a task for which simple comparison is not adequate. Models are better tools for this more advanced comparison.

Models operate to reduce the number of variables in a given study. Burke defines a model as "an intellectual construct which simplifies reality in order to understand it."[16] Lefebvre refers to such an approach as "reduction."[17] "Reduction is a scientific procedure designed to deal with the complexity and chaos of brute observations."[18] Reduction allows one to focus on certain elements of any given system, bracketing them to analyze their effect on other items within the system.[19] Social and natural scientists use such procedures in their everyday work in order to seek connections that are sometimes hidden by the multiplicity of "brute observations." This type of reduction is "necessary at first, but it must be quickly followed by the gradual restoration of what has thus been temporarily set aside for the

13. Ibid., 25–27.
14. Ibid., 26.
15. Ibid., 27.
16. Ibid., 28.
17. Lefebvre, *Production of Space*, 105–8.
18. Ibid., 105.
19. Burke, *History and Social Theory*, likens a model to a map.

sake of analysis."²⁰ If the other elements of a system are not restored after having been bracketed out, "the legitimate operation of reduction may be transformed into the abuse of *reductionism*."²¹ This reductionism amounts to a replacing of the fullness of the social system with an abstracted model. This danger always lies under the surface for those who use social-scientific models. Models are useful in that they help control the number of variables under consideration, but they are only an approximation of some aspects of a social system and cannot be substituted for the system itself.

The use of models can help to make clear the things assumed in approaching a particular cultural or social configuration and its interpretation. These models may be fully and consciously articulated, or they may lie below the surface of one's interpretation of a cultural event, production or pattern. It is always the case, however, that such models inform one's interpretation of events. "The hard fact is that we do not have the choice of whether we will use models or not. Our choice, rather, lies in deciding whether to use them consciously or unconsciously."²² Burke raises this point in his discussion of conspicuous consumption, symbolic capital, and reciprocity. He points out that a number of historians have dealt with ancient economies as if they are subject to Smith's classical laws of economics. These laws are based largely upon the idea that societies try to maximize production while limiting costs. This assumption, however, is contradicted in a number of societies in which symbolic capital such as honor or power is more valued than economic capital.²³ The issue, then, is that without an alternative model, scholars often import the basic "commonsense" assumptions of their own societies into those of different societies. Models help call attention to the differences in these "commonsense" assumptions between one society and another.

There are critics of a model-based approach.²⁴ There are three major issues to be addressed here:

---

20. Lefebvre, *Production of Space*, 105.

21. Ibid., 105–6.

22. Carney, *Shape of the Past*, 5. On these points in relation to biblical studies, see especially, Rohrbaugh, "Models and Muddles," 23–33.

23. Burke, *History and Social Theory*, 67–71. Here Burke suggests that of three basic types of economic systems, the market system, reciprocity and redistribution, "only one of them, the market system, is subject to the laws of classical economics" (70).

24. See Carney, *Shape of the Past*, 34–38.

- human agency and social change
- the proper use of models in research, and
- how social scientists and those who use social-scientific methods select their models.

The first issue has to do with the relationship between history and the use of social theory in general. Historians are often troubled by the fact that social theory frequently accounts neither for change nor human agency in a given society.[25] This argument basically involves the idea that "social construction is a human construction, and *only* a human construction, even if it may sometimes appear, to certain groups, as an unquestionable 'given.'"[26] It is certainly true that social theory, particularly functionalist and structuralist theory, stresses the order of the social world in such a way that it seems to take on an objective existence. The institutions of societies are then supposed to have an enduring position that is thought to "maintain the whole."[27] Horrell asserts that such models

> are based on a philosophy of human action that regards such behavior as predictable and regular, presentable in generalized and typical patterns that occur cross-culturally, and that might, albeit tentatively, enable the formulation of (social) laws, or at least generalizations, concerning human behaviour.[28]

Human agency can be ignored or significantly underappreciated in such theoretical systems. This criticism is significant and is a helpful reminder that social systems cannot be reified. While it is certainly true that humans can act in ways contrary to the socially constructed society, it remains the case that they more often act in ways that support the socially constructed society. Americans, for example, drive almost exclusively on the right side of the road. They are free to do otherwise, but social constructions prevent them from doing so in most cases.[29] That there are laws enforcing this social custom is in many ways irrelevant. Laws support many social customs. Esler responds to Horrell's criticism at this point by

---

25. Burke, *History and Social Theory*, 104–14. On this point see also Horrell, "Models and Methods," 94–99.

26. Horrell, "Models and Methods," 95.

27. Burke, *History and Social Theory*, 105.

28. Horrell, "Models and Methods," 86.

29. The arbitrary nature of this particular social custom is demonstrated by the fact that in the United Kingdom, drivers use the left side of the road.

asserting that his "belief is not based upon 'a philosophy of human action'" but rather his "observation that this is the way all human beings operate."³⁰ Esler argues that human behavior within particular settings is largely predictable, but such predictability does not rise to the level of social law.³¹

The second issue treats the proper use of models. Horrell argues that anthropologists have moved away from the idea of model-building and the objective results it suggests to the more "humanistic task of *interpreting*."³² They use deep immersion in native cultures and try to "listen" to the other. The use of models can prejudice the case from the beginning. Horrell suggests that models should be a result of research undertaken and not the thing that guides the research. "The problem with starting with a model is that—despite Esler's protestations—it can lead the researcher to view the evidence in a particular way, or to assume that a certain pattern of conduct must be present."³³ This critique is certainly substantive. There are, however, a few points to be made that mitigate its force somewhat. The first point is that Horrell himself suggests that while models are "generally formulated as a *result* of empirical research" they "serve to simplify, abstract or generalize the findings, such that they can be further tested elsewhere."³⁴ Biblical scholars who use social-scientific models are really actually engaged in this testing process. They are not themselves developing the models they use (any more than those who make use of social theory in other ways are producing the social theory themselves). This point, in part, answers the criticism of starting with a model. Secondly, the criticism works just as nicely without the use of a model. One's social background and interpretive context lead one to view information in a particular way or to assume that some behaviors would occur necessarily following on other behaviors even without using a specific model. Models

---

30. Esler, "Models in New Testament Interpretation," 110.

31. Ibid., 110–11. Esler goes even further on this point. "By and large, we write our lives in the cultural script given to us by the particular culture to which we belong. Even notable divergences, like those of ancient Cynics or modern hippies, are only comprehensible within the prevailing cultural framework" (111). See also the discussion in Sack, *Place, Modernity*, 56–62.

32. Horrell, "Models and Methods," 89.

33. Ibid., 90–91.

34. Ibid., 86.

are no more likely *a priori* to do that than the limited understanding of humanity in general.[35]

The final issue in dealing with the problem of using models, then, is how to best select models. The choice of a model can be problematic insofar as "model-building is a subjective activity fraught with many of the same difficulties inherent in the impressionistic/intuitive approach."[36] This problem can be overcome through testing a model's "goodness of fit" in a specific case.[37] A model ideally "specifies what parts of the data are being considered, from what aspects, and at what costs . . . Their explicitness, in fact, makes it possible to select a model to suit both the available data and the desired approach of pay-off."[38] The general principle is that one selects those models that are based on the closest societal analogues to the culture (or period) one is studying. For biblical scholars, then, the period and culture are those of ancient Palestine. An exact analogue for that particular cultural configuration does not exist. Ethnographers, further, are unable to immerse themselves into that culture, since it no longer exists. It is for this reason that Esler believes Geertz's notion of "thick description" is impractical for studying ancient texts.[39]

Biblical scholars have most often tended to adopt models developed from modern circum-Mediterranean societies. These models are adopted with the idea that they are closer analogues to ancient Palestine than models derived in studying modern Western cultures.[40] Models may have different levels of abstraction. The level of abstraction influences to what extent details of a particular historical setting are blurred. "The higher the level of abstraction, the more the specific details of a historical situation tend to lose their focus. The lower the level of abstraction, the more important such particularities become."[41] Circum-Mediterranean models operate at a very high level of abstraction. It is possible to study local variations in such models as honor/shame profitably. Honor is not everywhere the same and

---

35. Ibid., 87 concedes this very point when he says that "all our attempts to write history, ethnography, social science or whatever are perspectival, biased, creative constructions . . ."

36. Rohrbaugh, "Models and Muddles," 23.

37. Carney, *Shape of the Past*, 11–13.

38. Ibid., 12.

39. Esler, "Models in New Testament," 107–8.

40. For a good introduction to this approach, see Elliot, *What is Social-Scientific Criticism?*

41. Rohrbaugh, "Models and Muddles," 25.

the means of obtaining it vary from place to place. Again here, however, it is significant to note that the textual remains from the ancient world do not allow us much access to comparative material by which to discover these regional variations.

The use of models, then, is not undertaken without problems, but it is a justifiable and indeed useful corrective to the use of modern "commonsense" evaluations of ancient texts. Social theory and modeling allow scholars to understand the cultural distance between themselves and the interpreted texts. Social theory, however, must be combined with historical approaches in order to derive a full picture. Burke says that the "variety of human experience and institutions which theories inevitably simplify" suggests "that theory can never be 'applied' to the past."[42] The role of theory, rather, "is to suggest new questions for historians to ask about 'their' period, or new answers to familiar questions."[43]

Models in Geography

Before moving on it is necessary to note that there is an ongoing discussion in the field of geography about the appropriate use of models. This dispute is largely represented in the sub-disciplines of historical and social geography. Historical geography tends to focus on one historical setting and attend to its particular details. Social geography, on the other hand, tends to use theoretical approaches that take into account comparative data.

> Clearly these can be conceived as forming a continuum, and thus they need not in principle represent very different approaches. History and historical geography can use social theories and help reformulate them, and social theories can be made more precise and pertinent under the scrutiny of historians. Yet in practice—due perhaps to professional preferences in research, to styles of analysis, to the gap between fact and theory—the continuum has been a bit thin in the middle. Historians and historical geographers often criticize systematic social-science models as a-historical and claim that when the models are tested on the past, we learn very little about the period because these over-generalized models, rather than the historical contexts, select the facts to be explained. Social geographers and social scientists counter that many histori-

---

42. Burke, *History and Social Theory*, 164.
43. Ibid., 165.

cal geographers and historians are too unwilling to generalize and to accept the fact that even detailed descriptions must be based on generalizations about behavior and about the past. And of course, when one tries to bridge these differences by practicing in the middle of the continuum, one runs the risk of not satisfying either end.[44]

The issue in geography, then, between the use of a historical method and a method based on social theory is the same as the dispute between social scientists and historians in general. Sack asserts, as does Burke, that these two approaches need not be antithetical. Whether it is legitimate to use social-scientific models in historical research is the major question. The arguments above have demonstrated that it is, in fact, legitimate to use social-scientific models for understanding historical texts and societies provided one is aware of the problems associated with such an enterprise.[45] Since human behavior is largely regular and (somewhat) predictable, the present study is more inclined to the concerns of social geography. Insofar as the major text under consideration (the Gospel of Mark) is a historical document, however, this study attempts to operate as near as possible to the middle of the continuum described by Sack.

SPACE AND TIME

"Space and time are basic categories of human existence."[46] Indeed humans experience things only in space and time. Without an existence in either space or time (or both), perception of an object is virtually inconceivable.[47] Kant calls these two elements the "two pure forms of sensible intuition, serving as principles of *a priori* knowledge."[48] Space and time are complicated subjects of inquiry in science and philosophy, but are rarely acknowledged as such in everyday uses of these concepts; "we rarely debate their meanings; we tend to take them for granted and give them common-sense or self-evident attributions."[49] The lack of critical examination

---

44. Sack, *Human Territoriality*, 3.

45. This is not in any way to state that it is the only valid way to approach historical texts and societies.

46. Harvey, *Condition of Postmodernity*, 201.

47. On this point see Kant, *Critique of Pure Reason*, A21/B36–A22/B37.

48. Ibid., A22/B37.

49. Harvey, *Condition of Postmodernity*, 201.

is more substantial, however, for space than time. Casey says regarding the concept "place" that "it has been taken for granted, deemed not worthy of separate treatment."⁵⁰ Because humans move in and through space everyday, they seldom pause to reflect on the meaning or significance of that space. The present study is only indirectly concerned with the scientific or philosophic debates about place. The social element of space is of central importance here, and it is necessary to examine briefly the relationship of space to time in social theory.⁵¹

Time has been the predominant category for understanding human action in Western thought.⁵² This preoccupation with time may be due to the idea of progress that underlies much of the work in history and social sciences in the nineteenth and early twentieth centuries. This notion of progress focused the attention of historians and social scientists alike on the idea of "development." "Social theory has always focused on processes of social change, modernization, and revolution (technical, social, political). Progress is its theoretical object, and historical time its primary dimension."⁵³ Western historians and social scientists, however, have moved away from the idea that history is necessarily to be equated with progress. "The idea of progress . . . has run aground, so to speak on the shoals of the twentieth century, following the departure of the hopes or illusions that had accompanied the ocean crossing of the nineteenth."⁵⁴ The abandonment of this notion of progress in history has cleared the way for a reevaluation of space as an object of inquiry.

Foucault draws the point more sharply. He calls history the "great obsession of the nineteenth century" which "found its essential mythological resources in the second principle of thermodynamics."⁵⁵ He notes this period's "themes of development and suspension, of crisis and cycle,

---

50. Casey, *Fate of Place*, x.

51. For an excellent review of "place" in the history of philosophy see Casey, *Fate of Place*.

52. Pred, *Making Histories*, is instructive on this point. "Conventional social science texts have long been characterized by a privileging of history that either peripheralizes, subordinates, submerges, or devalues all that is spatial, or totally neglects any manifestation of humanly transformed nature and human geography, completely ignores the sit(e)-uated dimension of all social life" (6).

53. Harvey, *Condition of Postmodernity*, 205.

54. Augé, *Non-Places*, 24.

55. Foucault, "Of Other Spaces," 22.

themes of the ever-accumulating past."[56] Foucault assumed that the late twentieth century would be an "epoch of space" concerned with themes of "simultaneity," "juxtaposition," "near and far," "side-by-side," and "the dispersed."[57] Foucault overstates the case somewhat—at least in regard to social theory. Space still does not enjoy the same pride of place given to time in philosophical or social-scientific research.

Space as an interpretive category in the social sciences, then, has largely been underdeveloped due to this preoccupation with history. Space has been seen as a "neutral" backdrop in which the real action of "history" occurs.[58] Social theories, focused as they are on the notion of progress "broadly assume either the existence of some pre-existing spatial order within which temporal processes operate, or that spatial barriers have been so reduced as to render space a contingent rather than fundamental aspect to human action."[59] Space becomes the given while time is the "variable" in the equation. To put it another way, "action" takes place primarily in time and only tangentially in space.[60] Time, then, has been the predominant concern of social historians and social scientists for much of the history of these disciplines. Critical studies on spatiality are only now beginning to appear in more significant numbers.[61]

Nowhere is the privileging of time over space more apparent than in New Testament studies. The major questions surrounding historical Jesus research for much of its history have been related to Jesus and eschatology. *When* Jesus expected the kingdom of God has been the dominant question. This preoccupation with eschatology and apocalypticism has dominated the study of the Gospels as well. The relative paucity of studies addressing

---

56. Ibid.

57. Ibid.

58. On this point see especially Soja, *Postmodern Geographies*.

59. Harvey, *Condition of Postmodernity*, 205. Also Foucault, *Knowledge/Power*, 71: "Space was treated as the dead, the fixed, the undialectical, the immobile. Time, on the contrary, was richness, fecundity, life, dialectic."

60. Soja, *Postmodern Geographies*, 14. "The particular emphases may differ, but the encompassing perspective is shared. An already-made geography sets the stage, while the wilful (sic) making of history dictates the action and defines the story line."

61. See the various studies listed below and in the bibliography. Pred, *Making Histories*, 6, makes the point fully. "And yet, the prioritizing of history and the temporal is not universal. Increasingly the categories of space and time are being seen in a new light by social theorists, are no longer being unreflectingly separated from one another and social being. And, consequently, human geography has been assigned a new centrality by some."

the question of space in the Gospel of Mark attests to that fact. This fact is due in large part to the pride of place given to the historical-critical method in biblical studies.[62] The historical-critical method is structured largely to address historical questions (i.e. those relating to time). A social-scientific approach, however, can offer another starting point for examining space in the ancient world and in Mark in particular.

Theories of Space

An Inert Container for Human Action

The privileging of time over space in social theory resulted in an understanding of space as an inert container of human action. "New geography and new archaeology considered space as an abstract dimension or container in which human activities and events took place."[63] Human action left its imprint upon space, in this understanding, but was not really impacted by that space.

> Such a view of space decentred it from agency and meaning. It was something that could be objectively measured in terms of an abstracted geometry of scale. Space was quite literally a nothingness, a simple surface for action, lacking depth. This space was universal, everywhere and anywhere the same, and had cross-cultural impact on people and society . . . Space as container, surface and volume was substantial inasmuch as it existed in itself and for itself, external to and indifferent to human affairs. The neutrality of this space resulted in its being divorced from any consideration of structures of power and domination.[64]

Space, then, was a projection screen upon which the activity of history was played out. Lefebvre argued that these views of space constitute the "initial error" in thinking about space.[65]

---

62. The credibility of the historical-critical method is not in question here. It has been, is and will continue to be used to good end in biblical studies and other historical research. Other methods, however, may be used profitably to supplement and inform the historical-critical approach.

63. Tilley, *Phenomenology of Landscape*, 9.

64. Ibid.

65. Lefebvre, *Production of Space*, 94. "To picture spaces as a 'frame' into which nothing can be put unless it is smaller than the recipient, and to imagine that this container has no other purpose than to preserve what has been put in it—this is probably the initial error."

Part of the reason for this understanding of space comes from a rejection of environmental determinism. "Part of the story of the submergence of space in early twentieth-century social theory is probably related to the explicit theoretical rejection of environmental causality and all physical or external explanations of social processes and the formation of human consciousness."[66] Space, as an analytic category was subject to the same fate that befell much work done under the guise of positivism. As humanism developed and human agency was stressed, space was relegated to a subsidiary position. As a result, "critical social theory tended to project human geography on to the physical background of society, thus allowing its powerful structuring effect to be thrown away with the dirty bathwater of a rejected environmental determinism."[67] When the tenets of positivism fell, particularly its notion of direct causality, space was left off of the map of social theory.

Lefebvre argues for the predominance of space as an analytic category. He points out that time can only be apprehended through space. History is nothing more than time spatialized. "In nature, time is apprehended within space—in the very heart of space: the hour of the day, the season, the elevation of the sun above the horizon, the position of the moon and the stars in the heavens."[68] A similar point is made by Casey with respect to existence. "To exist at all as a (material or mental) object or as (an experienced or observed) event is to have a place—*to be implaced*, however minimally or imperfectly or temporarily."[69] The necessity of space as an analytic category, then, cannot be overstated.

What has been lost in viewing space as an inert container for human action, or merely as a projection screen for the important activity of history, then, is a truly social account of space. Space is a cultural element, produced by societies and replicating (though possibly occasionally subverting) those societies' power structures. A truly social account of the production of space is needed in order to reclaim space as an analytic category in social theory.

---

66. Soja, *Postmodern Geographies*, 34–35.

67. Ibid., 35. Or, as Giddens, *Giddens Reader*, 176, puts it, this "suppression of space in social theory derives . . . probably in some part from the anxiety of sociological authors to remove from their works any hint of geographical determinism."

68. Lefebvre, *Production of Space*, 95.

69. Casey, *Getting Back into Place*, 13.

Definitions

Before moving on to examine the nature of space as the result of social and cultural activity, it is necessary to define some of the key terms. Space is frequently distinguished from the concept of place. Place is a specified locale, a distinguished area. In the present context, however, space and place are thought to be synonymous when the former is "socially produced."[70] Undifferentiated space will be referred to as "natural space." This type of space would include the undeveloped areas both of the earth's surface and of the solar systems of the universe.

Socially produced space and place, as they are used here, are also similar to territory and region. A region or territory is a space defined by human intention and, as a result, distinguished from other space(s). A region or territory, however, usually involves some complex of structures, governance and relations to other regions or territories. A place or space may consist of something less than a region or territory.[71] A house, for example, is a place, but it is not a region.[72] A group of houses taken together to be a "neighborhood" could be considered a region on a small scale.

All of these concepts are related to the idea of the "built environment." The built environment "refers in the broadest sense to any physical alteration of the natural environment, from hearths to cities, through construction by humans."[73] This space is that which is in some way distinguished by human activity from the natural environment. The built environment, however, does not only include "architectural" spaces. The planting and reaping of crops, for example, alters the natural environment. Short makes the interesting point that the idea of "wilderness" only developed after agricultural practice began, because there was no difference between cultivated

---

70. Pred, *Making Histories*, uses the terms interchangeably much as they are being used here. For a brief discussion of the relation of place to space, see Sack, *Place, Modernity*, 11–16. See also Tilley, *Phenomenology of Landscape*, 14–17. There he adopts the same basic principle that is adopted here: "places *constitute* space as centres of human meaning" (14). These centers of human meaning are socially produced spaces.

71. Though Johnston, *Question of Place*, prefers the term place to territory in referring to the same entity.

72. Sack, *Place, Modernity*, 11, says of the terms area, region and place that while these "three terms are often use interchangeably . . . there is some implication about scale, with region being the largest area."

73. Lawrence and Low, "Built Environment," 454.

and uncultivated land before that.[74] In other words, without a landscape significantly altered by human activity, the concept of wilderness does not exist. It is only in its differentiation from territory marked off as "cultivated" or "domesticated" that the wilderness exists. It is an area unmarked by the normal social customs of the built environment. The built environment, then, even affects elements that are not themselves "built."[75] Even foraging and hunting communities changed the built environment any time they used natural resources for the production of shelter or developed paths on which they traveled regularly. Such spaces also include "uncovered areas in a compound, a plaza, or a street. Further they may include landmarks or *sites*, such as shrines which do not necessarily shelter or enclose activity."[76] This concept is related to the idea of landscape.

> The landscape is an anonymous sculptural form always already fashioned by human agency, never completed, and constantly being added to, and the relationship between people and it is a constant dialectic and process of structuration: the landscape is both medium *for* and outcome *of* action and previous histories of action.[77]

The landscape, rather than being a completely natural space, is influenced and determined, in part, by the social and cultural activity of humans. Prior generations have already impacted the landscape, and future generations will undoubtedly impact it further and in different ways. There are, then, "three components to the definition of a place—the physical environment, the built environment, and the people."[78]

Space as a Cultural Element

Geography is a social science. As such it is concerned with the "lived world" of humanity. Reality, for humanity, is not co-terminus with the physical world. Humans interpret their world and provide a structure of meaning to it. These "interpretations and meanings constitute" the "lived world" of humanity and "exist prior to, and independent of, any scientific

---

74. Short, *Imagined Country*, 5.
75. See the example of the nature park below.
76. Lawrence and Low, "Built Environment," 454.
77. Tilley, *Phenomenology of Landscape*, 23.
78. Johnston, *Question of Place*, 97.

explanations of them."[79] Geography, or space, comprises one part of the lived world. Understanding how humans conceive of space in a given society, then, and how that conception relates to the "natural space" of the physical world, illuminates the lived world of humans in a particular time and place.

Every society has its own way of understanding space.[80] This is due to the fact that "social practices are inherently spatial, at every scale and all sites of human behavior."[81] The relation of the built environment to nature varies from society to society. Categories such as "sacred" and "secular" or "profane" and "public" and "private" are attached to space by societies. The very idea of private space, including private property, reflects a certain understanding of space. Space is an element of culture that is negotiable in the same way as gender roles, child-rearing practices, religious customs and many other social elements.[82] Spatial practices, even when they remain the same, are under constant negotiation.

Method in the Study of Space

There are many disciplines involved in the study of space, including landscape studies, visual and cultural (including what is called "human") geography, architecture, geology, biology, anthropology, and sociology to name but a few.[83] This study is primarily interested in the cultural approach to geography, and its relation to historical geography.

> A cultural approach is principally concerned with the study of landscape as a product of those evolutionary processes by which successive communities have left an imprint, whether by design or accident, on the land they have occupied. It is the domain of archaeologists, anthropologists, sociologists, historical geographers,

79. Christensen, "Geography as a Human Science," 37.

80. Harvey, *Condition of Postmodernity*, 201–10. Lefebvre, *Production of Space*, 31, says, "every society—and hence every mode of production within its subvariants—produces a space, its own space."

81. Dear and Wolch, "How Territory Shapes Social Life," 9.

82. To be sure, not every society is as open to negotiation as the next. Many societies attempt to embed their understanding of space, like many other elements of culture, in the concept of a "natural order" to hide the fact that it is changeable.

83. Appleton, "Integrity of the Landscape," 189–99, suggests that while the convergence of so many disciplines in the "landscape movement" is in itself a positive development, this development raises methodological issues that threaten the very integrity of the movement. On fragmentation in the field of geography, see Johnston, *Question of Place*, 1–37.

and historians of various kinds (including social, economic, architectural, agrarian, and horticultural).[84]

The cultural approach, then, is concerned with how humans interact with and impact the landscapes in which they live. There is a dialectical relationship between these successive communities and the regions they inhabit. These regions themselves are the products of human design. Johnston notes three characteristics of regions that are of particular importance for a cultural understanding of space. The first of these characteristics is that the "creation of regions is a social act."[85] The social act of creating a region is deliberate. While differences between regions "may be underpinned by differences in the physical environment . . . similar physical environments can be associated with very different human responses and similar patterns of human organization can be found in very different physical milieux."[86] Humans can create very different social and spatial formations even in the same general environmental conditions. Or, conversely, they can create very similar social and spatial arrangements in very different environments. A second characteristic of regions is that they "are self-reproducing entities."[87] This fact should hardly be surprising since regions "are contexts in which people learn. They provide role models for socialization and they nurture particular belief sets and attitudes, if not values."[88] While it is not always the case, people by and large behave in ways that their cultural scripts tell them to behave. Reproduction works to reinforce spatial patterns and social practices. The spaces people occupy in their daily lives generally reinforce the patterns of spatial expression of the society. For example, people in American cities usually drive on roads and walk on sidewalks. To do otherwise would be to challenge a basic social construction of space. Every time that one drives a car on a road one is reinforcing the basic idea that roads are social spaces designed for cars and not pedestrians.[89] Johnston's third characteristic is that these "self-reproducing features of a region are not deterministic."[90] Regional social

84. Appleton, "Integrity of the Landscape," 193.
85. Johnston, *Question of Place*, 67.
86. Ibid.
87. Ibid.
88. Ibid., 67–68.
89. On the concept of reproduction, see Dear and Wolch, "How Territory Shapes," 5–6.
90. Johnston, *Question of Place*, 68.

behavior does not constitute social law, and it is never entirely predictable. Regions, then, are creations of human cultures. This fact is the basic premise of cultural approaches to landscape.

Historical geography arose within a period that was dominated by positivism and the search for laws that governed spatial relations.[91] Historical geography, however, "emerged partly in reaction to the view of geography as a spatial science."[92] As geography has become a more cross-disciplinary field, concerned with questions of culture, politics, and power, historical geography has developed along the lines of human geography.[93] Its interests have widened to include cultural systems. "Geography is becoming sensitive to culture as well as space, to the past, and to the changing spatial configuration of power."[94] Historical geography now encompasses many of the insights of cultural approaches to landscape theory.

Space as the Result of Social and Cultural Activity

Recent studies on territoriality and the production of social space have reevaluated the role of the social element and human action in space. Sack defines territoriality as a "spatial strategy to affect, influence, or control resources and people, by controlling an area."[95] It "is intimately related to how people use the land, how they organize themselves in space, and how they give meaning to place."[96] Sack understands territoriality to be culturally and socially, rather than biologically, produced. Three steps are part of the process of making a space into a territory: classification, communication, and control. One space must be differentiated from other spaces surrounding it, must be marked somehow to convey its classification, and an effort to control the territory must be made.[97]

---

91. Johnston cites positivism as one of four main approaches to geography. The elimination of metaphysics and the centrality of the verification principle are among its chief characteristics. These two elements lead to the rejection of all material that cannot be verified by an observable scientific method. The aim of the positivist approach is to create "geographic laws" in order to understand past events and predict future events.

92. Harris, "Power, Modernity," 671.

93. Indeed, Johnston notes that humanistic geography includes economic, social, political and historical geography. See Johnston, *Philosophy and Human Geography*.

94. Harris, "Power, Modernity," 671.

95. Sack, *Human Territoriality*, 1.

96. Ibid., 2.

97. Ibid., 21–22.

Tilley reaffirms the view that social space is produced. He argues that the alternative to viewing space as a container stresses that space is a medium for human action. "Space is socially produced . . . Space has no substantial essence in itself, but only has a relational significance, created through relations between peoples and places."[98] Tilley argues further that, "Space can only exist as a set of relations between things or places . . . Space is created by social relations, natural and cultural objects. It is a production, an achievement, rather than an autonomous reality in which things or people are located or 'found.'"[99]

Lefebvre argues that for a society to have its own space, several elements are necessary. The first of these elements is that "it is necessary for the society's practical capabilities and sovereign powers to have at their disposal special places: religious and political sites."[100] Some people have power to define specific places through which other spaces are defined and controlled. In the U.S., for example, local government officials establish public schools. Once an area is designated as a school, certain activities are prescribed while others are proscribed in that area and its surroundings. A tavern may not be established within a certain distance of a school. Drug and weapon charges are usually considered "aggravated" if they occur within a certain proximity to a school. Speed limits are drastically reduced around schools at certain hours of the day. A school, then, is a clear example of a site that takes a central role in defining other spaces. These sites are classified by authorities (be they informal or formal) and then become central in classifying further spaces.

Johnston refers to this classificatory process in somewhat different terms. The first criterion that he suggests is necessary for defining a region is "*the assumption of territorial awareness and shape.*"[101] A region can only exist when it has agreed upon boundaries. The creation of a region, however, "can take shape *only* after there are institutions capable of reproducing and maintaining them."[102] A region, then, becomes defined through a set of institutions that reproduce certain spatial conceptions and practices

---

98. Tilley, *Phenomenology of Landscape*, 10–11.

99. Ibid., 17.

100. Lefebvre, *Production of Space*, 34.

101. Johnston, *Question of Place*, 71.

102. Ibid. Families, governments and other institutions are responsible for establishing and maintaining schools. These schools, in turn, train children to reproduce specific values and behaviors necessary for the maintenance of the region.

and maintain its understanding to the larger public. It takes shape through a set of smaller scale spaces establishing enough coherence to reproduce a certain type of space.

When a space, territory or region is defined, it is not necessarily accepted by all members of a society or other groups outside the membership of society. Once a territory has been classified, communication of that classification is necessary. This communication can occur in any number of ways. Returning to the example of the school, school buildings are frequently labeled with their names upon the building. A fence or series of fences surrounds many schools. The streets around the schools are marked with traffic signs indicating that those streets are part of a "school zone." Locked gates prevent entry to school grounds after official school activities are completed for the day. Some schools employ security guards, closed circuit camera systems, or alarm systems to prevent unauthorized personnel from entering them. Local laws often prohibit "trespassing" on school grounds. All of these things are means of communicating the school's classification as a place of safety and learning for children.

In terms of regional development, two steps are at work here—"*the development of conceptual (symbolic) shape*" and "*the development of a sphere of institutions.*"[103] The first of these stages "promotes the inhabitants' regional consciousness,"[104] which becomes part of the region's symbolic landscape through "consciousness-creating acts such as the coining of a regional name."[105] The creation of a name or other regional symbols is part of the overt communication of the classification of the region. The "development of a sphere of institutions" helps to communicate and foster "a sense of regional membership for the inhabitants."[106]

The third stage in the production of a territory, according to Sack, is control. Control involves oversight of a territory. Sack says that a delimited space only becomes a territory "when its boundaries are used to affect behavior by controlling access."[107] It involves shaping and reshaping a space's meaning. Control suggests the ability to enforce the classification and communication of a territory. The concept of control involves power.

---

103. Ibid.
104. Ibid.
105. Ibid.
106. Ibid.
107. Sack, *Human Territoriality*, 19.

Socially produced space replicates and reproduces social power. Sack uses the example of a field to discuss control of a territory.

> A cultivated field is a place, but is it also a human construction and requires such efforts as plowing, fertilizing, and weeding to maintain it. Even more basic, such a place exists because certain decisions have been made that all else but certain specific processes and events will be excluded from that area: trees, bushes, and weeds will not be permitted there, nor will animals or even most humans. If this field were not tended, natural forces would eventually make it another kind of place entirely.[108]

A socially produced space, then, requires human social action to maintain or control it. Returning to the example of a school allows a fuller explication of this notion of control. Each classroom is a separate place. Different people or groups exercise different levels of control over the space. The school board or some other local (or sometimes state) governing board exercises control in the erection of buildings, the hiring of teachers, the limiting of class sizes, and the determination of curricula. Such a group also determines the appropriate ages or developmental levels for the students of each class. Within the classroom itself, the teacher exercises control. The teacher selects the way that he or she will present the determined curricula, often designates seating, allocates the class's resources (i.e. books and other educational materials), teaches the class and evaluates the results by assigning grades. The teacher is also responsible for giving passes that allow students to leave the classroom during the time in which they are normally expected to remain in the classroom. Within the school there are also other levels of control. The principal oversees the operation of the school. He or she is responsible for overseeing the conduct of both students and teachers, as well as other employees such as food servers, custodians, nurses, and the administrative staff. If any of these people violate the appropriate use of the place, the principal may remove them from the school (through dismissal, suspension or expulsion). He or she is also responsible for maintaining the boundaries of the school, thereby ensuring that no unauthorized personnel are found on the school grounds. He or she provides passes for visitors on school grounds to legitimate their presence there. Police also exercise control in some instances. They are responsible for ensuring that unauthorized personnel are prohibited from entering or are removed from

---

108. Sack, *Place, Modernity*, 41.

school property after hours. These principals, however, also are responsible to school boards and superintendents. Schools, at the same time they are controlled space, reproduce and maintain regions by developing students who adopt the same territorial practices as the wider region of which they are a part. Control over a socially produced space is always exercised to a greater or lesser extent. Such control need not be a negative thing. A fence around a school, for example, may prevent kids from running into a busy street. That fence involves control of territory by restricting access, in this case by preventing children from leaving a territory.

The definition of a place, then, involves these three elements of classification, communication and control. Through the study of territoriality and the use of cultural geography, it is possible to see how human societies produce bounded space. One of the major features of territory or place is "that it can be bounded, and thus readily communicated."[109] Such bounded spaces are "not simply the unintended outcomes of economic, social and political processes but are often the deliberate products of actions by those with power in society, who use space and create places in pursuit of their goals."[110] This process is the social production of space (in Lefebvre's terms) or territoriality (in Sack's terms). This social production of space is reproduced, thus providing a territory that socializes people to understand space in the way it has been defined by the culture.

How Space Replicates Power

The production of social space replicates power in a society. "The analysis of any space brings us up against the dialectical relationship between demand and command, along with its attendant questions: 'Who?', 'For whom?', 'By whose agency?', 'Why and how?'"[111] As an example of such a replication, one may consider zoning laws. Zoning laws determine what type of structures may be built and what types of activities may be pursued in certain areas. These laws are passed by local authorities (in the U.S.), but may be influenced by the constituents of those local authorities. Certain types of structures are not permitted within certain distances of one another (for instance, a school and a tavern). Certain types of structures may not be built in certain areas at all (for instance, a private house may not

109. Johnston, *Question of Place*, 189.
110. Ibid., 68.
111. Lefebvre, *Production of Space*, 116.

be built within a city park). There are also other laws that affect the use of space. Without proper documentation one may not enter the U.S. Laws concerning trespassing on private or public property restrict access to certain types of spaces. If one takes segregation in the US as an example, one can see how the social production of space works. Segregation was a strategy that separated African-Americans (variously defined) from Americans of European descent. The strategy involved the creation of spaces that were "black only" and "white only." These spaces were *classified* according to various criteria which were *communicated* (sometimes by means of signs, sometimes by means of word of mouth), and *enforced* (sometimes through arrests, sometimes through far more violent vigilante methods). Segregation was a social strategy that involved the production of social spaces that were then enforced through spatial means.

The question of whose interests are served in the production of space is often not raised. A major reason for this is the attempt to "hide" the social production involved. This is another major feature of territoriality. Along with the idea that space can be bounded and communicated, territory "can be used to displace personal relationships, between controlled and controller, by relationships between people and the 'law of the place'—territory is thereby reified in order to promote personal ambitions impersonally."[112] Instead of the social relationship being the focus of attention the rules regarding the space become paramount. This displacement of attention from the social relationship leads to an impersonal sense of control over the territory. The territory itself seems to be the entity wielding the power, and such control is frequently attributed to some "natural order." "Legal and conventional assignments of behavior to territories are so complex and yet so important and well understood in the well-socialized individual that one often takes such assignments for granted and thus territory appears as the agent doing the controlling."[113]

In other words, people act as if space controls their lives without looking past that idea in order to examine the social relations that remain latent within the social production of space. In order to understand fully the social production of space it is necessary to look past the idea that

---

112. Johnston, *Question of Place*, 189. See also Lefebvre, *Production of Space*, 32, "Symbolic representation serves to maintain these social relations in a state of coexistence and cohesion. It displays them while displacing them—and thus concealing them in symbolic fashion—with the help of, and onto the backdrop of, nature."

113. Sack, *Human Territoriality*, 33.

territory controls behavior. Social relationships control behavior, and they do so sometimes through the control of space, which is itself a social and cultural action.

When place is considered impersonal it makes territory appear neutral. It also presents opportunities for space to be "empty." Empty space is space that is not designated for a purpose by those controlling it.[114] Sack gives the example of a vacant lot. "It is empty because it is devoid of socially or economically valuable artifacts and meanings."[115] Empty spaces, then, are also defined by the social production of space, since their standing as "empty" relies on a relational definition within the social structure of a society.

Power may be spatialized in a number of ways. "In small-scale societies the major axes of spatial domination are usually organized along the axes of age, gender, kin and lineage."[116] It is probably fair to say that economic, political and military factors are major axes in modern spatial domination. Spaces may be multivalent. Different people can interpret spaces differently. Those who control space are only able in a limited way to control the meaning of that space.[117] The same space can mean two (or more) completely different things to different groups or people. One might consider here the idea of gang "turf." The gang's area (usually effectively classified, communicated, and sometimes controlled) is, to the local government officials, part of the taxable space in their districts. It is also a "crime-ridden" area necessitating the need for more police action. At the same time, the area is the space that others call home (or perhaps in which they work). The space is at one and the same time all of these things. Several different levels of power are operative here, and different means are used to enforce such power. At the level of those who call this space "home" parents may be reluctant to let their kids out to play in front of houses or on the streets for fear of harassment either by gangs or police. Parents exercise power spatially by restricting access to certain areas (outside, in the street, etc.) for their children. For those who work in such a space, it would be inconceivable for many of them to be in such a place after working hours, though they exercise power over the space

114. Sack, *Human Territoriality*, 32–34.
115. Sack, *Place, Modernity*, 42.
116. Tilley, *Phenomenology of Landscape*, 26.
117. On this point see especially Eade and Sallnow, eds., *Contesting the Sacred*.

during the days and nights by restricting access to some people (i.e. those who are not "customers") and allowing it to others (customers or clients) during business hours. The gangs themselves exercise power, patrolling the streets looking for members of other gangs who might violate their turf. The police patrol the streets looking for things that would threaten the "order" of the wishes of the local government officials. Foucault addresses the role of the government in overseeing space. In speaking of the role of the Attorney-General in Paris, he notes that this person and those who serve this office constitute "one and the same gaze" that "watches for disorder, anticipates the danger of crime, penalising every deviation. And should any part of this universal gaze chance to slacken, the collapse of the State itself would be imminent."[118] This type of vigilance may be practiced at all levels of social space. Each person or group that produces a space must control it in some way. Every deviation from the order that that group imposes upon its space threatens the very space that is socially produced.

Space as Changeable

The history of the social production of space limits the way and the extent to which social space may be produced in the present. This is not to say that a socially produced space may not be changed, but it is more difficult and requires more effort to change previously produced space. At the extreme end one might note Tilley's point that places "can never be exactly the same places twice, although there may be ideological attempts to provide 'stability' or perceptual or cognitive fixity to a place, to reproduce a set of dominant meanings, understandings, representations and images."[119] The reason that places can never be exactly the same twice is that social configurations also are never exactly the same twice. Spaces, in so far as they are produced and reproduced, however, do attain a relative fixity in the imagination. Shields notes that the "spatial is thus an area of intense cultural activity . . . the empirical datum of geographical space is mediated by an edifice of social constructions which become guides for action and constraints upon action, not just idiosyncratic or pathological fantasies."[120] Societies and cultures create "place-images" which lead to the creation of "place-myths."

118. Foucault, "Questions on Geography," 72.
119. Tilley, *Phenomenology of Landscape*, 27–28.
120. Shields, *Places on the Margin*, 30. Shields contrasts himself with geographers and

> Collectively a set of place-images forms a place-myth. Thus, there is both a constancy and a shifting quality to this model of place- or space-myths as the core images change slowly over time, are displaced by radical changes in the nature of a place, and as various images simply lose their connotative power, become 'dead metaphors', while others are invented, disseminated, and become accepted in common parlance.[121]

Place-myths sometimes change. Changes occur when the social relationships that produced or maintained the place-myth of the place change.[122] For the most part, however, these place-myths remain fairly constant over long periods of time. Shields argues further concerning the function of these space myths.

> Space myths—aligned and opposed, reinforcing or mutually contradictory—form a mythology or formation of positions which polarises and dichotomises [sic] different places and spaces. Place- and space-myths are united into a system by their relative differences from one another even while they achieve their unique identities by being 'set-off' against one another. Even if split by inconsistencies and in continual flux, this formation works as a cosmology: a more emotionally-powerful understanding of the world than that represented by rational, cartographic techniques and comparative statistics. Through these contrasts of spatialised identity, communities may distinguish themselves from other social collectivities.[123]

These place-myths create the illusion in the social production of space that spaces and places continue to be the same over long periods of time. It can happen that a place myth can change relatively rapidly (due to a natural disaster, famine, disease, war, etc.), but overall the socially and culturally shared understanding of the meaning of places remains relatively fixed generally, even though these spaces are always changing in subtle ways.

Again there is the question of human agency in the process of change. Humans do not behave according to social laws, but they do behave in

---

psychologists who "have emphasized the individual and subjective nature of spatial images and 'cognitive maps'" (29).

121. Ibid., 61.

122. The place-myths that insiders construct can be substantially different from those constructed by people outside the region or territory. On this point, see Sack, *Place, Modernity*, 11–12.

123. Shields, *Places on the Margin*, 62–63.

relatively predictable ways within social configurations. Change is possible, however, due to human agency and other factors. "Change can be brought about by . . . the need for people to respond to new stimuli (physical and/or human), contact with people from other regions, and the determined actions of individuals who wish to promote change."[124]

Spaces in Texts

Texts represent space in a slightly different way from the way space is represented in the everyday social world. In a text, space acquires a fixed meaning that does not change in the same way social or cultural space changes. A text, however, does interact with the actual space of a society insofar as the author is a product of that space. The author passes along those social codes that are embedded in space, but he or she may assume them and pass them on uncritically or critically engage them, challenging them, modifying them or rejecting them.

Representational Spaces

It is useful here to consider Lefebvre's distinction between "spatial practice," "representations of space," and "representational spaces."[125] Spatial practice is the space actually lived in by a society that attempts to secrete itself. It is perceived space.[126] Representations of space are "conceptualized space, the space of scientists, planners, urbanists, technocratic subdividers and social engineers . . . all of whom identify what is lived and what is perceived and what is conceived."[127] Representations of space tend to reproduce the social relations of spatial practice, but may sometimes offer alternatives to them. Representational space "is the dominated—and hence passively experienced—space which the imagination seeks to change and appropriate. It overlays physical space, making symbolic use of its objects."[128] Lefebvre says that "artists—painters, sculptors or architects—do not show space, they create it."[129] The same can be said for authors. Authors create space

---

124. Johnston, *Question of Place*, 68.
125. Lefebvre, *Production of Space*, 38–39.
126. Ibid., 38.
127. Ibid.
128. Ibid., 39.
129. Ibid., 124.

in that the spatial presentation of their material might either reinforce or challenge conventional notions about socially produced space. They are not, like the scientists, planners and others that Lefebvre mentions, bound by spatial practice. They do not necessarily have to mold their presentation of space to reflect the everyday lived space of their society, though this everyday space is presumed to be a general point of departure for authors.

Maps, Texts, and Space

Maps provide a clear example of representational spaces. They are selective, highlighting the interests and concerns of their producers.

> Maps cease to be understood primarily as inert records of morphological landscapes or passive reflections of the world of objects, but are regarded as refracted images contributing to the dialogue in a socially constructed world . . . Maps are never value-free images; except in the narrowest Euclidean sense they are not in themselves either true or false. Both in the selectivity of their content and in their signs and styles of representation maps are a way of conceiving, articulating, and structuring the human world which is biased towards, promoted by, and exerts influence upon particular sets of social relations.[130]

Maps are embedded in the power relations of a society of their producers. This is true since "the cartographer has never been an independent artist, craftsman, or technician. Behind the map-maker lies a set of power relations, creating its own specification."[131] Here Harley notes that maps have been used to legitimate imperial seizures of lands and even to help "create myths which would assist in the maintaining of the territorial status quo."[132] Maps are generally socially conservative documents that "tended to favour the status quo."[133] In this sense, maps take for granted the social relationships that underscore the production of space. While it is true that authors may challenge the status quo, maps rarely, if ever, do so. Maps are able to communicate by "manipulating scale, by over-enlarging or moving

---

130. Harley, "Maps, Knowledge, and Power," 278.
131. Ibid., 287.
132. Ibid., 282.
133. Ibid., 294.

signs or topography, or by using emotive colours."[134] Maps almost always represent the interests of the powerful in society.

Leyerle has shown how the understanding of space can be defined both by and within texts. The first point to note is that "the perceived world differs significantly from the so-called 'real' world."[135] In discussing the earliest texts of Christian pilgrimage, Leyerle notes how the biblical texts provided itineraries for these Christian pilgrims. The biblical text itself, however, was not always sufficient. Some of these pilgrims traveled to areas that were significant because of their (historical and cultural) designation in the biblical texts. The biblical texts themselves, however, only told part of the story of the pilgrims' routes. The ritual attention paid to sites in the period in which they traveled also helped to determine their itinerary. For instance, "the Bordeaux pilgrim didn't go to Nazareth or to the Sea of Galilee because there was nothing to be seen there."[136] For many biblical sites it was only after the conversion of Constantine and with the "rediscovery" of (especially) New Testament sites that pilgrims became interested in these sites.[137] Leyerle argues, then, that for the Bordeaux pilgrim physical locale was not important, but rather the biblical texts together with the ritual activity (i.e. the erection of shrines, monuments, churches, etc) dictated the significance of certain sites. "The importance of geographical locale is implicitly denied. In terms of terrain these holy places could be anywhere."[138] Egeria's case is somewhat different. She traveled to sites exclusively on the basis of the biblical text and "obscures the fact that no monuments, in the conventional sense of the term, punctuate the desert landscape."[139] There are monks who guide her and identify the holy sites for her. While the biblical texts classify the territories, these monks perform the communicative aspect of territoriality.[140]

134. Ibid., 287. Harley notes that Africa is consistently proportionally smaller than Europe and North America on maps with no regard for the actual physical size of these continents. See also Newstead, Reid and Sparke, "Cultural Geography of Scale," 485–497.
135. Leyerle, "Landscape as Cartography," 120.
136. Ibid., 124.
137. On this point see especially Smith, *To Take Place*, 74–95.
138. Leyerle, "Landscape as Cartography," 124.
139. Ibid., 128.
140. One might also say that they perform the "controlling" aspect insofar as they control access to the sites by guiding visitors there. Also, the identification of "biblical" sites in the ancient world was an oft-contested procedure. The monks controlled the site by

Texts, then, can control the interpretation of space. For the pilgrims, the space through which they traveled to get to the biblical sites was largely undifferentiated. It had no meaning. The meaningful sites were those where biblical events occurred, according to their guides.[141] The texts produced by Egeria and the Bourdeaux pilgrim also became texts that influenced the social definition of the Holy Land for their readers. Texts, like maps, produce a textual space that replicates social and cultural (and therefore also power) relations. Unlike maps, texts may either support or challenge the status quo. They may offer alternative definitions of space that subvert or challenge the dominant definitions.

Texts, then, produce their own type of social space. Lefebvre calls attention to this type as "representational space." These spaces, since they are abstract, "need obey no rules of consistency."[142] Though they are "redolent with imaginary and symbolic elements," however, "they have their source in history."[143] It is significant to understand these representational spaces within a triad including spatial practice and representations of spaces. The representational spaces, however, are the most useful for thinking about the Gospel of Mark insofar as it is a text that creates its own abstract world.[144]

Conclusion

Social-scientific research has produced numerous insights into biblical texts. While there is still some concern over how best to use social theory in examining biblical texts, its use is now considered justified (in most cases). The use of models offers a way to isolate and to control some variables in a given study. Though there are pitfalls involving the use of models, such an approach can yield both new questions and new results for biblical studies.

Interpretation of space through methods of geography and landscape studies have multiplied in the last twenty years. While once subordinate to time as an interpretive category, space and place are now treated as objects

---

"ensuring" its validity as the "true" site.

141. Many of these sites were contested during the fourth century.

142. Lefebvre, *Production of Space*, 41.

143. Ibid.

144. The relationship of this abstract world to the actual physical and socially produced space of first century Palestine will be examined in chapter five.

worthy of their own investigation both in philosophical and social-scientific circles. The study of space has provided important insights into the formation of societies and cultures. Scholars inquiring about the nature of socially produced space and territoriality have clearly spelled out the reciprocal relationship between the maintenance of a society and its spatial configurations.

That space is socially produced is now a commonplace among cultural geographers and landscape theorists. Space is among the "webs of significance" that constitute culture. The shift from understanding space as a causative element subject to certain laws (i.e. in positivism) to a social space that is deeply embedded in the place-myths of cultures is by now a fait accompli in studies of space. Texts interact with this cultural and social notion of the social significance of space, sometimes affirming and sometimes undermining other understandings of space. They represent a static picture of socially produced spaces that give an apparent fixity of meaning to that space when, in fact, the meaning of any given socially produced space is not permanent, but is always subject to change and negotiation.

Greek and Roman authors brought their own spatial conceptions to writing texts. The next two chapters will examine some of the spatial practices and conceptions of Greek, Roman and early Jewish cultures and texts in order to note patterns of spatial understandings that will be useful for understanding the Gospel of Mark. By defining themselves as the center of spatial conceptions of the world, the Greeks and then the Romans privileged their own spatial practices and judged all other civilizations by how their practices mimicked or differed from Greek and Roman practices.

CHAPTER 3

Space in Ancient Texts

Defining the *Oikoumenē*

PRIOR STUDIES OF MARK'S space have not addressed the wider question of how ancient Greeks, Romans and Jews perceived the space in which they lived. The concern of the present chapter, then, is to develop an understanding of the way that these ancient peoples thought about the spatial elements of the world in which they lived. The primary focus in this chapter will be on the space of the *oikoumenē* (οἰκουμένη), that is, the inhabited world, and the discussion of the elements surrounding it. These ancient peoples believed that the territorial region in which one lived defined their essence—their personality, their appearance, their constitution, and their modes of community living. All of these elements of a peoples' makeup were determined by their geographical locale.

The Greeks and Romans were especially interested in the concept of the οἰκουμένη [γῆ], literally the "inhabited world," in their discussions of space.[1] The Greeks and Romans used this term to refer to the extent of land in which it was possible (according to their knowledge and understanding), due to climatic conditions, for people to live. Outside of the *oikoumenē*, activity leading to the generation and maintenance of human life was not possible, primarily due to excessive cold or heat.[2]

---

1. Though it it is sometimes translated as "known world," the term *oikoumenē* literally refers only to the part of the world in which people dwell. Strabo means only these inhabited regions to be included in the *oikoumenē*. See Pothecary, "Strabo and the Inhabited World," 10–11, 51–52.

2. See the discussion below. The existence of other oikoumenai remained a possibility for Strabo (and others), but these other oikoumenai were cut off from interaction with the *oikoumenē* of the Greeks and Romans. See ibid., 54–55, 243–44.

Scientific/Geometric Space and Geographical Tradition

The Greeks were among the first civilizations to conceive of geography in scientific terms.[3] This type of geography seems to have begun with Eratosthenes in Alexandria, though to be sure he drew on some earlier sources.[4] It is with Eratosthenes (in the third century BCE) that this development began in earnest. Burnbury says that during Eratosthenes' direction of the Alexandrian library, "geography first began to assume something of a regular and systematic character; and to be based, however imperfectly, upon fixed scientific principles."[5] It is this systematic character and these "scientific" principles, including the use of astronomy, that marked the beginnings of scientific geography.

Scientific geography in the ancient world consisted of discussions about the shape of the earth and (sometimes) the cosmos, the extent of the known world, some major topographical features and the distance of the length and width of the entire world.[6] By the time of Eratosthenes, the earth was widely thought to be spherical, and most philosophical movements consider the earth to be the center of the universe.[7] Eratosthenes "measured" the earth's circumference as 250,000 stadia.[8] The primary concern of scientific geography, then, was measurements and distances, with much of its information derived from astronomy. While these things

---

3. A purely "scientific" understanding of geography in the ancient Greek or Roman world did not exist. A "scientific" geography in the sense of a work unencumbered by the preconceptions of the geographer is not possible now any more than it was in the Greek or Roman world. It is only because, particularly in the 19th and early 20th centuries, geography was conceived of as a bare description of the land that produced a picture of what actually was, that analysts of ancient geography have tended to focus on these scientific details to the exclusion of others.

4. Burnbury, *History of Ancient Geography*, 1.615, "It is to the Alexandrian school that we are indebted for the first steps in this direction; and Eratosthenes, who presided over that school during the space of more than forty years, may be regarded as the parent of scientific geography."

5. Ibid., 1.615.

6. On the idea of space in an abstract sense in the Greek world see Algra, *Concepts of Space in Greek Thought*; and Sambursky, *The Concept of Place in Late Neoplatinism*.

7. See Aristotle *Cael.* 2.13–14. The Pythagoreans are the one school of contrary opinion. They believed, according to Aristotle, that fire was the element in the center of the universe.

8. For other measurements of the earth's circumference, see Burnbury, *History of Ancient Geography*, 1.620–25.

concern all ancient geographers to some extent, there are some notable attempts to limit geography to only this type of information.

Agathemerus's *Sketch of Geography*

An account of a scientific type is found in Agathemerus's *Sketch of Geography*.[9] This text sets out the various distances that the continents cover and attempts to summarize prior geographic thought. The text begins by relating the prior attempts to map the earth, such as those by Anaximander and Hecataeus, whom Agathemerus calls a "widely traveled man" (1.1).[10] The text next describes the various winds that blow upon the earth and relates that Timosthenes, "who wrote the circumnavigations . . . says nations dwell on the borders (τὰ πέρατα) of the earth" (2.7).

After giving the measurement of various sections of the earth in chapters three and four, Agathemerus sets out to "give the perimeters of the islands of our earth" (5.20). He says that the Ocean is so named because it quickly encircles the earth (ὠκεανὸς δὲ διὰ τὸ ὠκέως ἀνύειν κύκλῳ τὴν γῆν, 1.4). Agathemerus shows considerable interest in what prior geographers said concerning the shape of the earth. He notes that the ancient Greeks thought the earth was round with Delphi as its navel (ὀμφαλός). Democritus held the length to be half again as much as the width (ἡ γῆ ἡμιόλιον τὸ μῆκος τοῦ πλάτους ἔχουσα) and was followed by the Peripatetic Dicaearchus. Eudoxos argued that the length was twice as much as the width, Eratosthenes that the ratio was even greater, while Crates thought the earth to be a semi-circle and Hipparchus a trapezoid (1.2). This text contains sustained discussion on the earth's measurement, the size and shape of the *oikoumenē* and an interest in maps and astronomy.

---

9. For an introduction, text, translation and brief commentary see Diller, "Agathemerus, '*Sketch of Geography*.'" Its likely date is the first or second century CE.

10. The text's divisions are those found in Diller's translation. The Greek phrase used here is ἀνηρ πολυπλανὴς, calling to mind the traveller *par excellence*, Odysseus. Seeing for oneself through travel was considered a reliable, indeed the most reliable, source of information about far off places in both geographical and historical traditions. See, for example, Diodorus Siculus 1.1.2 who also cites *Od.* 1.3 as a paradigm of information gathering. He contrasts the reading of universal histories with actual travel and says: "the understanding of the failures and successes of other men, which is acquired by the study of history, affords a schooling that is free from the experience of actual ills" (1.1.2).

Ptolemy's *Geography*

This more scientific approach to geography culminated, in the Greek tradition, with Ptolemy, in the middle of the second century CE.[11] Romm suggests that Ptolemy's *Geography* was the first to approach our modern way of perceiving geography.

> Earlier geographers, such as Hecataeus, Herodotus, and Strabo, went about their task chiefly by way of narratives: They sifted through a vast storehouse of traveler's tales in order to separate fact from fiction, then retold those which they thought credible enough to claim a reader's attention. More important, they often retold even those they deemed incredible—revealing that the geographer's science and storyteller's art, in many periods of antiquity, could not be fully detached from each other.[12]

Ptolemy seeks to remove elements of the fantastic as well as ethnographic information regarding the specific peoples that inhabited various regions. He is primarily interested in the shape, the size, and the general topographic features of the *oikoumenē*. Ptolemy specifically rejects as part of his *Geography* the idea of describing the peculiarities and novelties of the inhabitants of various regions of the known world. "We shall expand our 'guide' for so far as this is useful for the knowledge of the location of places and their setting upon the map, but we shall leave out of consideration all the many details about the peculiarity of the peoples" (*Geogr.* 2.7)[13] He sets out to construct a map of the world that would locate individual places according to their longitude and latitude based on astronomy.[14]

> Our present object is to map our *oikemenē* as far as possible in proportion with the real [*oikemenē*]. But at the outset we think it is necessary to state clearly that the first step in a proceeding of this kind is systematic research, assembling the maximum of knowledge from the reports of people with scientific training who have toured the individual countries; and that the inquiry and reporting is partly a matter of surveying, and partly a matter of astronomical observation. The surveying component is that which indicates the relative positions of localities solely through measurement of distances; the astronomical component [is that which does

---

11. van Paassen, *Classical Tradition*, 1–3.
12. Romm, *Edges of the Earth*, 5.
13. Quoted in van Paassen, *Classical Tradition*, 2.
14. Burnbury, *History of Ancient Geography*, 2.548–50.

the same] by means of phenomena [obtained] from astronomical sighting and shadow casting instruments. Astronomical observation is a self-sufficient thing and less subject to error, while surveying is cruder and incomplete without [astronomical observation]. (*Geogr.* 1.2)[15]

Ptolemy sets out to base his mapping project solely on "surveying" and "astronomical observation." He prefers astronomical measurements where they were available, since "surveying is cruder and incomplete." The kind of astronomical information that Ptolemy intended to use was certainly more available in the second century CE than it had been to authors like Homer and Herodotus. Ptolemy, however, did not have access to enough of the kind of astronomical detail that was necessary for such a map to be produced. "Unfortunately, the number of such observations at his command was so small that it would have been utterly impossible to construct a map based on these materials."[16] Ptolemy's casting of his positions in scientific terms concealed "the fact that they were in reality nothing more than the approximate results arrived at by a comparison of authorities, of distances given by itineraries, of the reports of voyagers, and other such materials."[17] Nevertheless, he is far more interested in a scientific description of geographical features, such as measurements and the shape of the *oikoumenē*, than in a description of the inhabitants and the wonders relating to the places that he describes. Ptolemy is perhaps the most scientifically oriented among the ancient Greek and Roman geographers.[18]

---

15. Quoted in Berggren and Jones, *Ptolemy's Geography*, 59.

16. Burnbury, *History of Ancient Geography*, 2.549.

17. Ibid., 2.551. Burnbury goes further to note that these "approximate results" were "corrected frequently in a very summary and arbitrary manner to suit with his own preconceived opinions."

18. See, however, ibid., 2.551. Burnbury goes much further in his critique of those who anoint Ptolemy as a "scientific geographer" on a par with what is considered scientific geography in the modern world. "The blind, almost superstitious, reverence, with which Ptolemy was regarded throughout the Middle Ages, has descended in some degree to our own days' and it is not uncommon to find writers referring to his statements, as if his *apparently* definite and scientific results must necessarily be based upon definite information and scientific calculation" (ibid., 2.553).

Scientific Geography in Early Judaism

Early Jewish geographic descriptions of the *oikoumenē*, with some variations, are very similar to those of the Greeks and Romans.[19] There are no texts in early Jewish tradition (or Israelite tradition) that correspond to the scientific geography outlined above. There is no Jewish text in this period to which the title *Geography* is ascribed. Neither is there a text that gives the dimensions of the entire earth's surface, nor a text that gives the dimensions of the *oikoumenē*. That is not to say that the Israelites and early Jews were not interested in geographical matters. Indeed, quite the opposite is the case. Much of their geographical information (particularly by the Hasmonean period), including the idea of the shape of the world, is simply taken over from Greek and Ionic geography.

A Purely Scientific Geography?

Although there is evidence among many ancient Greek geographers of a concern with scientific geography, there is far more interest in what might be termed "human or cultural geography." Even though Ptolemy, in his *Geography*, was unconcerned about the ethnic characteristics of peoples, there remains in other of his works a clear indication of a more social concern. Additionally, though the purpose of Ptolemy's *Geography* was the establishment of a cartographic description of the entire known world on the basis of astronomical and mathematical information, the prerequisites for such an undertaking involved "assembling the maximum of knowledge from the reports of people with scientific training who have toured the individual countries" (*Geogr.* 1.2).[20] While Ptolemy is specifically interested in measurements and astronomical detail that these scientifically minded people might provide, he is dependant for his information on the same travelers' reports that the other ancient geographers use. These traveler's reports were full of details about peoples and the social significance which they bestowed upon certain geographic features. Also, Ptolemy's limiting his description to the size and shape of the *oikoumenē* reflects his interest in only those areas inhabited by humans. Furthermore, despite stating his

---

19. On the whole question of Jewish geography in this period see Scott, *Geography in Early Judaism and Christianity*.
20. Quoted in Berggren and Jones, *Ptolemy's Geography*, 59.

intentions to the contrary, Ptolemy did in fact show interest in human geography.

> Even the work of the "scientific" geographer par excellence, Claudius Ptolemaeus, reveals concern with what might be termed "ethnography." His latitudinal and longitudinal divisions of the earth were ethnographically characterized. His description of Taprobane and eastern India included the ethnographical notes on the size and appearance of the inhabitants, and the treatment of India provided details of some of the minerals and other natural resources, such as diamonds and beryls (*Geog.* 7.4). The Fish-Eaters of Agatharchides and of Nearchus appear in Ptolemaeus' descriptions of the west coast of Libya and of southern India.[21]

Describing the peculiarities of the inhabitants of various regions certainly fits under the heading of human geography. Ptolemy's text indicates an interest in the inhabitants of regions that marks human geography even within the most "scientific" geography of the Roman world.[22] This fact leads Clarke to question the neatness with which a distinction can be made between scientific and human geography in the ancient world. Both types of geographer were interested in both types of information to greater or lesser degrees. "It is clear both that so-called 'human geographers', the authors of periplus texts, were interested in scientific observations, and that 'theoretical' geographers relied on the reports of sailors, as well as taking an interest in ethnography."[23] Even the most notable of the scientific geographers, Eratosthenes and Ptolemy, make use of information gathered from sources whose primary interest is in human geography.[24] Characterizing ancient geographers, then, should be conceived more in terms of a sliding scale than an absolute categorization.

---

21. Clarke, *Between Geography and History*, 141–42.

22. As van Paasen notes, "There is indeed a remarkable contrast between the scientific way in which Ptolemy goes to work when he restricts himself to his proper aim, and the naïve uncritical way in which, sporadically it is true, curiosities found in tales of travel are taken over" (*Classical Tradition*, 2).

23. Clarke, *Between Geography and History*, 142.

24. See the discussion in ibid., 141–44.

The Shape and Extent of the Oikoumenē

The shape and extent of the *oikoumenē* was a matter of speculation among the Greek and Roman geographers.[25] The earliest geographers, including Hecataeus of Miletus, envisioned the *oikoumenē* as a circular landmass encircled by Oceanus. The entire idea of a circular land mass surrounded by Oceanus seems to have derived from Homer.[26] Herodotus was among those who rejected the concept of Oceanus encircling the entire *oikoumenē*. "I do not know of the existence of any River Ocean, and I think that Homer or one of the other poets from past times invented the name and introduced it into his poetry" (*Hist.* 2.23).[27] He further questioned the exact circularity of the earth's inhabitable landmass. "They show Ocean as a river flowing around the outside of the earth, which is as circular as if it had been drawn with a pair of compasses, and they make Asia and Europe the same size" (*Hist.* 4.36). Herodotus says that none of these geographers has presented a sensible picture of the world. Herodotus himself, however, was not free of geographical difficulty, holding that Europe was larger than Asia and Africa.[28]

Pliny considered the earth to be round and surrounded by Ocean. "Our own portion of the earth (pars nostra terrarum) . . . swims as it were in the ocean by which, as we have said, it is surrounded" (*Nat.* 2.112.242). He rejected the idea that the earth was twice as long as it was wide. "As a matter of fact I do not think that there is this reduction in the earth, or that it is not the shape of a globe, but that the uninhabitable parts (*inhabitabilia*) on either side have not been explored" (*Nat.* 2.112.245). These areas to the north and the south are cut off by heat and cold, but they still exist making the landmass a circle. Pliny claims to accept the testimony of Eratosthenes on this point (*Nat.* 2.112.247). These areas are part of the known world but fall outside the limits of the *oikoumenē*. Strabo, too, stresses that exploration of these areas is impossible, but he still considers

---

25. Much of this discussion and debate is preserved in Books 1–2 of Strabo's *Geogr.*

26. On Homer's influence on ancient geography, see below.

27. On his rejection of Ocean, see, *Hist.* 2.23; 4.8; 4.36. All quotations of Herodotus, unless otherwise indicated, are taken from Herodotus, *The Histories* (trans. Robin Waterfield).

28. "Europe extends lengthwise the same distance as both of the other continents together, and there is no comparison between their widths, in my opinion" (*Hist.* 4.42).

the landmass that contains Africa, Asia and Europe to be encircled by Ocean (*Geogr.* 1.1.8; 1.2.26).

Africa,[29] Asia, and Europe were the three known continents of the *oikoumenē*,[30] although this division seems to have been known neither to Homer nor Hecataeus.[31] By the time of Pliny the Elder, however, the threefold division of the continents was well-established.

> The whole circuit of the earth is divided into three parts, Europe, Asia and Africa. The starting point is in the west, at the Straits of Gibraltar, where the Atlantic Ocean bursts in and spreads out into the inland seas. On the right as you enter from the ocean is Africa and on the left Europe, with Asia in between them; the boundaries are the river Don and the river Nile . . . At the narrowest part of the Straits stand mountains on either side, enclosing the channel, Ximiera in Africa and Gibraltar in Europe; these were the limits of the labours of Hercules, and consequently the inhabitants call them the Pillars of that deity, and believe that he cut the channel through them and thereby let in the sea which had hitherto been shut out, so altering the face of nature. (*Nat.* 3.1.3–4)[32]

As Pliny's text shows, the *oikoumenē*'s westernmost boundary was to be found at the Straits of Gibraltar, commonly known as the Pillars of Heracles, which served as the westernmost point of travel in the inhabited world. Although by Pliny's time sailing through the Pillars was not uncommon, beyond this boundary one was forced to sail along the coast because there was no certainty of land away from the coast. Those who attempted to sail away from the coast always turned back without ever coming to

---

29. Commonly referred to as Λιβύη in the Greek sources.

30. See Dillon, "Agathemerus' '*Sketch of Geography*,'" 59–76. See also Strabo *Geogr.* 2.5.26.

31. "It is hardly necessary to mention that the primitive geography of the Homeric times knew nothing of a division of the world into three continents: and that the names of Europe, Asia and Africa, in this sense were wholly unknown to the poet. He indeed mentions the name of Libya (as Africa was always called by the Greeks) as that of a particular region of great fertility, doubtless referring to the country west of Egypt which always continued to be known by this special designation. But he never mentions the name of Asia, even as that of a country: and though he speaks of the Asian meadows on the banks of the Cayster, this was evidently a mere local appellation. The name of Europe does not occur in his poems at all" (Burnbury, *History of Ancient Geography*, 1.38). On Hecataeus' understanding of the two great continents, see Burnbury, *History of Ancient Geography*, 1.145–47.

32. Also, *Nat.* 2.112.242–113.248. All quotations from Pliny's *Natural History*, unless otherwise indicated, are taken from Rackham's translation in the LCL.

land because "the sea still continued open as before" and "because of their destitution and loneliness" (Strabo *Geogr.* 1.1.8).³³ The eastern edge of the *oikoumenē* was formed by India. "Its [that is, the *oikoumenē*] longest extent is from East to West, i.e. from India to the Pillars consecrated by Hercules at Gadiz" (Pliny *Nat.* 2.112.242). That part of Asia that is east of India was unknown even to the Romans. As we shall see below, Greeks and Romans speculated regularly on what might lie on and past the easternmost edge of India.

Josephus and Philo accept the tripartite division of the earth's surface into Asia, Europe and Africa. The earliest Israelite text that might be labeled "geographic" is Genesis 10.³⁴ In this text, the earth is apportioned into three sections for the three sons of Noah. The earth, just rid of its human inhabitants, is now free for the taking. Rather than living in a single territory, the sons of Noah are each given a portion of the world which they and their descendants are to occupy. This text explains how the various peoples of the world came to inhabit the various regions of the *oikoumenē*. Genesis 10 became the object of much attention in the Second Temple period. The Genesis text itself, however, leaves a problem unresolved. Genesis 10 assumes that the entire *oikoumenē* is populated by the descendants of Japheth, Ham, and Shem, while in Genesis 11, all peoples still live in one place with one language. Josephus's *Jewish Antiquities* 1.109–112 describes why the people had not departed for the lands to which they had been assigned.

> The three sons of Noah—Shem, Japhet and Ham . . . were the first to descend from the mountains to the plains and make their abode there; the rest, who by reason of the flood were sore afraid of the plains and loath to descend from the heights, they persuaded to take courage and follow their example. The plain where they first settled is called Senaar. God bade them, owing to increasing population, to send out colonies, that they might not quarrel with each other but cultivate much of the earth and enjoy an abundance of its fruits; but in their blindness they did not hearken to Him, and in consequence were plunged into calamities which made them sensible of their error. For when they had a flourishing youthful population, God again counselled them to colonize; but they,

33. All quotations of Strabo, unless otherwise indicated, are taken from the translation of Jones in the LCL.

34. VanderKam, "Putting Them in Their Place." See also the discussion in Westermann, *Genesis 1–11*, 495–530.

never thinking that they owed their blessing to His benevolence and regarding their own might as the cause of their felicity, refused to obey. Nay, to this disobedience to God's will they even added the suspicion that God was plotting against them in urging them to emigrate, in order that, being divided, they might be more open to attack. (*Ant.* 1.109–112)

Philo more explicitly lists Europe, Asia and Libya as the three continents of the *oikoumenē*. In his *Embassy to Gaius* he suggests that any benefits Gaius might confer on the Jews in Alexandria would be felt by the Jewish community worldwide. "So that if my own home-city is granted a share of your goodwill the benefits extend not to one city but to myriads of the others situated in every region of the inhabited world whether in Europe or in Asia or in Libya . . ." (*Legat.* 283).[35] Philo accepts the Greek and Roman division of the *oikoumenē* is into the three traditional continents.

Homeric Influence on the Discussion of the *Oikoumenē*

The impact of the Homeric poems on geographic questions is profound. Geographers normally debated whether Homer accurately relayed geographic information. There is more at stake in these questions, however, than whether Homer is an accurate geographer. Ancient authors of all genres were particularly indebted to Homer as a model and source of material.[36] It is no surprise, then, that ancient geographers engaged the epic poems of Homer.

There was an ongoing debate between the Alexandrian school and Roman traditions concerning the merits of Homer as a geographer. The Alexandrians, led by Eratosthenes, denied to Homer any real geographical knowledge. Eratosthenes, according to Strabo, held that the major purpose of epic was entertainment (ψυχαγωγία) rather than education (διδασκαλία).[37] Eratosthenes points to geographical errors on the part of Homer. He is especially critical of Homer as a source of geographical information. Indeed, Strabo quotes Eratosthenes as saying, "You will find

---

35. All quotations of Philo's *Embassy to Gaius*, unless otherwise indicated, are taken from Colson's translation in the LCL.

36. See, for example, Marrou, *History of Education*; Zeitlin, "Visions and Revisions of Homer," 195–266; MacDonald, ed., *Mimesis and Intertextuality*.

37. Strabo *Geogr.* 1.2.3.

the scene of the wanderings of Odysseus when you find the cobbler who sewed up the bag of winds" (*Geogr.* 1.2.15). In this way, Eratosthenes dismisses much of the geographical tradition before him. Strabo is at pains to defend Homer on this point and does so at length (*Geogr.* 1.2.3–40).

Homer's location of Ocean surrounding the *oikoumenē* was among the major points of disagreement between Eratosthenes and Strabo.[38] That the *oikoumenē* had definite limits preventing travel and exploration into certain areas was widely accepted in the ancient world even for those who dismissed the notion of Oceanus. Herodotus, for example, eventually "discovers" uninhabitable deserts surrounding the *oikoumenē*.[39] Aristotle preserves both the concept of Ocean and that of desert regions limiting the habitable world.[40] These limits at the edges of the *oikoumenē* became objects of fantastic literary description. The nearer one journeyed to the limits of that known world, the more wondrous and amazing things they could expect to see. Over a long period of time, the idea that the edges of the earth were filled with marvelous things unseen in the more central regions (whether they be Greek or Roman) developed into a literary topos that established stereotypical categories for reporting about those areas.[41] These tales of the fantastic at the outer limits of the *oikoumenē* begin with Homer's *Odyssey* and continue throughout the period with which this study is concerned.[42]

It is important for Strabo that Homer be correct because his poems "educate (παιδεύσιν) the young, at the very beginning of their education, by means of poetry; not for the mere sake of entertainment (ψυχαγ-

---

38. Strabo attributes the origin of this concept to Homer; "In the first place, Homer declares that the inhabited world is washed on all sides by Oceanus, and this is true" (*Geogr.* 1.1.3).

39. For the description of the deserts at the ends of the *oikoumenē*, see *Hist.* 3.98 (on the desert to the east of India); 4.17 (on the desert to the north of the Neuri people); 4.185 (on the desert to the south of Libya); and 5.9 (on the desert to the north of the Thracians). See the discussion in Romm, *Edges of the Earth*, 35–41.

40. Aristotle, *Mete.* 2.5.362b, "Yet we know the whole breadth of the habitable world up to the uninhabitable regions which bound it, where habitation ceases on the one side because of the cold, on the other because of the heat; while beyond India and the Pillars of Heracles it is the ocean (Greek: θάλατταν) which severs the habitable land and prevents it from forming a continuous belt round the globe." All quotations of Aristotle's *Meteorologica*, unless otherwise indicated, are taken from Lee's translation in the LCL.

41. See Romm, *Edges of the Earth*. Also Rhianon Evans, "Ethnography's Freak Show," 54–73. Almost all Greek thought about space involved some type of stereotyping.

42. Such tales continued for many centuries. See Romm, *Edges of the Earth*, 215–22.

ωγίας), of course, but for the sake of moral discipline (σωφρονισμοῦ)" (*Geogr.* 1.2.3). Thus, Homer must be a true geographic authority.[43] For Strabo, then, Homer's reliance as a geographer is related to his veracity in other respects. If Homer is a liar, a mere inventor of tales, he cannot and should not be used as the basis of an educational system whose purpose is the development of moral discipline.[44]

> You may be right, Eratosthenes, on that point, but you are wrong when you deny to Homer the possession of vast learning, and go on to declare that poetry is a fable-prating old wife, who has been permitted to "invent" (as you call it) whatever she deems suitable for purposes of entertainment. What, then? Is no contribution made, either, to the excellence of him who hears the poets recited? I again refer to the poet's being an expert in geography, or generalship, or agriculture, or rhetoric, the subject in which the poet naturally "invests" the reader with special knowledge. (*Geogr.* 1.2.3)

Homer represents everything that is good about Greek (and Roman) society. He has "acquaintance with all that pertains to public life" (*Geogr.* 1.1.2). Furthermore, he "made himself busy not only about public activities, to the end that he might learn of as many of them as possible and give an account to posterity, but also about the geography both of the individual countries and of the inhabited world at large, both land and sea" (*Geogr.* 1.1.2). His purpose in doing these things was to become an expert in all matters and so to be able to educate people in every way.[45] Homer, therefore, besides being the "founder of the science of geography" (ἀρχηγέτην εἶναι τῆς γεωγραφικῆς) is the model of a Greek educator. Everything he says, therefore, must be true and useful for educating citizens. Homer's accuracy in geography, then is a test case for his accuracy in "generalship, agriculture, rhetoric" and all other subjects.

Josephus assumes the conception of the *oikoumenē* as circular and surrounded by Ocean. His conception of the shape of the *oikoumenē* is clearly indicated in *Ant.* 1.38–39. "Now the garden [Eden] is watered by a single

---

43. "Strabo's defense of Homer's geographical knowledge is a necessary prerequisite for the belief, held by Strabo, that the places mentioned by Homer are real places; that their descriptions are accurate; and that not only can the places mentioned by Homer be identified, they can be identified by virtue of what Homer tells us about them" (Pothecary, "Strabo and the Inhabited World," 35).

44. See the discussion of these points in Romm, *Edges of the Earth*, 183–96.

45. On the idea of travel and seeing things with one's own eyes as a prerequisite to teaching, see below.

river whose stream encircles all the earth and is parted into four branches" (*Ant.* 1.38). Furthermore, Josephus states that the sash which encircled the priest was representative of ocean (*Ant.* 3.185). Josephus adopts the same general conception of the earth's shape as had Homer before him.

Strabo's Two Views of the *Oikoumenē*

As noted above, Strabo held the world to be surrounded by Oceanus.[46] "We may learn both from the evidence of our senses and from experience that the inhabited world is an island" (*Geogr.* 1.1.8). Strabo, however, also held another understanding of the *oikoumenē*. This understanding is of a "chlamys-shaped" (χλαμυδοειδές) *oikoumenē* (*Geogr.* 2.5.14).[47] This conception presents the *oikoumenē* in the shape of a parallelogram (*Geogr.* 2.5.14–16). This theory is dependant on the theory of climatic zones (which number five, according to Strabo) that mark inhabitable areas from uninhabitable areas. The northernmost part of the inhabited world is Ierne and the southernmost part is the Cinnamon-Producing Country (Κινναμωμοφόρου) and the island of the fugitive Egyptians (τῆς τῶν Αἰγυπτίων τῶν φυγάδων νήσου; *Geogr.* 2.5.14). There are people known to inhabit such places, but they are wild and not like the Romans. Since such places have unfavorable climactic conditions, social configurations like those of the Romans are impossible. Ierne "is the home of men who are complete savages (ἀγρίων τελέως) and lead a miserable existence (κακῶς οἰκούντων) because of the cold" (*Geogr.* 2.5.8).[48] Since all places at a given latitude are assumed to be climatically the same, life north of this latitude is considered impossible by Strabo.[49] The Iernians exist at the margins of the *oikoumenē* and at the margins of human existence since they are savages and not refined like the Romans. This type of existence is also true for the Kimmerians.[50]

46. See Pothecary, "Strabo and the Inhabited World," 51–57.
47. Ibid., 57–64.
48. See also *Geogr.* 2.1.13.
49. Pothecary, "Strabo and the Inhabited World," 67.
50. Homer *Od.* 11.13–19: "She came then to the ultimate bounds of the deep-flowing Ocean, where the Kimmerian people are found, their country and city shrouded about by the mist and the clouds, so that never does shining Helios look down over the land with his radiant sunbeams—neither whenever he climbs on high to the star-filled heaven, nor indeed when again out of heaven to the earth he is turning—but a maleficent night spreads over the miserable mortals." All quotations of the *Odyssey*, unless otherwise indicated, are

Strabo's understanding of the inhabited world, then, led him to conclude that it was inhabited west to east from the Pillars of Hercules to India and north to south from Ierne to southern Egypt. Small segments of land existed outside of the *oikoumenē* to the north and south of the inhabitable areas, but these were not very large and could be circumnavigated save for the difficulties of being "hindered by many perplexing circumstances" (πολλῶν ἀποριῶν κωλυόμενοι) because Ocean surrounded the entire landmass which consisted of Africa, Europe, and Asia (*Geogr.* 1.2.26).[51]

Expansion of the *Oikoumenē* under Alexander and the Romans

Before beginning a fuller explication of the ancient Greek and Roman understanding of space, it is necessary to discuss briefly the changing notions of the conception of the world during the Hellenistic and Roman periods. Strabo sets out as a reason for his *Geography* the changed conditions of world knowledge during, and shortly prior to, his lifetime. Strabo notes that geography is a sub-discipline of philosophy and that its utility is "not only as regards the activities of statesmen and commanders but also as regards knowledge both of the heavens and of things on land and sea, animals, plants, fruits, and everything else to be seen in various regions" (*Geogr.* 1.1.1). Strabo is better equipped to speak about these things because of recent developments. "Indeed, the spread of the empires of the Romans and of the Parthians has presented to geographers of to-day a considerable addition to our empirical knowledge of geography, just as did the campaign of Alexander to geographers of earlier times, as Eratosthenes points out" (*Geogr.* 1.2.1). Knowledge of the world was expanding at a fairly rapid rate in the Hellenistic and Roman periods. Military conquests and increased travel allowed for much new information to be gathered and new territories to be discovered.[52]

---

taken from Homer, *The Odyssey* (trans. Rodney Merrill).

51. All three of these continents were known to Strabo in a much more limited sense than we know them today. See Pothecary, "Strabo and the Inhabited World," 51.

52. Although the geographical knowledge of the Greeks and Romans had increased exponentially during the expansions under Alexander and the Romans, from the modern perspective, their understanding of geography was still quite limited. Moynihan, "Geographical Mythology," lists "all of the stock elements of the Greek geographical tradition" that are still to be found in the description of Agrippa's map contained in Pliny's *Nat.* 3: "Germany is smaller than Gaul; Dacia abuts the Northern Ocean. The area north of the Black Sea is very small; the Caspian Sea opens onto the ocean. Armenia is only a

The conquests of Alexander the Great, for example, brought much new information that rendered older geographic traditions irrelevant. Further, the campaigns of Romans and Parthians also revolutionized geographic understanding.

> For Alexander opened up for us geographers a great part of Asia and all the northern part of Europe as far as the Ister River; the Romans have made known all the western part of Europe as far as the River Albis (which divides Germany into two parts), and the regions beyond the Ister as far as the Tyras River; and Mithradates, surnamed Eupator, and his generals have made known the regions beyond the Tyras as far as Lake Maeotis and the line of coast that ends at Colchis; and, again, the Parthians have increased our knowledge in regard to the Scythians who live north of Hyrcania and Bactriana, all of which countries were but imperfectly known to earlier geographers. (*Geogr.* 1.2.1)

During the period from Alexander's conquests until the time of Strabo, the geographical knowledge of the Greeks (and then the Romans) had been expanding. Much more of Asia and Europe had been "discovered" by such expansion. While Alexander's conquests made known much of central and east Asia, the Romans' conquests revealed much new information regarding western Europe, particularly regarding Britian and Ierne. It is because of such expansion that Strabo remarks, "I therefore may have something more to say than my predecessors" (*Geogr.* 1.2.1).

The vastness of the empire was a source of pride for the Roman empire. Aristides, in comparing the kingdom of the Persians with that of the Romans, remarks, "what the Atlantic Ocean now means for you, was then simply the Mediterranean for the King" (*Or.* 26.16).[53] In fact, the Romans believed that their empire was the greater part of the known world and corresponded to the extent of the *oikoumenē*. Moynihan argues that their limited understanding of the vastness of Europe, Asia and Africa led them to believe that they could conquer the entire known world. "For them, the Empire was not a vulnerable band of land circling the Mediterranean at

---

step away from China; India is at the end of the world; Africa is truncated into a narrow island" (155).

53. See also Diodorus, 1.4.3, "For the supremacy of this city, a supremacy so powerful that it extends to the bounds of the inhabited world . . ." All quotations of Diodorus, unless otherwise indicated, are taken from Welles's translation in the LCL.

one tip of the Eurasian land-mass. Rather, it was the larger portion of the habitable earth, poised on the verge of world rule."[54]

There were those, however, who were more guarded in their estimation of Rome's expanse. In a more critical reflection on Rome's expanse, Cicero writes: "the earth is inhabited in only a few portions, and those very small, while vast deserts lie between those inhabited patches, as we may call them" (*Rep.* 6.19.20). It is characteristic of the inhabitants of such an earth that they "are so widely separated that there can be no communication whatever among the different areas" (*Rep.* 6.19.20). And further,

> Examine this northern zone which you inhabit, and you will see what a small portion of it belongs to you Romans. For that whole territory which you hold, being narrow from North to South, and broader from East to West, is really only a small island surrounded by that sea which you on the earth call the Atlantic, the Great Sea, or the Ocean. (*Rep.* 6.20.21)

Cicero accepts the idea of other *oikoumenai*, but these do not belong to the *oikoumenē* of the Romans since they are cut off by vast deserts. Cicero, like Aristotle before him, contains a combination of the concept of the *oikoumenē* as an island surrounded by the sea and the idea of vast deserts preventing travel and communication between the various *oikoumenai*.[55]

The *oikoumenē*, despite its expansion under Greece and Rome, covered only one quarter of the globe according to the geographers. This quarter was not the only one known to Greek and Roman geographers, inasmuch as they intuited the presence of other *oikoumenai*, but it was the only one with which they could be concerned, because there was no way to reach the others. Strabo believed that voyages made before and during his lifetime left a portion of the landmass that included Africa, Asia and Europe "not of very great extent" to explore (*Geogr.* 1.1.8). Beyond these small unexplored regions of the known world, however, it was impossible to travel. The other *oikoumenai* were permanently cut off from the Greeks and Romans. The geographic tradition of the Greeks and Romans, then, led to the conclusion that their *oikoumenē* was an expanse of land surrounded by unnavigable Ocean, uncrossable deserts (or tundras) or some combination of these things.

---

54. Moynihan, "Geographical Mythology," 151.

55. See also Cicero *Nat. d.* 1.10.24. All quotations of Cicero's *Republic*, unless otherwise stated, are taken from Keyes's translation in the LCL.

Josephus also provides a description to the extent of the Roman world.

> For, not content with having for their frontiers on the east the Euphrates, on the north the Ister, on the south Libya explored into desert regions (τῶν ἀοικήτου), on the west Gades, they have sought a new world (ἑτέραν οἰκουμένην) beyond the ocean and carried their arms as far as the Britons, previously unknown to history. (B.J. 2.363)

Josephus highlights that the Roman empire stretches to the south and the north in the same places that one would expect based on Strabo's description of the Roman *oikoumenē*. In the south the world has been explored until the Romans reached uninhabitable territory. These uninhabitable regions reflect the Greek and Roman concept of the climatic zones. Below the southernmost part of the temperate northern zone, the land is uninhabitable on account of the heat. Similarly, above the Ister, the earth is uninhabitable because of the severe cold. Gades as the western extreme of the Roman empire is also well-established. It is there that the Pillars of Hercules are located, and thereafter lies the great Ocean. The interesting and somewhat surprising elements of Josephus' description of the Roman world involve his location of the eastern edge of the empire and his description of Britain as a new *oikoumenē*.

Josephus lists the Euphrates as the easternmost boundary of the Roman *oikoumenē*. This delimitation recognizes the kingdom of the Parthians to the east of the Romans. The Parthians, however, were subject to Rome through a treaty. Josephus elsewhere acknowledges this fact (B.J. 2.388–390). There Josephus stresses that "in the habitable world (οἰκουμένης) all are Romans" (B.J. 2.388). Furthermore, Josephus calls "Caesar, the lord of the universe" (ὁ τῆς οἰκουμένης προστάτης Καῖσαρ, B.J. 1.633). Josephus, then, while acknowledging other powers in the *oikoumenē*, is clear that the Romans control the entire *oikoumenē*.

Unlike several of the Greek and Roman authors who accepted Britain as the northern most part of the Roman *oikoumenē*, Josephus calls it a "new *oikoumenē*" unknown in history prior to the Roman conquest of it. Upon its conquest by the Romans, it becomes part of their empire and part of the single *oikoumenē* of the Roman world, but Josephus seems aware of the idea that the world contains [potentially] more than one *oikoumenē*. Rather than conceiving of Roman expansion in terms of bringing peace to the one known *oikoumenē*, however, Josephus seems to understand the expansion of the Romans as the conquest of new worlds.

Another early Jewish text also discusses lands outside of the *oikoumenē*. The *History of the Rechabites* describes islands that exist beyond the limits of the *oikoumenē* that can be reached only by traversing Ocean (*Hist. Rech.* 3:4). This land contained the "blessed ones" and was located "in the midst of the sea" (*Hist. Rech.* 3:5).[56] *When the Rechabites refused to break their vows to God and conform to the practices of the people of Jerusalem, they were spirited away by angels to the island land in which they are now located (Hist. Rech.* 10:5–7). There their women live separately among them, and God "commanded and the waters rose up from the deep abyss and encircled this place" (*Hist. Rech.* 10:7). This island, then, is cut off from the *oikoumenē*, and travel to it from the "world of vanity" is ordinarily impossible (*Hist. Rech.* 5:1). This idea, of course, is a fairly common Greek geographical concept. Beginning with the Isles of the Blest in the *Odyssey*, the Greeks and Romans presented several different ideas concerning island *oikoumenai* that existed beyond Oceanus. These islands were generally thought to contain peoples who lived in idyllic conditions and were not subject to the same whims of fate and history to which all other peoples were subjected.

Human Geography:
Historiography, Ethnology, and Geography

The *oikoumenē* is a social as well as a geographical concept. Indeed, it is "above all a social space."[57] The inhabited world set the limits on human activity in space, even as it acknowledged other fringe groups that existed either at or beyond the limits inhabited by normal humans; "the boundaries of Strabo's *oikoumenē* do not simply mark the separation of the 'known' from the 'unknown'. Rather, they mark the separation of the 'habitable' earth from the 'uninhabited' or 'uninhabitable' areas around it."[58]

---

56. All translations from the *History of the Rechabites* are taken from the translation in *OTP*.

57. "*Oikoumenē* ist demnach nicht nur geographisch, sondern zunächst sozialer Raum, der durch die zumindest grundsätzlich vorausgesetze Möglichkeit der Bewohner konstituiert ist, untereinander in Verbindung zu treten" (Schmidt, "*Oikoumenē*," 1138).

58. Pothecary, "Strabo and the Inhabited World," 52.

Ancient geography developed largely from the ethnological literature that described the various regions of the earth.[59] There is a close relationship between storytelling and ancient history and geography. Ancient historiography and geography are, in many instances, difficult to distinguish.[60] Both of these types of literature are dependant upon the travel reports of others, for no single person so far as is known, traveled the entire surface of the known world except in epic and story (so, for example, Odysseus and Apollonius of Tyana).[61] These travel reports contained information about the distinctive elements of the peoples of various places. Consider, for example, books 9–12 of the *Odyssey*, where Odysseus relates his stories of wandering to Alcinous. He tells of the various peoples who inhabited each of the lands to which he came and of his adventures in dealing with each of them. Instead of relating only, or even primarily, cartographic information, he describes the social customs of the people whom he encounters. As Malina puts it, "movement through space was an adventure with various people and the environs in which they were embedded providing travelers with unexpected experiences as they passed from place to place."[62] Places, even as presented by the geographers, were notable for the people, animals, plants and wonders contained in them.[63]

---

59. Pausanias, for example, drew on the historian Herodotus, whose account of the Scythians in book 4 of his *Hist.* served as an model for much of Pausanias' own work. On this point see Elsner, "Structuring 'Greece'," 3–20.

60. At least some authors made a distinction between these two types of literature in antiquity, as Strabo, in addition to his *Geography*, wrote a now lost *History*. See the excellent discussion in Clarke, *Between Geography*, 1–76.

61. There were also a number of traditions concerning Alexander in this regard, especially the Romance tradition. Alexander, it is supposed, would have investigated every area of the world had he lived long enough to do so. See Romm, *Edges of the Earth*, 109–20. See also Pearson, *Lost Histories of Alexander the Great*.

62. Malina, "'Apocalyptic' and Territoriality," 370. Or as Gurevich, *Categories of Medieval Culture*, 31, notes "for the Greeks, the perception of time remained deeply affected by the mythological interpretation of reality. Time was neither homogeneous nor chronologically sequential; like space, it had not yet become an abstraction." Clarke, *Between Geography*, contests this point by arguing that Greeks did, in fact, have abstract conceptions regarding geometrical space. It seems obvious that Gurevich has overstated the case, but his point is still well taken that Greeks and Romans were more interested in cultural space than in geometric space.

63. See Jacob and Mullen-Hohl, "Greek Traveler's Area of Knowledge," 65–85.

Primacy of Sight

Much of what could be called human geography in the ancient world relied on the primacy of sight. The experts, even for the more scientific geographers, were those who had seen for themselves the things they reported. Strabo notes that "the poets declare that the wisest heroes were those who had visited many places and roamed over the world; for the poets regard it as a great achievement to have 'seen the cities and known the minds of many men'" (*Geogr.* 1.1.16).[64] For this reason, Odysseus was considered the foremost expert in geography among those who later wrote about the *oikoumenē* because he had seen everything.

> Odysseus was the man who had seen and who knew because he had seen. This, right from the start, alerts us to a relation to the world that is central to the Greek civilization: here, the seeing eye was the means of knowledge valued above all others. Seeing, seeing for oneself, and knowing "came to the same thing."[65]

The same idea can be found also in Philostratus' *Life of Apollonius*. Here, however, the sage not only travels throughout the known world, he also "corrects the rites and lectures the priests" at each stop.[66] Travelers throughout the ancient world were considered experts in the field of geography because they were themselves witnesses to the things they described.[67] Diodorus says concerning the veracity of his *Library of History* that "we have visited a large portion of both Asia and Europe that we might see with our own eyes all the most important regions and as many others as possible" (1.4.1). It is necessary to undertake such travel because "many errors have been committed through ignorance of the sites" (1.4.1). Seeing with one's own eyes became a criterion for reporting truthful information.[68]

---

64. The quotation is from Homer *Od.* 1.3. The Greek text is πολλῶν ἀνθρώπων ἴδεν ἄστεα καὶ νόον ἔγνω. The obvious implication here is that to travel involved meeting others and "knowing their minds." Travel is a personalized phenomenon that involves others rather than being a journey through abstract space.

65. Hartog, *Memories of Odysseus*, 4.

66. Elsner, "Hagiographic Geography," 27.

67. Romm, *Edges of the Earth*, 35, notes this same feature in Herodotus who "makes room for a new kind of distant-world geography, based not on geometry but on what can be learned from reliable informants."

68. Lucian *Ver. Hist.* 1.3–4 parodies this tradition. In 1.4 he says, "Be it understood, then, that I am writing about things which I have neither seen nor had to do with nor

Borders of the Earth

The most basic act that the ancient Greeks undertook was labeling the boundaries of the world. "These peirata or 'borders' are purely an imaginative construct and are conceived only in the vaguest of terms."[69] In the eleventh book of the *Odyssey*, Odysseus relates his own journey through the Pillars into the house of Hades. He travels "off the map" and into an area outside of the *oikoumenē*. The *oikoumenē* did not necessarily encompass all the peoples of the earth "since lands which were thought to contain men (like the Antipodes) were not necessarily included within its scope, while other, uninhabited spaces might so be included."[70] Romm suggests that a more appropriate way to envision the *oikoumenē* is "as a region made coherent by the intercommunication of its inhabitants, such that, within the radius of this region, no tribe or race is completely cut off from the peoples beyond it."[71] It is significant to note that some *ethnoi*, however, fell outside the limits of the *oikoumenē*, however it was defined.

The borders of the inhabited world were of particular significance among the ancients because marvelous and strange things, persons and events were thought to occur beyond the ends of human habitation.[72] For example, Herodotus relates that certain Indians living "at the border of the town of Caspatyrus and Pactyican territory" are aided in unearthing gold through ants "which are bigger than foxes, although they never reach the size of dogs" that bring sand to the earth's surface that contains gold in it (*Hist.* 3.102). Herodotus further says that "the outer reaches of the inhabited world were allotted the most attractive features . . . in the first place, living creatures, both animals and birds, which are far larger than those to be found in other countries" (*Hist.* 3.106). There is also an unlimited supply of gold and wild trees which produce wool better than that of sheep (*Hist.* 3.106). Elsewhere, Herodotus relates tales of the Libyan tribe of the Maxyes. These people claim descent from the Trojans, have

---

learned from others—which, in fact, do not exist at all and, in the nature of things, cannot exist. Therefore my readers should on no account believe them." All quotations from Lucian's *Ver. Hist.*, unless otherwise indicated, are taken from Harmon's translation in the LCL. As noted above, Strabo considered Homer's wide travel as a guarantor of his veracity.

69. Romm, *Edges of the Earth*, 11–12.
70. Ibid., 37.
71. Romm, *Edges of the Earth*, 37.
72. Ibid.

developed agriculture and houses, but shave half of their heads while letting the hair grow long on the other side. Their portion of Libya "has far more wildlife and more trees than the rest of Libya" (*Hist.* 4.191). Among the more amazing creatures in this region are horned donkeys, dog-headed creatures, headless creatures "and a large number of other creatures whose existence is not merely the stuff of fables" (*Hist.* 4.191). There are many other examples of these types of descriptions of wondrous animals, peoples, and natural goods at the edges of the *oikoumenē*.[73]

The peoples that existed on the periphery of the inhabited world were often considered savages by ancient Greek and Roman authors. So, for example, Strabo suggests that many European cultures were savages according to their nature because of the poor quality of the land that they inhabited and also because they did not have communication with the rest of the inhabited world (*Geogr.* 2.5.26).[74] Coës tells Darius not to dismantle the bridge his men have constructed over the Ister in case they need to retreat hastily. Coës gives these instructions because Darius "is about to invade a land where agriculture is completely unknown and there are no settlements" (*Hist.* 4.96). The Cannibals are found among the more northerly tribes of the Scythians. They are the "most savage people in the world; they have no sense of right and wrong, and their life is governed by no rules or traditions" (*Hist.* 4.106). Among all Scythians they are "the only one of these tribes to eat human flesh" (*Hist.* 4.106). The Cannibals represent the worst savagery to be found in humanity.[75] They are, however, a part of the larger Scythian people.

Some African peoples were also presented as fantastic and extraordinary. Pliny, for example, discusses the peoples of southwest Ethiopia in these terms. He describes these regions as containing the Nigroi, who have a one-eyed king, the wild-animal eaters (*Agriophagi*), who eat primarily the flesh of panthers and lions, the *Pamphagi*, who eat everything, a group of cannibals (*Anthropophagi*), the dog milkers (*Cynamolgi*), who have dog

73. So, for example, book 3 of Diodorus' *Library* is full of fabulous descriptions of the customs, animals and resources of the Ethiopians. Herodotus' book 4 also contains many such accounts. Romm, *Edges of the Earth* contains numerous other examples. Lucian's *Ver. Hist.* parodies these fantastic elements of far off travel.

74. It is important to note that defining these cultures in such a way reflects the lack of control that the Romans had over these people. The element of control and power is at issue in the description of the cultures at the edges of the *oikoumenē*.

75. Roman geographers tended to portray all Scythians as cannibals. See Evans, "Ethnography's Freak Show," 59.

heads themselves, and a group of Ethiopians who eat only dried and salted locusts and do not live more than forty years (*Nat.* 6.35.195). These people are all savage insofar as they do not cultivate the soil. Such cultivation is the mark of civilization for the Greeks and Romans.[76] In most instances, remote cultures are considered savage by the Greeks and Romans.

In other cases, however, positive characteristics of these cultures could be highlighted to show deficiencies in Greek and Roman culture. The Ethiopians, for example, were thought to inhabit a region that was frequented by the gods. Poseidon was visiting among the Ethiopians when the other Olympian gods convened to allow Odysseus his homecoming (*Od.* 1.20–24). Diodorus notes that the quality of Egyptian soil and climate makes it the most likely candidate for the genesis of humanity (1.10.3).

In another case, Herodotus relates the story of Cambyses' failed attack on the Ethiopians.[77] According to Herodotus, the Persians were a very ethnocentric people.

> After themselves, they hold their immediate neighbours in the highest regard, then those who live the next furthest away, and so on in order of proximity; so they have the least respect for those who live furthest from their own land. The reason for this is that they regard themselves as by far the best people in the world in all respects, and others as gradually decreasing in goodness, so that those who live furthest away from them are the worst people in the world (*Hist.* 1.134).

He turns the tradition of the Persians as the most civilized and best people on its head when he describes Cambyses' attempt to overthrow the Ethiopians. Cambyses, in his anger at the Ethiopians, attacks without securing proper provisions. His men ran out of food less than one-fifth of the way into the journey and ate all the pack animals. Without meat to eat, they resorted to eating wild grasses. Finally, when they encountered a desert where the grasses did not grow, they turned to cannibalism and ate one out of every twenty men (*Hist.* 3.25). Cambyses' men, rather than the Ethiopians who live outside the boundaries of the *oikoumenē* are the ones who resorted to the abnormal behaviors expected of primitive and

---

76. See Hartog, *Memories of Odysseus* 24–25. Standard social practices do not occur in non-cultivated areas: "hospitality, as a general rule, has no place. Strangers are not welcomed" (ibid., 25).

77. See the discussion of these passages in Romm, *Edges of the Earth*, 55–59.

uncivilized cultures. The very people who considered themselves to be the paragons of civilization became the savages when they tried to force their way of life on a people favored by the gods. Herodotus frequently employs this type of ethnological satire in order "to show the master races of the world humbled in the eyes of indifferent aliens."[78]

Rhetoric

Rhetoricians offered instruction to others on describing space. Menander provides direction on how to praise a city. "Praises of cities, then, are combinations of the headings discussed in connection with countries (περὶ χώρας) and those related to individuals (περὶ ἀνθρώπους)."[79] Under the first heading, one should discuss all things related to the site of the city, including its "relation to the sky and the seasons...in terms of cold, heat, mistiness, clearness of atmosphere, or the balance of all seasons" (1.347.14–16). Included under the second heading are descent (τὸ γένος), the deeds (τὰς πράξεις), and the practiced habits (τὰς ἐπιτηδεύσεις) of the city (1.346.30–31). These things are all part of the encomiastic tradition for praising people.[80] In discussing a city's origins, Menander cites five topics that should be addressed: the founders of the city (οἰκιστάς), its settlers (τοὺς οἰκήσαντας), its time (τὸν χρόνον),[81] its changes (μεταβολάς) and its causes of origin (τὰς αἰτίας ἀφ᾽ ὧν αἱ πόλεις οἰκοῦνται, 1.353.6–8). Clarke suggests that "writing the life of a city was parallel to writing a human biography."[82] A city's race or descent, its deeds and its practiced habits are all part of describing the inhabitants that lived there. Each of the inhabitants of the city reflects all these characteristics, both positive and negative, of people from that place. Libanius, in his *Oration in praise of Antioch*, stresses that it is necessary to praise the past of a city in order to show that the present praiseworthy characteristics of that city are deserved because of its illustrious past.[83] The close relationship between

---

78. Romm, *Edges of the Earth*, 59.

79. Menander Rhetor 1.346.27–29. All quotations from Menander, unless otherwise specified, are taken from Russell and Wilson's translation in *Menander Rhetor*.

80. So, Menander 1.353.5–367.8.

81. This reference likely indicates a city's founding date.

82. Clarke, *Between Geography*, 41.

83. Libanius *Or.* 11.11. See Downey, "Libanius' Oration in Praise of Antioch," 652–86.

people and places is demonstrated in the fact that writing the "story" of a city is done in the same manner as writing a biography.

Maps

Greek and Roman maps also reflected interest in human geography. Despite the interest in more scientific approaches to geography among some Greek and Roman authors and the detailed attempts to measure and map the world, it is highly unlikely that the Greeks and Romans regularly used scale maps for travel. Brodersen argues that, though the popular opinion among scholars has always held that the Romans drew and used scale maps for travel, there is little evidence to support this case. Travel was conducted through itineria rather than through the use of scale maps.[84] Bekker-Nielsen draws this point somewhat further, inasmuch as he argues that ancient perceptions of place (particularly for travelers) related to "strip" maps. These maps are mental images "indicating how to get to different places but giving no clear indication of their location in relation to each other."[85] This type of map "gives only a hazy idea of geographical direction and of the relative locations of surrounding towns and geographical features; distances between points on the route, on the other hand, will be precise."[86] These types of maps are also drawn from the itineraries common among the Romans and Greeks.[87] The itineraries followed the road systems of Rome, and the points they discussed were, generally speaking, those places of human habitation that one would encounter when traveling upon these roads.

These types of itinerary maps, however, were not the only attempts to picture the world. Beginning with Homer's description of Achilles' shield in *Il.* 18.480–610, numerous Greek and Roman authors sought to draw the world of the Greek and Roman *oikoumenē*. Homer's descrip-

---

84. Brodersen, "Presentation of Geographical Knowledge," 7–21. See also Sundwall, "Ammianus Geographicus," in 619–43.

85. Bekker-Nielsen, "Terra Incognita," 153. On the idea of mental images and mapping, see Gould and White, *Mental Maps*.

86. Bekker-Nielsen, "Terra Incognita," 155.

87. A good example of this type of travelogue in a slightly later period is Egeria's travelogue. Bekker-Nielsen says that "the itinerary was the standard form of road guide or 'road map' used by European travellers, and itineraries continued to be produced as late as the 18th century" (ibid., 154).

tion is of a round earth surrounded by Ocean.[88] Diogenes Laertius says that Anaximander "was the first to draw (ἔγραψεν) on a map the outline (περίμετρον) of land and sea, and he constructed a globe (σφαῖραν)"[89] as well (*Lives* 2.1). Hecataeus followed Anaximander, and he produced a circular map with the continents of Europe and Libya surrounded by Ocean. From Homer onward, the Greeks believed that the earth was in the middle of the universe.[90]

Much of the discussion about the size and shape of the world and its place in the universe was restricted to discussions among philosophers. There is, however, some indication in Aristophanes' comedy *The Clouds* that a broader audience had at least limited familiarity with maps. Strepsiades discusses with a student at Socrates' school the representation of the earth on a map (*Nub.* 200–217). Strepsiades, who in the story is a bumbling fool from the countryside, does not understand the purpose of the map. When the student informs him that through astronomy and geometry they "mete out lands" (γῆν ἀναμετρεῖσθαι), Strepsiades understands this to mean that the whole earth is surveyed so every person may take a portion of if for his or her own. When the student points out Athens on the map, Strepsiades replies, "I see no dicasts sitting. That's not Athens." When the student reassures him that it is, in fact, Athens, Strepsiades asks to see his fellow townspeople on the map. Finally, Strepsiades laments that Sparta is so close to Athens on the map and asks the student to move it further away. When the student responds that the request is impossible to grant, Strepsiades says, "the worse for you" (οἰμώξεσθ᾽ ἄρα). This comedic presentation of a map of the world conveys the idea that maps were the province of philosophers and not easily understood by ordinary people. While Aristophanes likely overstates the case to some extent, maps of the entire world were likely not widely known among most people since long distance travel was restricted to a relatively small segment of the population.[91]

88. The idea of a circular world surrounded by Ocean, however, was not without its critics. As discussed above, Herodotus rejected this notion. For a discussion of these points, see Harley and Woodward, *Cartography*, 131–35.

89. σφαῖραν here probably refers to a round land mass rather than a spherical earth encircled by the heavens, though the concept developed c. 530 BCE with Pythagoras. See Harley and Woodward, *Cartography*, 136.

90. So Plato *Phaedo* and Aristotle *Meteorologica* among other works. See Harley and Woodward, *History of Ancient Geography*, 1136–47.

91. The relatively limited information available to Ptolemy in constructing a world

Strabo and Personalized Space

> Again, we wish to know about those parts of the world where tradition places more deeds of action, political constitutions, arts, and everything else that contributes to practical wisdom; and our needs draw us to those places with which commercial and social intercourse is attainable; and these are the places that are under government, or rather under good government. (Strabo, *Geogr.* 2.5.18)

This text clearly indicates Strabo's concern with human settlements and, more specifically, those human settlements that interact with the Roman world. The description of "deeds of action" (πράξεις), "political constitutions" (πολιτεῖαι), "arts" (τέχναι) and "everything else" (τἆλλα) related to "practical wisdom" (φρόνησιν) is indicative of a concern for human settlement and what geography might contribute to the life of the Roman empire. Elsewhere, Strabo says of geography that "its utility is manifold, not only as regards the activities of statesmen and commanders but also as regards knowledge both of the heavens and of things on land and sea, animals, plants, fruits, and everything else to be seen in various regions" (*Geogr.* 1.1.1). The very purpose of geography, for Strabo, is a description of the inhabited world and the peoples, places, and things it contained.[92] It has a practical value that is especially significant to politicians and military commanders.

Those parts of the world that are unattainable for commercial and social interaction are unimportant to Strabo's geographical concern.[93] Strabo is more interested in geography's relationship to human activity.[94] He states "the geographer, however, need not busy himself with what lies

---

map should be taken to indicate the limited availability of any type of map.

92. The underlying idea in Strabo is that if a region remains uninhabited, there must be some defect about that part of the earth. One of the tasks of examining the "earth as a whole" was to discover "likewise how large the uninhabited part is, what its nature is, and why it is uninhabited" (*Geogr.* 1.1.15).

93. Van Paassen, *Classical Tradition* says, "The object of Strabo's geography is not a fixed theoretically abstracted enity, but the selected concrete reality of society and environment in which nature forms an integral part, the whole seen in a spatial perspective. In this, the structure of the object and the criterion of selection are both irreducible facets of one and the same reality, the total and concrete human reality, and geography is consciously conceived as an anthropocentrical science" (23).

94. Ibid., 14.

outside of our inhabited world" (*Geogr.* 2.5.34). Here Strabo is explicitly contrasting the work of astronomers and geographers. His point, however, can be taken more broadly. "Not only was Strabo's interest confined to the portion of the globe inhabited by man, but also, within that portion, Strabo was not concerned with empty landscape."[95] For Strabo, geography was about the *oikoumenē* and the people it contained. Everything outside of that space was inconsequential to his work.

Human Geography in Early Judaism[96]

There are many indications that the Jews of the Second Temple period were aware of traditions regarding fantastic elements at the ends of the earth. Several Jewish authors simply take from Roman geographical traditions the "savageness" of other peoples. The ethnographic and geographic stereotypes common to many genres of Greek and Roman literature are passed along by early Jewish authors with little modification. Philo, for example, in his description of Gaius' ascension to power, relates a description of the earth in which he conveys the personalized geography that marks much of the Greek and Roman traditions treated above.

> For who that saw Gaius when after the death of Tiberius he succeeded to the sovereignty of the whole earth and sea . . . a dominion not confined to the really vital parts which make up most of the inhabited world, and indeed may properly bear that name, the world, that is, which is bounded by the two rivers, the Euphrates and the Rhine, the one disservering us from the Germans and all the more brutish nations (ὅσα θηριωδέστερα ἔθνη), the Euphrates from the Parthians and from the Sarmatians and the Scythians, races which are no less savage than the Germans (ἅπερ οὐχ ἧττον ἐξηγρίωται τῶν Γερμανικῶν), but a dominion ending, as I said above, from the rising to the setting sun both within the ocean and beyond it. (*Legat.* 8–10)

Philo describes the peoples of the more northern climates as "brutish" (θηριωδέστερα) and "savage" (ἐξηγρίωται). Greeks and Romans commonly used these terms to describe the peoples who live outside of the temperate zone. Their inability to practice cultivation in the same way as

---

95. Clarke, *Between Geography*, 29.

96. On the relationship between ethnography and historiography in Greek and its development in Jewish texts, see Sterling, *Historiography and Self-Definition*.

those who live in the temperate zone leaves them unable to have the same type of civilized life. They are, therefore, wild and savage, prone to war, and incapable of self-governance in peaceful fashion.

Josephus describes the Germans in a similar fashion. He says of them that they have "stalwart and burly figures" (ἀλκὴν καὶ μεγέθη σωμάτων) and that "their rage [is] fiercer than that the most savage beasts" (τοὺς δὲ θυμοὺς τῶν ἀγριωτάτων θηρίων σφοδροτέρους, B.J. 2.376–377). Again the stereotype, common among the Greeks and Romans, that the Germanic peoples are savage and uncivilized, is seen. Due to the fact that they live at some distance from the civilized world, however, they are thought to be fierce fighters. The Romans, however, according to Josephus, "tamed" (δαμαζόμενοι) the Germans with eight legions (B.J. 2.377).

Descriptions of African peoples in the Hebrew Bible/LXX and elsewhere also are similar to the personalized descriptions of space found in the Greco-Roman sources. Ethiopia[97] was considered a land rich in resources such as gold and precious stones (so, for example, Job 28:19). The Ethiopians are called a "lofty people and strange and difficult people" (ἔθνος μετέωρον καὶ ξένον λαὸν χαλεπόν, Isa 18:1)[98] and pictured as a warlike people in the Hebrew Bible/LXX.[99] Being on the periphery of the civilized world as they are, they do not share the same characteristics that mark those of the temperate region which is dominated by crop-producing, peaceful and well-governed people. This presentation matches that of Herodotus concerning the Ethiopians and many other Greek authors.

There are also some descriptions of more exotic peoples to which normal humans do not have regular access. *Third Baruch* describes some such types of people. The first of these peoples are described in *3 Bar.* 2:3 where Baruch sees "men dwelling. . .with faces of cattle and horns of deer and feet of goats and loins of sheep."[100] In *3 Bar.* 3:3, Baruch sees humans whose "appearance was like (that) of dogs, and their feet (like those) of deer."[101] When Baruch questions his angelic guide about the identity of

97. Typically the Hebrew word כוש is translated by the Greek word Αἰθίοψ.

98. Translation my own.

99. So, for example, 2 Kgs 19:9; 2 Chr 12:3; 14:9; 16:8; Jer 46:9; Ezek 27:10; 38:5; Nah 3:9. On this point see, Lavik, "'African' Texts of the Old Testament," 43–53.

100. This quotation, and all others from *3 Baruch*, are taken from the translation in *OTP* according to the Greek text, unless otherwise stated.

101. The Slavonic reads "faces of dogs, the horns of deer, and the feet of goats." This text brings to mind discussions of the dog-headed people of India.

these people, he discovers that they are the people who attempted to build the tower of Babel. These texts are reminiscent of those Greek texts that discuss peoples who live outside of the boundaries of the *oikoumenē*, at the edges of the earth. They resemble humans in most respects, but are grotesque and distorted in some obvious fashion. Baruch is able to see them on his heavenly journey, but like in the Greek texts examined above, most people never have access to these humans that share features with other species.

The ethnographic and geographic stereotypes so common among the Greeks and Romans are carried over into Israelite and early Jewish literature. People from various places are known by the characteristics of their lands, and all of the inhabitants of a region share these character traits. The further a people lives from the "civilized center" the more likely they are to be bellicose and savage. Such peoples ultimately must be tamed, either by another human force (such as the Romans) or by divine intervention.

Summary

In general ancient Greek, Roman, and Jewish authors demonstrate much more interest in human geography than in scientific geography. Human geography is chronologically prior, deriving, as it does, from Homer's epics. In describing places, this tradition of geography alludes to mythical and "biographical" elements of each place. It is concerned with the peoples that inhabit various regions, their customs, their specific attributes and their relations with the center of the world (whether it be Greece or Rome). The type of geography, while not entirely uninterested in questions of the more "scientific" type, is substantially more concerned with human life and its varieties. Space, in this type of geography, is thoroughly imbued with the characteristics of its inhabitants, while at the same time it endows those people with its own characteristics.

This human geography, then, is characterized by a concern for the types of people one discovers in certain types of climates. It is based largely on the idea that the physical environment determines the character of people. Furthermore, it places the center of the world within Greek and then Roman territory, thereby creating a situation in which all other cultures are measured by their adherence to Greek or Roman cultural traditions. The more remote a country is from Greek or Rome, the less likely it is to be considered "civilized" by Greek and Roman authors. Human geography in antiquity is primarily concerned with a blend of chorography and ethnography. This type of geography became established in all genres of literature in the ancient world. It is not limited to those works specifically called "geography" and it is by far the most common way of describing space in antiquity.

Environmental Determinism and Regional Variations

Human geography in antiquity involved stereotyping. The inhabitants of certain regions, as seen above, were thought to share similar constitutions and characters.[102] The environment of each area was supposed to play a large role in determining the makeup of its inhabitants. One's place of origin and its particular configuration of environmental factors were thought to determine one's character. Several environmental factors contributed to determining a person's constitution and character: the influence of the environment as a "character" in antiquity, the role of climatic zone theory, and the nature of civilization's benefits and drawbacks. The effect of these factors combined to shape the stereotypical character of the inhabitants of each region.

Space as a Personified Actor in History

Space itself was personalized and sometimes presented as an actor at particular moments of human history in the ancient world.[103] To the ancient mind, humans were subject to nature's whims, and nature was considered a personalized thing.[104] Various elements of nature were thought to control, restrict and sometimes aid human abilities and efforts. There are multiple examples of such phenomena, and a few will suffice here to illustrate the point. When the Phoenicians and Egyptians had finished bridging the Hellespont under the order of Xerxes, "a violent storm erupted which completely smashed and destroyed everything" (*Hist.* 7.34). In response,

---

102. The issue of geographical stereotyping is related to the attempt to hide the power relations at issue in the understanding of space. See chapter two above.

103. See Clarke, *Between Geography*, 27–33. While modern cultural geography has come into conflict with the notion of environmental determinism, it is important to note the ancient Greeks and Romans, though substantially interested in human impact upon their landscapes, readily accepted the idea of environmental determinism.

104. See Pilch, "Sickness and Healing in Luke-Acts," 181–209. Nature could either consist of personalized forces itself or it could be a personal agent of the gods or God.

Xerxes "ordered his men to give the Hellespont three hundred lashes and to sink a pair of shackles into the sea," and he told the men who were lashing the sea "to revile it in terms you would never hear from a Greek" (*Hist.* 7.35). Finally, Xerxes told the Hellespont that "King Xerxes will cross you, with or without your consent. People are right not to sacrifice to a muddy, brackish stream like you" (*Hist.* 7.35). Clearly the example is a comedic one, but the point remains that in the ancient world storms were thought to be active agents intervening in human affairs. When others of Xerxes' army approached Delphi in order to destroy it, "thunderbolts crashed down on them from the sky, and two crags broke off from Mount Parnassus, hurtled towards them with a terrible noise, and hit a large number of them" (*Hist.* 8.37). These things made the Persians abandon their assault on Delphi.

Nature could also be a positive force in aiding people. For example, when the Athenians were under attack by the Persian fleet, they appealed and offered sacrifice to Boreas, the north wind, to destroy the fleet. "Now, whether or not this was why Boreas struck the Persians as they were laying at anchor I cannot say. In any case, the Athenians say that Boreas had come to their help in the past and that on the occasion in question what happened was his doing" (*Hist.* 7.189). In response for his deliverance, the Athenians built a sanctuary on the River Ilissus to honor Boreas.

Sometimes nature could cause the creation of a people. Diodorus relates that the Ethiopians were the first people to arise on the earth since the sun dried up their land before any other land. So, "it is reasonable to suppose that the region which was nearest the sun was the first to bring forth living creatures" (3.2.1). Since the Ethiopians were the first people on the earth, they were "the first to be taught to honor the gods and to hold sacrifices and processions and festivals and the other rites by which men honour the deity" (3.2.2). It is for that reason that their piety is renowned throughout the world and they are essentially unconquerable; "they manifestly enjoy the favour of the gods, inasmuch as they have never experienced the rule of an invader from beyond" (3.2.4). The natural phenomenon of their land being the first to dry up and being arable enables the Ethiopians to be closest to the gods by virtue of their origins.

As in Greek and Roman thought, the Israelites often conceived of the environment as a personalized actor. There are again many examples of such phenomena, and a few will suffice here to demonstrate the point. Perhaps the most famous examples are to be found in the Exodus traditions. The plagues of the water turned to blood, the frogs, the gnats, the flies, the diseased livestock, the boils, thunder and hail, locusts and darkness could all be counted of examples of the environment's mastery over human affairs (Exod 7:14—10:29). Another example in the Exodus tradition is the parting of the Reed Sea and its subsequent drowning of the Egyptian armies (Exodus 14). While all of these examples clearly indicate that God is in charge of environmental elements, it is clear that humans are subject to environmental forces in the minds of the ancient Israelites. Job 37 expresses that God uses the elements of nature for his own purposes; "whether for correction, or for his land, or for love, he causes it to happen" (Job 37:13).

The first chapter of Jonah is another example of human's subjection to the environment. There God uses a storm and the great fish in order to force Jonah to prophesy to the Ninevites. Those sailing with Jonah clearly know that the storm has come against them on account of someone's actions (Jonah 1:7). When they realize Jonah is to blame, they are loathe to compound the problem by doing as Jonah suggests and tossing him overboard (1:10–13). Finally, they agree to do as he requests, and the storm is quieted when Jonah is cast overboard (1:15).

These examples show that, like the Greeks and Romans, the Israelites believed that they were subject to nature. It was beyond the control of ordinary human beings to manipulate the environment to a very great extent.[105] God was capable of that type of manipulation.[106] In certain cases, humans might also be able to manipulate the environment with God's help. So, for example, Moses is able to bring forth water from a rock (Exod 17:1–6). Nevertheless, in general circumstances, humans were incapable of controlling the elements of nature.

Zone Theory

Beyond the idea that humans were subject to the forces of nature, ancient Greeks and Romans believed that one's place of origin played a signifi-

---

105. Certainly things like cultivation of land are types of manipulations, but only certain areas were arable. Other lands were not arable and could not, through human manipulation, become so.

106. In Greek and Roman traditions a variety of gods and goddesses had abilities to manipulate various aspects of the environment for their own ends. See, Collins, "Rulers, Divine Men," 207–27.

cant role in determining one's character.[107] The Greeks developed a system of κλίματα or zones to "order" the world.[108] These climate zones seem to have originated with Hipparchus (Strabo, *Geogr.* 2.5.34). While the number of zones varied slightly (from five to seven), by Strabo's time it was widely accepted that there were five such zones. "Now it is one of the things proper to geography to take as an hypothesis that the earth as a whole is sphere-shaped,—just as we do in the case of the universe—and accept all of the conclusions that follow this hypothesis, one of which is that the earth has five zones" (πεντάζωνον; *Geogr.* 2.2.1). Pliny's *Natural History* describes these zones.

> For this has five divisions called zones, and all that lies beneath the two outermost zones that surround the poles at either end—both the pole named from the Seven Oxen and the one opposite to it called after Auster—is all crushed under cruel frost and everlasting cold. In both regions perpetual mist prevails, and a light that the invisibility of the milder stars renders niggardly and that is only white with hoarfrost. But the middle portion of the lands, where the sun's orbit is, is scorched by its flames and burnt up by the proximity of its heat: this is the torrid zone. There are only two temperate zones between the torrid one and the frozen ones, and these have no communication with each other because of the fiery heat of the heavenly body. (2.68.172)[109]

This account of two polar zones that are uninhabitable because of the cold, two temperate regions inhabited by the world's population, and a torrid zone uninhabitable because of the heat of the sun is common among ancient geographers and scientists. The northernmost region of the Roman *oikoumenē* is not habitable as it lies too close to the north pole.[110] It is perpetually covered in frost and allows neither the cultivation of crops nor the growth of plants that would enable animal husbandry. The southernmost regions, those lying to the south of Egypt and Ethiopia, are uninhabitable due to being "scorched by its flames and burnt up." Again, this area permits no growth of crops or wild plants, and therefore, human habitation is impossible.

107. On this point, see especially Malina and Neyrey, *Portraits of Paul*, 113–25.

108. On the origin of these climate zones, see Hicks, "*KLIMATA* in Greek Geography," and "Strabo and the *KLIMATA*." See also the discussion in Aujac, *Strabon et la science*, 149–79.

109. See also Seneca, *Nat.* 5.2–4.

110. Recall Strabo's description of the Iernians above.

The social implications of the climate zones and the lack of the possibility of communication between the two temperate zones are clearly described in Cicero's account of Scipio's dream in book six of his *Republic*. Africanus says "that the earth is surrounded and encircled by certain zones" (*Rep.* 6.20.21). Two of these zones are the poles and are not fit for human habitation, and the central zone is "scorched by the heat of the sun" (*Rep.* 6.20.21). This leaves only two zones, one northern (which the Romans inhabit), and one southern which "has no connection with your zone" (*Rep.* 6.20.21). The speech is given in the context of seeking honor. Africanus stresses that a return to one's heavenly origin by virtue of rendering service to the state is the proper way to spend one's life. This is so since "some of the inhabitants live in parts of the earth that are oblique, transverse, and sometimes directly opposite your own; from such you can expect nothing surely that is glory" (*Rep.* 6.19.20). Without news of the exploits of the Romans being able to travel to the other temperate zone, honor received from those dwelling in the southern *oikoumenē* is not a possibility.

Those people who lived in the southern *oikoumenē* were called the "antipodes" or "antichthones" by the Greeks and Romans.[111] The tradition can be traced at least as far as Aristotle. "Since, then, there must be a region which bears to the other pole the same relation as that which we inhabit bears to our pole, it is clear that this region will be analogous to ours in the disposition of winds as well as in other respects" (Aristotle, *Mete.* 2.5.362b).[112] This other half of the world was inaccessible to the Greeks and Romans. "Thus there are seas encircling the globe and dividing it in two, so robbing us of half the world, since there is no region affording passage from there to here or from here to there" (Pliny, *Nat.* 2.68.170). Describing the earth, Cicero reports in his *Tusculan Disputations* that it is "habitable and cultivated in two separate zones . . . the one in which we dwell" and "the other, the Southern, unknown to us, called by the Greek ἀντίχθονα: all other parts are uncultivated, because we gather they are either frozen with cold or parched with heat" (*Tusc.* 1.28.68–69). Manilius describes these antipodes as "unknown nations of mankind" who "draw from the same Sun light that we share and [have] shadows which fall contrary to ours; in an inverted sky they behold signs which set on the left and rise on the right" (Manilius *Astr.* 1.377–381). The antipodes are op-

111. Romm, *Edges of the Earth*, 128–35.

112. Diogenes Laertius *Lives* 3.24, says that Plato was the first to speak about the antipodes.

posites of the Greeks and Romans. For example, "our 'down' is their 'up'" (Diogenes Laertius *Lives* 8.26). Lucian parodies the idea of the antipodes. "When a scientist was talking of the Topsy-turvy people (ἀντιπόδων), he made him get up, took him to a well, showed him their own reflection in the water and asked: 'Is that the sort of topsy-turvy people you mean?'" (Lucian *Demon.* 22). The idea of the antipodes was still current in the time of Augustine. Augustine, however, rejects their existence on the basis that it is contrary to scripture (Augustine *Civ.* 16.9).

While Ptolemy had denied the relevance for geography of the characteristics of peoples in his *Geography*, he elsewhere held that geographical location was the chief criterion by which one might understand ethnic characteristics (τῶν ἐθνικῶν ἰδιωμάτων). Such national characteristics were in large part determined by where upon the earth one's homeland was located. Ptolemy describes how these climate zones affect national characteristics.

> The demarcation of national characteristics is established in part by entire parallels and angles [that is, latitude and longitude] . . . the region we inhabit is in one of the northern quarters, the people who live under the southern parallels, that is, those from the equator to the summer tropic, since they have the sun over their heads and are burned by it, have black skins and thick, wooly hair, are contracted in form and shrunken in stature, are sanguine in nature, and in habits are for the most part savage because their homes are continually oppressed by heat . . . Those who live under the more northern parallels, those, I mean, who have the Bears over their heads, since they are far removed from the zodiac and the heat of the sun, are therefore cooled; but because they have a richer share of moisture, which is most nourishing and is not exhausted by heat, they are white in complexion, straight-haired, tall and well-nourished, and somewhat cold by nature; these too are savage in their habits because their dwelling places are continually cold. . .The inhabitants of the region between the summer tropic and the Bears, however, since the sun is neither directly over their heads nor far distant at its noon-day transits, share in the equable temperature of the air, which varies, to be sure, but has no violent changes from heat to cold. They are therefore medium in colouring, of moderate stature, in nature equable, live close together, and are civilized in their habits. (*Tetrabiblos* 2.2.56–57)[113]

---

113. All quotations of Ptolemy's *Tetrabiblos*, unless otherwise indicated, are from Robbins's translation in the LCL. See also Vitruvius *Arch.* 6.1.1–12.

According to Ptolemy, more than just the appearance of peoples was determined by their position on the earth. Those who live in the extreme northern or southern parts of the Greek *oikoumenē* are "savage" (ἄγριοι). Those who live in the temperate climate (i.e. Greeks and Romans in this case) are, by contrast, "civilized" (ἥμεροι) because of the excellence of their region. The Hippocratic tract, *Airs, Waters, Places* reveals to what extent the region in which one dwelt affected character.

> For in general you will find assimilated to the nature of the land both the physique and the characteristics of the inhabitants. For where the land is rich, soft, and well-watered, and the water is very near the surface, so as to be hot in summer and cold in winter, and if the situation be favourable as regards the seasons, there the inhabitants are fleshy, ill-articulated, moist, lazy, and generally cowardly in character. Slackness and sleepiness can be observed in them, and as far as the arts are concerned they are thick-witted, and neither subtle nor sharp. But where the land is bare, waterless, rough, oppressed by winter's storms and burnt by the sun, there you will see men who are hard, lean, well-articulated, well-braced, and hairy; such natures will be found energetic, vigilant, stubborn and independent in character and in temper, wild rather than tame, of more than average sharpness and intelligence in the arts, and in war of more than average courage. The things also that grow in the earth all assimilated themselves to the earth. Such are the most sharply contrasted natures and physiques. Take these observations as a standard when drawing all other conclusions, and you will make no mistake. (24.43–67)[114]

The geographic locale of a people is the first and most important clue to their identity and ethnos. Indeed, if this is taken as a standard by which to assess people it will admit of "no mistake." Geography was, at least for this author, the primary criterion of identity. The region of origin, therefore, determined not only what individuals would look like (literally their forms: εἴδεια), but also what type of character (τρόπους) they

---

114. All translations of Hippocrates's *Airs, Waters, Places*, unless otherwise indicated, are taken from Jones' translation in the LCL. That inhabitants of various regions and climates shared similar character traits and constitutions was a widely held view in antiquity. See Plato *Leg.* 5.747D, "some districts are naturally superior to others for the breeding of men of a good or bad type . . . Some districts are ill-conditioned or well-conditioned owing to a variety of winds or to sunshine, others owing to their waters, others owing simply to the produce of the soil . . ." All translations of Plato's *Leg.*, unless otherwise indicated, are taken from Bury's translation in the LCL. See also Pliny *Nat.* 2.80.189–90.

had. Cicero, for example, relates that the Carthaginians were fraudulent because merchants regularly sailed into their harbors.[115]

The rhetoricians also held that geography in large part determined personal characteristics.[116] Menander Rhetor conveys instructions on how to praise an emperor's geographical origins.

> After the prooemia, you will come to the topic of his native country. Here you must ask yourself whether it is a distinguished country or not [and whether he comes from a celebrated and splendid race or not]. If his native country is famous, you should place your account of it first . . . This encomium is not peculiar to the emperor, but applies generally to the inhabitants of the city . . . If the city has no distinction, you must inquire whether his nation as a whole is considered brave and valiant, or is devoted to literature or the possession of virtues, like the Greek race, or again is distinguished for law, like the Italian, or is courageous, like the Gauls or Paeonians. You must then take a few features from the nation, instead of from the native city, associating the emperor's praise with this also, and arguing that it is inevitable that a man from such a [city or] nation should have such characteristics . . . (*Or.* 2.369.18–370.3)

To be sure, Greek and Roman authors allowed for variations within regions, but one's regional status was largely constitutive of one's character. In fact, in praising the emperor, Menander allows that "he stands out among all his praiseworthy compatriots" (2.370.4–5). There is an inevitability, however, to which Menander refers insofar as he, like most Greeks and Romans, assumes that people from various places are generally the same in their constitutions, with little individual difference. This way of thinking about character and geography was not limited to the Greeks and Romans in the ancient world. Indian health systems also relied on these types of generalizations in the treatment of patients.[117]

Strabo follows this tradition vigorously. In *Geogr.* 3.1.6–2.15 he discusses the Turditanians (also known, according to Strabo, as the Turdulians). These people occupy the best land of the Iberians for cultivation. Strabo calls it a blessed region (τῇ δὲ τῆς χώρας εὐδαιμονίᾳ, *Geogr.* 3.2.15) and "wondrously well endowed" (θαυματῶς εὐτυχεῖ, *Geogr.* 3.2.4). These people, like the Romans (and because of Roman intervention) are

---

115. Cicero *Agr.* 2.35.95. See also Tit 1:12 in reference to the Cretans.

116. Malina and Neyrey, *Portraits of Paul*, 70–72; and Neyrey, *Honor and Shame*, 95–97. See also Vasaly, *Representations*.

117. Sargent, *Hippocratic Heritage*, 1–80.

"civilized" (ἥμερον) and "political" (πολιτικὸν, *Geogr.* 3.2.15). Because of the land's natural endowments, these people were the most peaceful among their neighbors and "completely changed over to the Roman way of life" and became "wearers of togas" (τογᾶτοι, *Geogr.* 3.2.15). The cultivation of the land leads to a Romanization of the Turditanians.[118] Forsaking cultivation, alternately, could lead to ruin for a civilization. This is what happened to the Artabrians.

> . . . although the country was blest in fruits, in cattle, and in the abundance of its gold and silver and similar metals, still, most of the people had ceased to gain their livelihood from the earth, and were spending their time in brigandage and in continuous warfare both with each other and with their neighbours across the Tagus, until they were stopped by the Romans, who humbled them and reduced most of their cities to mere villages, though they improved some of their cities by adding colonies thereto. It was the mountaineers who began this lawlessness, as was likely to be the case; for, since they occupied sorry land and possessed but little property, they coveted what belonged to the others. And the latter, in defending themselves against the mountaineers, were necessarily rendered powerless over their private estates, so that they, too, began to engage in war instead of farming; and the result was that the country, neglected because it was barren of planted products, became the home only of brigands. (*Geogr.* 3.3.5)

Without cultivation, a people falls into lawlessness (ἀνομίας). They are no longer bound by the customs of civilized (that is, Roman) society. Fortunately, according to Strabo, the Romans relieved the Artabrians of this burden of incessant warfare by "civilizing" them and returning their focus to agriculture. One can easily see here the power relations hidden within this way of describing the spaces of Roman spatial practices and the alternative spatial practices of their neighbors.

At least some early Jewish authors were aware of the Greek geographic theory of zones. *Jubilees* 8–9 presents a picture of the world that reflects this zone theory familiar to the Greeks and Romans. In its description of the inhabited world divided among the three sons of Noah and their offspring, *Jub.* 8:29–30 describe the lands to which each of Noah's sons was assigned.

---

118. On the relationship between cultivation and civilization see, Hartog, *Memories of Odysseus*, 21–26. On the discussion of other people in Strabo, see Sherwin-White, *Racial Prejudice*, 1–13.

This is the land which came to Japheth and to his sons as the portion of his inheritance which he will possess for himself and for his sons and for their generations forever: the five great islands and a great land in the north. But it is cold, and the land of Ham is hot, but the land of Shem is not hot or cold because it is mixed with cold and heat.

Ham's assigned portion is Africa, a region difficult to inhabit because of its oppressive heat, while Japheth is given the northern parts of Europe. Shem is given the temperate zone in the middle of the hot and cold zones. This understanding of the *oikoumenē* clearly is indebted to Greek geographical traditions concerning the five zones.[119] Jubilees, while accepting the notion of the zones, does not go on to describe the types of inhabitants of each zone, but it is likely that this author would have accepted the notion of ethnographic stereotypes so prevalent in Greek and Roman texts.[120]

Omphalos and Centrality

The Greeks believed themselves to inhabit the middle position of the *oikoumenē*. Delphi was considered to the be the exact middle of the earth. Strabo describes Delphi and its temple as "almost in the centre of Greece taken as a whole . . . and it was also believed to be in the centre of the inhabited world, and people called it the navel of the earth" (*Geogr.* 9.3.6). Plutarch also notes that Delphi is the center of the earth (*Def. Orac.* 409E–410A). The tradition is first recorded, according to Strabo, in Pindar's *Pythian Ode 6*. There Pindar calls Delphi "the shrine that is the centre of the loudly echoing Earth" (*Pyth.* 6.3–4). Greek maps reinforced the idea of the Greek peninsula as the center of the earth with Delphi as the center of Hellas.[121] Pausanias also relates the idea that Delphi was a sacred site because of its location at the center of the earth. The Delphians had a white marble marker that they said is "the centre of all the earth" (*Descr.* 10.16.2). The earliest Greeks, as discussed above, understood the *oikoumenē* to be circular and surrounded by Ocean. This way of conceiving of the world placed Greece in the middle and everything outside of it on

---

119. See the discussion in Scott, *Geography in Early Judaism*, 23–35.

120. Philo *Heir* 147 describes the zones of the earth in terms similar to those discussed above. Also Philo *Mos.* 114.

121. Dilke, *Greek and Roman Maps*, 24.

the periphery to varying degrees. Much like Aristotle's claim that Greece lay in the middle of the earth according to its latitude, the tradition of Delphi as the center of the earth placed Greece, and Delphi in particular, in the most significant position on the earth.

Aristotle believed the Greeks, by virtue of their global position, to be the most advanced humans. Europeans were "full of spirit but somewhat lacking in intelligence and skill, so that they continue comparatively free, but lacking in political organization and capacity to rule their neighbors" (*Pol.* 7.6.1).[122] Those residing in Asia, on the contrary, were "intelligent and skillful in temperament, but lack spirit, so that they are in continuous subjection and slavery" (*Pol.* 7.6.1). Finally, Greece "participates in both characters, just as it occupies the middle position geographically, for it is both spirited and intelligent" (*Pol.* 7.6.1). This middle position of the Greeks is, according to Aristotle, why the Greeks are able to maintain their freedom and rule over other peoples.

The Romans spoke of Rome in much the same manner. Vitruvius, for example, argues that Rome lies in the most favorable location according to climate zone theory. He says that "it is in the true mean within the space of all the world and the regions of the earth, that the Roman people holds its territories" (*Arch.* 6.1.10). Those to the north, according to Vitruvius, lack intelligence, while the more southerly peoples lack courage. The Romans, on the contrary, "are exactly tempered in either direction, both in the structure of the body, and by their strength of mind in the matter of endurance and courage" (*Arch.* 6.1.11). It is due to this most favorable combination of elements that the Romans are able to rule the entire world. "Thus the divine mind has allotted to the Roman state an excellent and temperate region in order to rule the world" (*Arch.* 6.1.11). The Romans were able to take over this line of reasoning straight from the Greeks insofar as those who occupied the same latitude were thought to share the same constitution and character.

The Romans, however, could not argue that Rome occupied the middle position in terms of the entire *oikoumenē*. They lived near the westernmost edge of the *oikoumenē* and were well aware that the vast majority of the land lay to the east of them. There is a sense, nevertheless, in which the Romans could argue for Rome as the center of the world. Rome was the central city of the world insofar as it drew resources from

---

122. All quotations of Aristotle's *Politics*, unless otherwise indicated, are taken from Rackham's translation in the LCL.

all other parts of the world.¹²³ These resources could consist of goods or peoples. Rome imported meat from the Sequana (*Geogr.* 4.3.2), textiles from Patavium (*Geogr.* 5.1.7), plants, reeds and papyrus from Tyrrhenia (*Geogr.* 5.2.9), and several wines and grain from Campania (*Geogr.* 5.4.3). There are numerous tales also of Roman elites being collectors of cultural artifacts (e.g. *Geogr.* 5.2.2; 6.3.1; 10.2.21; 12.5.3; 13.1.19; 14.1.25). Rome is central insofar as it is the place to which all things come. "By saying that Rome was centrally placed in Strabo's conception of the world, I refer to its position at the point where the various lines of movements of goods, people, and ideas met."¹²⁴ It is not the center of the earth in terms of physical geography, but its centrality is in its symbolic geography as the place to which all things flow.¹²⁵

Early Jews considered Jerusalem the center of the *oikoumenē*. The idea that Jerusalem is the center of the world, or its omphalos, is first preserved in Ezekiel. Ezekiel 5:5 reads, "Thus says the Lord God: This is Jerusalem; I have set her in the center of the nations, with countries all around her." This is the beginning of a prophetic pronouncement of judgment upon Jerusalem, but it clearly claims that God placed Jerusalem in the middle of the *oikoumenē*. The text of Ezekiel further stresses the centrality of Jerusalem and its coming destruction in 38:12. The Lord is coming "to seize spoil and carry off plunder; to assail the waste places that are now inhabited, and the people who were gathered from the nations, who are acquiring cattle and goods, who live at the center of the earth (τὸν ὀμφαλὸν τῆς γῆς)." Jerusalem, then, is the center of the *oikoumenē* according to Ezekiel. *Jubilees* 22:11–14 preserves the same idea, probably based in large part upon Ezekiel.¹²⁶

Josephus and Philo also preserve traditions regarding the centrality of Jerusalem.

> On the frontier separating them lies the village called Anuath Borcaeus, the northern limit of Judaea; its southern boundary, if one measures the country lengthwise, is marked by a village on

---

123. See the discussion in Clarke, *Between Geography and History*, 210–28.

124. Ibid., 223.

125. On Rome as a cultural center see Jaeger, *Livy's Written Rome*; Kraus, "'No Second Troy.'"

126. See Scott, *Geography of Early Judaism*, 33–34; and *Tan., Kedoshim* 10. See Hanson, "Transformed on the Mountain," 151–52. In addition to those texts listed above, Hanson discusses Judg 9:37; *Jub.* 8:19; and *1 Enoch* 26:1–4.

the Arabian frontier, which the local Jews call Iardan. In breadth is stretches from the river Jordan to Joppa. The city of Jerusalem lies at its very centre, for which reason the town (τὸ ἄστυ) has sometimes, not inaptly, been called the 'navel' (ὀμφαλὸν) of the country. (Josephus, *B.J.* 3.51–52)[127]

Both of these authors show the centrality of Jerusalem, but they limit its centrality to the land of Judea. Neither author makes the same claim as Ezekiel. Whereas Ezekiel states the Jerusalem is centrally located among all the nations of the world, Josephus and Philo locate it centrally among the Jewish territories. Both authors were well aware of Rome's claim to centrality, and neither author would have expected a favorable response had they claimed that Jerusalem instead was the center of the *oikoumenē*. Josephus clearly recognizes Rome's claim to centrality elsewhere in the *Jewish War*. In describing the temple dedicated to Pax in Rome, Josephus says that in it are collected the most precious things from everywhere in the *oikoumenē*.

> ... indeed, into that shrine were accumulated and stored all objects for the sight of which men had once wandered over the whole world, eager to see them severally while they lay in various countries. Here, too, he laid up the vessels of gold from the temple of the Jews, on which he prided himself; but their Law and the purple hangings of the sanctuary he ordered to be deposited and kept in the palace. (*B.J.* 7.160–162)

The Roman temple and the imperial palace now held the objects most sacred to the Jewish people. More than that, however, the temple in Rome "stored all objects for the sight of which men had once wandered over the whole world." There is no longer need to travel across the *oikoumenē* to see the most spectacular artifacts contained in it. They have all been moved to the new center of the *oikoumenē*, that is, Rome. This temple is the *oikoumenē* writ small. It is the world in microcosm.

Isaiah envisions a time when Israel will be the middle of a new world. Isaiah 19:24 states, "On that day Israel will be the third with Egypt and Assyria, a blessing in the midst of the earth" (בקרב הארץ). The es-

---

127. Compare Philo *Legat.* 294: "But why should I cite the testimony of strangers when I can set before you that of many of your closest kinsmen? For instance your maternal grandfather M. Agrippa, being in Judaea when Herod my grandfather was king of the country (χώρας), saw fit to come up from the coast (ἀπὸ θαλάττης) to the capital city (μητρόπολιν) situated in the centre of the land (ἐν μεσογείῳ κειμένην ἠξίωσε)."

chatological centrality of Israel, Jerusalem, and the Jerusalem temple, of course, are well known. Many texts contain the idea of the nations coming to Jerusalem to worship with the Judeans at Mount Zion.[128] The end of the present era, then, marks a new phase in which all the nations will recognize the centrality of Jerusalem.

Civilization and Softness

Because of their central location, then, the Greeks and Romans believed themselves to hold the best position for ruling in terms of the balance of their geographical zone. In some instances, however, good land could be seen as a problem rather than a benefit. At the end of his *Histories*, Herodotus relates the proposal of a certain Artacytes to Cyrus to allow the Persian people to emigrate from their native homeland into a more prosperous and fruitful country. In response, Cyrus "advised them to be prepared, in that case, to become subjects instead of rulers, on the grounds that soft lands tend to breed soft men" (*Hist.* 9.122). Even for a people as hardened by war and conquest as the Persians, it was impossible to remain militarily strong in the face of the easy living provided by a land that produced plenty. Cyrus stated further, "It is impossible, he said, for one and the same country to produce remarkable crops and good fighting men" (*Hist.* 9.122). The Persians' response to such logic was that they "admitted the truth of his argument and took their leave . . . and they chose to live in a harsh land and rule rather than to cultivate fertile plants and be others' slaves" (*Hist.* 9.122). Dio Chrysostom also notes this dichotomy between hard and soft peoples. He says that Indians, Spartans, Phrygians and Lydians all experience pain from wounds or burns, "yet while the Indian and the Spartan refuse to flinch because they have been hardened to it, the Phrygian and Lydian do flinch, because they are weak and not hardened" (*Or.* 68.2).

Sometimes nearness to a developed civilization produces this type of softness in people. Caesar notes that the Belgae are "the most courageous (*fortissimi*), because they are the farthest removed from the culture and civilization of the Province, and least often visited by merchants introducing the commodities that make for effeminacy" (*Bell. gall.* 1.1). These Gauls are made valiant (*virtute*) on account of their continuous warfare with the

---

128. The texts are too numerous to mention in full. Some examples include Isa 66:20; Jer 3:17; Mic 4:2; Zech 8:22; 14:16.

Germans. That civilization could weaken a people is a stock idea in Roman literature. Cicero, in fact, thinks that the location of Greece allows for its present state of decline since it lies on the seacoast. This creates a situation in which the inhabitants "are constantly being tempted far from home by soaring hopes and dreams" (*Rep.* 2.7). Luxury items are particularly notorious for causing "ruin to states" (*perniciosa civitatibus*; *Rep.* 2.8).[129]

CREATING DIVISIONS

The ancients believed that the world was divided into a certain order by God or gods.[130] This order was represented in the divisions made on the land between the various peoples who inhabited it. A country or even the earth itself could be divided into smaller pieces which were then assigned certain characteristics. Greek and Roman mythology held that these units most often were divided by the gods/God or their agents and assigned to individual peoples or nations.

Gods divided and assigned territory in the Greek and Roman worlds. Homer relates that the cosmos is divided into three parts for the sons of Cronus (*Il.* 15.187–99). Aelius Aristides says, "Zeus created everything, and all that exists is the work of Zeus" (*Or.* 43.7).[131] Moreover in his creation, "he made a proper division of each thing and gave out lots in which to dwell" (*Or.* 43.14). Finally, he assigns to the gods the four regions of the earth.

> And he gave the four regions of the earth to the gods, so that nothing anywhere might be without gods, but that they might everywhere attend upon all things which are and all things which are coming into being, having divided up among themselves, like prefects and satraps, first as their homeland the region of heaven and then that in the air and in the sea and on the earth. He caused that man most of all share in their providence, since everywhere he preserved the proper due of the races and thought that their rank should not be unprofitable. (*Or.* 43.18–19)

---

129. Also Hippocrates *Airs, Waters, Places* 12 says of the temperate section of Asia that "courage, endurance, industry and high spirit could not arise in such conditions, either among the natives or among immigrants, but pleasure must be supreme."

130. So, for example, Aelius Aristides *Or.* 37.5; Pausanias *Descr.* 2.1.5–6; Arrian *Indika* 7.5–6.

131. All translations from Aelius Aristides, unless otherwise indicated, are taken from Behr's translation in *P. Aelius Aristides*.

The gods behave like prefects and satraps, dividing and overseeing the lands. It is from the gods, particularly Zeus, that humans come to understand the divisions of the land which are already in place when they are created. Each people has a proper place in the divine *oikoumenē*, over which Zeus rules as the "father of all, rivers, heaven, earth, gods, mankind, animals, and plants" (*Or.* 43.29).

In Virgil's *Aeneid*, Jupiter assigns not only Rome and Latium to the Trojan ancestors, but "empire without end" (*imperium sine fine*; *Aen.* 1.255–279). The Romans are to become "lords of the world" (*rerum dominos*; *Aen.* 1.282). Julius Caesar would extend the empire to the ocean (*imperium Oceano*; *Aen.* 1.287), with Ocean here representing the edge of the world. For this to happen, however, Aeneas has to abandon his city of origin. Hector appears to him in a dream allowing him to do just that. "'Ah, flee, goddess-born,' he cries, 'and escape from the flames'" (*Aen.* 2.289–290). He is to take Troy into its glorious future. "Troy entrusts to you her holy things and household gods; take them to share your fortunes: seek for them the mighty city, which, when you have wandered over the deep, you shall at last establish!" (*Aen.* 2.293–295). The fullness of this vision of the new empire is found in book 6. Augustus Caesar will "again set up the Golden Age in Latium amid fields where Saturn once reigned, and shall spread his empire past Garamant and Indian, to a land that lies beyond the stars, beyond the paths of the year and the sun, where heaven-bearing Atlas turns on his shoulders the sphere, inset with gleaming stars" (*Aen.* 6.792–797). Roman rule recreates the order of Saturn since Caesar is of divine stock. His empire will go beyond the zones of the *oikoumenē* (that is, beyond the territory marked out by the zodiac). The divisions of land will change when the Roman empire rises to its height, and the new divisions are to be marked out by the Roman ruler acting in Saturn's place.

In the Roman world, then, the emperors were thought to be responsible for dividing the world into its constituent parts. These parts could then be changed according to the will or need of Caesar. According to the geographer Strabo, Caesar Augustus made two major divisions between territories.

> . . . for when his native land committed to him the foremost place (προστασίαν) of authority . . . he divided the whole of his empire into two parts, and assigned one portion to himself and the other to the Roman people; to himself, all parts that had need of

> a military guard (that is, the part that was barbarian and in the neighbourhood of tribes not yet subdued, or lands that were sterile and difficult to bring under cultivation, so that, being unprovided with everything else, but well provided with strongholds, they would try to throw off the bridle and refuse obedience), and to the Roman people all the rest, in so far as it was peaceable and easy to rule without arms ... (*Geogr.* 17.3.25)

Clearly this text is meant to praise Caesar for acting on behalf of the people. He has granted the people (more specifically the Roman Senate) control over territory that requires no standing army to defend and only taken possession for himself of those territories that are in need of protection from uncivilized or non-pacified neighbors. These territories he divides in such a way that he is able to pacify the people living in them and bring them under Roman rule. From Strabo's point of view, then, Augustus acts only with the best interests of Rome in mind in dividing the land.

Dionysius of Halicarnassus places the Roman division of the earth in an even earlier period. He relates how Numa, the legendary second Roman king apportioned out the land.

> First, to the end that people should be content with what they had and should not covet what belonged to others, there was the law that appointed boundaries (κτήσεων) to every man's possessions. For, having ordered everyone to draw a line around his own land and to place stones on the bounds, he consecrated these stones to Jupiter Terminalis and ordained that all should assemble at the place every year on a fixed day and offer sacrifices to them; and he made the festival in honour of these gods of boundaries among the most dignified of all. This festival the Romans call Terminalia, from the boundaries, and the boundaries themselves, but the change of one letter as compared with our language, they call *termines*. He also enacted that, if any person demolished or displaced these boundary stones he should be looked upon as devoted to the god, to the end that anyone who wished might kill him as a sacrilegious person with impunity and without incurring any stain of guilt ... For they looked upon these boundary stones as gods and sacrifice to them yearly ... (*Ant. rom.* 2.74.3–5)

After fixing the boundaries of the land, Numa reinforced these boundaries by means of religious festivals. The boundaries in effect became part and parcel of the gods' allotment of territory. Those who violated these boundaries by moving the stones were subject to death without the opportunity for vengeance. The boundary stones themselves were thought to be gods. Even the distinctions made by human beings were actually, at base, part of the divine order of the world.

In his discussion of the art of measuring, Frontinus says that "the truth about sites or area cannot be expressed without lines that can be geometrically measured."[132] The very idea that a place has a "truth" (veritas) suggests that divisions are considered an inherent feature of the land that is made explicit in the act of measuring. For Frontinus, those areas that are geometrically divided reflect their truth. Unmeasured land, however, violates its truth, or its fundamental way of being. The measuring out of a territory allows the calculation of its size. These "two operations of mapping out the territory and calculating its size—of measuring and counting, of *mathematizing* the territory—are made to equate truth, or, in other words, are seen as amounting to an expression of the real nature of the territory."[133] A territory's truth, then, is expressed when it has been officially measured and allotted by the Roman land surveyors (agrimensores). This allotment of land is especially crucial to Roman interests in times of conquest where it "provided a public and highly visible demonstration of Roman power and the humiliation of the enemy" and "announced complete Roman control of the disposal of the land."[134]

For early Jews, it was God or God's agents that created such divisions in the land. "When the Lord created his works from the beginning, and, in making them, determined their boundaries, he arranged his works in an eternal order, and the dominion for all generations" (Sir 16:26–27).[135] The primordial act of creation is fixing the boundaries of the things created. Everything has a place in the creation, and this includes the various nations of people. Indeed, in Israelite tradition Yahweh held the first position as a divider of territories. This is hardly surprising insofar as Yahweh is the creator of territory. Deuteronomy 32:8 states, "When the Most High apportioned the nations, when he divided humankind, he fixed the boundaries of the peoples according to the number of the gods . . ." Here Yahweh is seen as the one who established the territories of the various

---

132. Julius Frontinus *De Arte Mensoria* 2–3. The text and translation is found in Campbell, *Writings of the Roman Land Surveyors.*

133. Cuomo, "Divide and Rule," 193.

134. Campbell, "Surveyors in Ancient Rome," 81.

135. See also Acts 17:26.

human inhabitants of the earth. He is the divider of the land. He also fixes the boundaries of Israel in the land (Num 33:50—34:15). Yahweh is responsible for the division of people also in Genesis 11. Yahweh scatters the descendants of Noah all over the world in Genesis 11 and confuses their speech so that humans are no longer able to live together in one "nation."

In Yahweh's case, he also is free to change the boundaries. Isaiah 10:13 reads in part, "I have removed the boundaries of peoples . . ." Yahweh is not bound by the divisions of the land, but the people are bound by them. Yahweh is also presented as a granter of lands. "He gave them the lands of the nations, and they took possession of the wealth of peoples" (Ps 105:44).[136] Similarly he is free to take the land away. "Therefore he raised his right hand and swore to them that he would make them fall in the wilderness, and would disperse their descendants among the nations, scattering them among the lands."[137]

Failure to respect the divisions God makes in the land may result in terrible consequences. Yahweh assigns the Israelites land (Exod 23:31; Num 33:50—34:15). Other nations, however, violate the distinctions that Yahweh establishes, and according to Joel 3:2, they will be judged "because they have scattered them among the nations. They have divided my land . . ."

The book of Jubilees explains that the Israelites were due the land that God had set apart for them, and that the Canaanites had taken possession of it wrongly in the first place.

> And Ham and his sons went into the land which was his possession, which he found in his portion in the land of the south. But Canaan saw that the land of Lebanon as far as the river of Egypt was very good. And he did not go into the land of his inheritance toward the west, that is the sea, but he dwelt in the land of Lebanon, eastward and westward, from the bank of the Jordan and from the shore of the sea. And Ham, his father, and Cush and Mizraim, his brothers, said to him, "You have dwelt in a land which is not yours nor did it come forth for us by lot. Do not do this, because if you do this, you and your children will fall in the land and be cursed with sedition because by sedition you have dwelt and by sedition your children will fall and you will be uprooted forever. Do not dwell in the dwelling of Shem because it came to Shem and his sons by lot. You are cursed and you will

---

136. Also Pss 107:3–9; 135:12.
137. Also Ezek 20:23.

be cursed more than all of the sons of Noah by the curse which we swore with an oath before the holy judge and before Noah, our father." But he would not listen to them and he dwelt in the land of Lebanon from Hamath to the entrance of Egypt, he and his sons, until this day. (*Jub.* 10:28–33)[138]

There were strong prohibitions as well for the Israelite who might be tempted to move his neighbor's boundary markers. "You shall not move your neighbor's boundary marker, set up by former generations, on the property that will be allotted to you in the land that the Lord your God is giving you to possess" (Deut 19:14).[139] One who does so is cursed in the sight of the community (Deut 27:17).[140] Hosea contends that the "princes of Judah have become like those who remove the landmark" (Hos 5:10). Distinctions in the land are to be maintained unless God changes them.

Israelite rulers also had authority to divide land. David decides to divide land between Mephibosheth and his servant Ziba (2 Sam 19:19). Joshua is told to divide the land that the Israelites possess between the nine and a half tribes (Josh 13:7), and Yahweh gives him specific directions for doing so (Josh 13:8—21:45). Ezekiel also is instructed in apportioning the land to the tribes (Ezekiel 47). A further Israelite tradition attributes the authority to divide territory to Moses. Artapanus presents Moses as a *Kulturbringer*. Of Egypt he relates that Moses "also divided the state into thirty-six nomes, and to each of the nomes he assigned the God to be worshipped."[141] Here Moses shares the same role as Yahweh in the text from Deuteronomy.

The distinctions made by God's agents had the same force as those made by Yahweh. They were also held to be inviolable. After dividing the land among his three sons, Noah "made them all swear an oath to curse each and every one who desired to seize a portion which did not come to his lot" (*Jub.* 9:14). The sons agree to the oath and said "So be it and so let it be to them and to their sons forever in their generations until the day of judgment in which God will judge them with a sword and with fire on account of all the evil of the pollution of their errors which have

---

138. All translations of *Jubilees*, unless otherwise stated, are taken from Wintermute's translation in *OTP*. See Blenkinsopp, "The Bible, Archaeology and Politics."

139. See also Prov 22:28.

140. Those who do so are called "wicked" (Job 24:2).

141. All translations of Artapanus, unless otherwise stated, are taken from Holladay, *Fragments from Jewish Hellenistic Authors: Vol. 1.*

filled the earth with sin and pollution and fornication and transgression" (*Jub.* 9:15). Those who violated the borders of another's land stood under God's judgment. Beyond that, however, the text implies that the violation of another's boundaries brings with it sins of several types. Violation of boundaries led to total corruption insofar as living within one's boundaries was to live in a civilized (and therefore pure) manner.

Uniting Territory

At the other end of the spectrum are texts that present rulers uniting previously divided territory.

> And what was said by Homer, "The earth is common to all," you have made a reality, by surveying the whole inhabited world, by bridging the rivers in various ways, by cutting carriage roads through the mountains, by filling desert places with post stations, and by civilizing everything with your way of life and good order. Therefore I conceive of life before your time as the life thought to exist before Triptolemus, harsh, rustic, and little different from living on a mountain; yet if not entirely so, still that while Athens initiated our present, cultivated existence, this has been confirmed by you "with second attempts better" as they say. And now, indeed, there is no need to write a description of the world, nor to enumerate the laws of each people, but you have become universal geographers for all men by opening up all the gates of the inhabited world and by giving to all who wish it the power to be observers of everything and by assigning universal laws for all men and by stopping practices which formerly were pleasant to read about, but were intolerable if one should actually consider them and by making marriage legal between all peoples and by organizing the whole inhabited world into a single household. (*Or.* 26.102)

Aristides goes on to compare the rule of Rome with that of Zeus, likening the primordial chaos of the world before Zeus banished the Titans to the world before the order of Rome was established. Rather than dividing the world, then, the universal order of Rome "has been given to the earth itself and those who inhabit it" (*Or.* 26.103). The order that Rome imposes on the world, then, becomes the established order of the gods for the Romans.

For Josephus, God had granted the Romans their domination of the *oikoumenē*. Josephus appeals to the idea of God's divisions when he attempts to dissuade his fellow Judeans from open revolt against Rome. Josephus' *Jewish War* contains a speech of Agrippa trying to convince the Jews of Jerusalem who are disposed toward war to submit to Roman authority (*B.J.* 2.345–401). Josephus describes the entire inhabited world that is under Rome's control. Toward the end of the speech, Agrippa asks where the Jews would look for allies to fight Rome.

> What allies then do you expect for this war? Will you recruit them from the uninhabited wilds (ἀοικήτου)? For in the habitable world (οἰκουμένης) all are Romans—unless, maybe, the hopes of some of you soar beyond the Euphrates and you count on obtaining aid from your kinsmen in Adiabene. But they will not, for any frivolous pretext, let themselves be embroiled in so serious a war, and, if they did contemplate such folly, the Parthian would not permit it; for he is careful to maintain the truce with the Romans, and would regard it as a violation of the treaty if any of his tributaries were to march against them. The only refuge, then, left to you is divine assistance. But even this is ranged on the side of the Romans, for, without God's aid, so vast an empire (ἡγεμονίαν) could never have been built up. (*B.J.* 2.388–390)

Since Rome dominates the entire inhabited world (and another in Britain), there is nowhere to look for help in the *oikoumenē*. Furthermore "God's aid" granted them this "vast empire." Agrippa wonders if those who wish to fight Rome might look outside the *oikoumenē* (that is, outside of the areas controlled by Rome) for assistance. Even those wild nations beyond the *oikoumenē* represent no significant source of help because of their distance from Judea. No one else, including those to whom the Judeans are related, will become embroiled in an open war with Rome since the consequences would be disastrous. In the end, Agrippa's conclusion is that no nation can control the sizeable empire that Rome controls without the aid and approval of God.

Critiquing Empire

Not everyone accepted the claims to control of space made by the Greeks and Romans. Critiques of space and empire were sometimes preserved in the literature of antiquity. The famous example of Diogenes' meeting with Alexander is one example. Alexander offered to give Diogenes anything when he encountered him in Greece, but "Diogenes answered that he needed nothing else, but told him and his followers to stand out of the sunlight" (Arrian, *Anab.* 7.2.1).¹⁴² This story of Arrian follows the report that Alexander would not have stopped his expansion "even if he had added Europe and Asia and the Britannic Islands to Europe, but that he would always have searched far beyond for something unknown, in competition with himself in default of any other rival" (*Anab.* 7.1.4). At their core, both texts suggest that Alexander did not control the territories through which he traveled and challenged the notion that Alexander's campaigns represented a new control over space previously uncontrolled by Alexander. The sophists of India also critiqued Alexander's understanding of space and empire. When Alexander found these sophists "in the open air in a meadow ... they did nothing more than beat with their feet upon the ground they stood on" (*Anab.* 7.1.5). The interpretation given to this action was that "each man possesses no more of this earth than the patch we stand on; yet you, though a man like other men ... are roaming over so wide an area away from what is your own, giving no rest to yourself or others" (*Anab.* 7.1.6). The end result of Alexander's conquests is "very soon you too will die, and will possess no more of the earth than suffices for the burial of your body" (*Anab.* 1.6). The critique cuts at the very heart of the notion of empire. Despite Alexander's wide conquests, he occupies no more land than when he started, and the land which he now occupies is far from his home.

Divisions of space were a fact of life in antiquity as they are today. Those with power were able to impose their own vision of the landscape onto it through military conquest, taxation and outright usurpation of land. Often these divisions were supported through ideologies that legitimized the current arrangement.¹⁴³ Sometimes, however, the idea of a future erasure of the divisions or a return to previous divisions challenged the current divisions. For the most part, however, those who lacked the power to make divisions understood these divisions as a fact of life. Locating these divisions within divine and legal mythologies, however, hides the power relations contained therein. They are considered to be "the way things are" and so inviolable.

---

142. There are similar reports in Diogenes Laertius' *Life of Diogenes* 6.38; Plutarch *Alexander* 14; and a *Cynic Epistle* of Diogenes to Phanomucs.

143. See, for example, Bonz, "Beneath the Gaze of the Gods."

Cosmology[144]

The ancient Greeks and Romans believed that the earth was at the center of the cosmos. Indeed, this is one of the most unified points of Greek cosmology. That is not to say the position was without its critics. Aristarchus, for example, argued as early as the third century BCE for a heliocentric understanding of the universe. His views, however, were not widely accepted in antiquity.[145] Lloyd argues that Greeks believed that the earth was the center of the universe because of their anthropomorphic cosmology. Humans were considered by the Greeks to be "the highest member of the animal kingdom."[146] It followed, then, that humans be located in a "privileged position" at "the centre of the universe."[147] Much as the earth itself had a navel, or center, out of which it grew, the universe also had a center. Not surprisingly, the center of the cosmos was the earth upon which the humans who wrote about it dwelt.

A Three-Tiered Universe

The earliest Greek accounts of the cosmos assumed that the earth was a flat disk which rested on water. Above it were the sky/heavens and below, the underworld. This conception of the universe is found in the writings of Homer and Hesiod. The cosmos according to the Homeric tradition was "a simple one of earth as a circular disk around which flowed the freshwater river Ocean; the hemisphere of the vault of the sky was above, and the matching realm of Tartarus below."[148] The Greeks received this understanding of the universe from the ANE civilizations that surrounded them, most notably from the Babylonians, Assyrians, and Egyptians.[149] The Israelites adopted the tradition of the three-tiered universe from these same ANE cultures. They understood the heavens above to con-

---

144. Strabo *Geogr.* 1.1.1 considered "knowledge both of the heavens and things on the earth" as part of geography. See also Menander *Or.* 1.347.14–16.

145. Lloyd, "Greek Cosmologies." The view of the earth as the center of the universe was also challenged by some Pythagoreans.

146. Ibid., 212.

147. Ibid.

148. Wright, *Cosmology in Antiquity*, 16.

149. Ibid., 16–18.

tain the firmament beyond which God dwelled.[150] Sheol was the place of the dead underneath the world.[151] Indeed, "the great majority of biblical texts assume the three-storied universe so clearly assumed in other, ancient traditions."[152]

Concentric Circles of the Heavens

Various other cosmologies developed in the Greek and Roman worlds. Chief among these alternatives was the idea of a series of concentric circles of "heavens" surrounding the earth. The number of these heavens varied from as few as three to as many as eight.[153] From the outermost heavenly realm the supreme God ruled over the other realms. Various stars and divine beings were located in the realms between this outermost realm and the earth, which maintained its place in the center of the cosmos. These elements were eternal and not subject to the same decay as the material beings on the earth. The heavens clearly bore more importance than the earth, since the earth was sublunar. According to Cicero, everything that is sublunar is perishable, while those things that exist above the moon are eternal, such as the stars, the sun, the planets and the supreme God.[154] Cicero's cosmos consists of nine spheres. The outermost of these spheres "is that of heaven; it contains all the rest, and is itself the supreme God, holding and embracing within itself all the other spheres" (*Rep.* 6.17). By the first century BCE, the Stoics believed that the dead ascended into the supralunar spheres upon their death. Without being weighed down by the flesh, they were able to ascend to the lofty heights from which their souls originated.[155] This understanding of the cosmos is represented in early Christian literature in 2 Cor 12:2–4. There Paul speaks of being taken up into the third heaven, where Paradise is located. The fact that Paradise is located in this heaven likely indicates that it is the highest heaven in Paul's cosmological framework.

---

150. Deut 4:39; 1 Kgs 8:27; 2 Kgs 19:15; 2 Chr 20:6.

151. Job 33:18, 22, 24, 30; Ps 16:10 [15:10 LXX]; 28:1 [27:1 LXX] to cite but a few examples.

152. Oden, "Cosmogony, Cosmology."

153. Aune, *Revelation*, 2.317–19.

154. So, for example, Cicero *Rep.* 6.17. Cicero mentions that the one sublunar thing that is incorporeal and not subject to decay is the human soul.

155. Cicero *Rep.* 6.17; see also Plato *Resp.* 10.616B–617C; and *Tim.* 36–38.

Microcosm of the Universe in Architecture and Art

Roman architecture and art sometimes mimicked the shape of the cosmos. In doing so, it provided architectural/artistic representation of Rome's cosmic centrality. Ovid's description of Vesta's Roman temple (*Fast.* 6.267–282) is an example of how the Romans used the idea of the earth as a sphere in architecture. Vesta's temple is a architectural microcosm of the universe. The temple is round because "Vesta is the same as the earth" (*Fast.* 6.267). Vesta represents the earth in Ovid's description, and she, like the earth, is round. Her round temple, therefore, represents the shape of the earth. As the earth stands in the center of the spherical universe, so too, the temple of Vesta stands in the middle of the earth. The temple has "no projecting angle" (*Fast.* 6.281–282), just as the model of the universe produced by Archimedes of Syracuse (*Fast.* 6.276–279). Vesta's temple, like the earth, contains perpetual fire underneath it (*Fast.* 6.267). For this reason, Ovid likens both the hearth (which is Vesta's temple)[156] and the earth to "symbols of the home" (*Fast.* 6.268).[157]

The Romans also used the symbol of the globe to show that they had become masters over the entire earth. The fact that Vesta's temple was built in Rome replicated this idea. Since in the spherical conception of the universe the earth occupied the middle position, the microcosm of the earth represented in Vesta's temple legitimated Rome as the center of the earth. Since the earth is center of the universe, and Rome the center of the earth, Vesta's temple became (or was) the center of the entire universe.

The rule of Rome over the entire inhabited world is also represented in the form of statues according to the testimony of Dio. His *Roman History* contains a description of a statue of Caesar "mounted upon a likeness of the inhabited world" (εἰκόνα αὐτὸν τῆς οἰκουμένης χαλκοῦν ἐπιβιβασθῆναι; *Rom. Hist.* 43.14.6) and another of "the image of the inhabited world lying beneath his feet (τὴν εἰκόνα τῆς οἰκουμένης ὑπὸ τοῖς ποσὶν αὐτοῦ; *Rom. Hist.* 43.21.2). The ruler of Rome, rather than being small in comparison to the earth, stood over it as its ruler.

Microcosmic representation of the universe, as found in Vesta's temple, served to justify Rome's rule of the inhabited world. Such representations furthered the idea of Rome's centrality on the earth, and therefore, in

---

156. Vesta's name is derived from the Greek goddess Hestia. See Gee, *Ovid, Aratus and Augustus*, 115–16.

157. See the discussion in ibid., 92–125.

the cosmos. Architectural shapes, however, are not "natural." By building the temple in this shape, the Romans laid claim to a place in the cosmos that had not previously been theirs. As the earth is the "central weight" of the universe (Ovid *Fast.* 6.276), so Rome becomes the central axis of the world, from which everything stretches out across the *oikoumenē*.

Cosmic Travel

Realm of the Dead

The underworld or the realm of the dead was, in special circumstances, accessible to the living. Thus, Odysseus travels to the underworld, as does Aeneas.[158] There are many other accounts of Greek and Romans, themselves still alive, descending into the realm of the dead.[159] Lucian parodies these accounts in his *Menippus*. Menippus goes to the underworld to consult with Teiresias of Boeotia in order to find out how to live his life. His means of arriving in the underworld is through "the gates of Hades" which are opened by a Babylonian *magos* (*Men.* 6). Rather than sailing to the edge of the earth and encountering the realm of the dead there, Menippus is able to have the gates of Hades opened for him by means of magical incantation.[160] Trips to the underworld are not uncommon among early Jewish and Christian sources.[161] In the *Acts of Thomas* 6:55–57, a woman who had been killed and raised by the prayers of the apostle relates the details of her journey to the underworld. As in the Greek traditions, dying was not the only means by which one could travel to the underworld. The *Apocalypse of Paul*, for instance, relates the story of the apostle's travel to the third heaven and then his tour of the underworld.

In some circumstances, then, a living human being could access the realm of the dead. In the three-tiered universe, the land below the earth was part of the universe to which humans could (but ordinarily did not) travel. Even though such travel was possible, in no instance does it appear

---

158. *Od.* 11 and *Aen.* 6.

159. So, for example, Aristophanes *Ran.*; Plutarch *Gen. Socr.*; Pausanias, *Descr.* 9.39.5–12; Isocrates *Or.* 10.20; Herodotus *Hist.* 2.122; Diodorus 4.63.4; *Homeric Hymn to Demeter* 7; Ovid *Metam.* 4.432ff.; Lucian *Ver. hist.* 2.21–22; Philostratus *Vit. Apoll.* 8.19.

160. Psyche is also able to find a portal through the upper world into the underworld (Apuleius *Metam.* 6.17–19). For further tales of underworld journeys in the Greek and Roman traditions, see Himmelfarb, *Tours of Hell*, 41–48.

161. Ibid., 8–40.

to be a desirable thing. Humans only traveled to the underworld under divine compulsion or under some other substantial compulsion, and divine assistance was necessary in returning from the underworld.

Travel to the underworld relativized human affairs on earth. Achilles sees life on earth as preferable to that in the house of Hades. He tells Odysseus that he "would prefer to be working the earth, hired out to another, even a landless man, whose living is far from abundant, than to be lord over all of the phantoms of those who have perished" (*Od.* 11.488–91). Life on earth, while better, is vastly shorter than life in the underworld. The realm of the dead, even for the lord of the phantoms, is less pleasant than even the meanest life on earth. At least by the fifth century BCE, however, there was a special part of the realm of the dead reserved for those who performed heroic deeds on earth. This area, known as Elysium among the Romans, was later thought to contain all of those dead who had lived pious lives on earth.[162]

In the underworld, distinctions that mattered on earth eventually fade away. Indeed, Menippus relates to his friend that none of those distinguishing features which mark people on earth such as wealth or beauty are recognizable when they are merely skeletons in the underworld: "for none of their former means of identification abode with them, but their bones were all alike, undefined (ἄδηλα), unlabelled (ἀνεπίγραφα), and unable ever again to be distinguished by anyone" (Lucian *Icar.* 15). Each person is given a part to play by Fate, as it were, and in the end must return the "costume" to Fate before assuming a place in the underworld. Earthly distinctions cease to matter after death (*Men.* 16). Philip of Macedon, for instance, is seen by Menippus "cobbling worn-out sandals for pay" (*Men.* 17). In this way, tours of the underworld suggest that life on earth is a relativized condition that is fleeting. Interestingly, though it is difficult to distinguish them, the dead are found "living by nations and clans" (κατὰ ἔθνη καὶ κατὰ φῦλα: *Icar.* 15). These are primary markers of identity in the geographical material surveyed in chapter three. According to Lucian, the one thing that does matter even in the underworld is one's ethnos and tribe.

---

162. Solmsen, "The World of the Dead," 31–41.

Heavenly Travel

Travel into the heavenly spheres was also a possibility. When looking down at the world from his lofty vantage point, Menippus ridicules those who possess lands considered vast by the inhabitants of earth.

> I was especially inclined to laugh at the people who quarreled about boundary-lines, and at those who plumed themselves on working the plain of Sicyon or possessing the district of Oenoe in Marathon or owning a thousand acres in Acharnae. As a matter of fact, since the whole of Greece as it looked to me then from on high was no bigger than four fingers, on that scale surely Attica was infinitesimal. I thought, therefore, how little there was for our friends the rich to be proud of; for it seemed to me that the widest-acred of them all had but a single Epicurean atom under cultivation. And when I looked toward the Peloponnese and caught sight of Cynuria, I noted what a tiny region, no bigger in any way than an Egyptian bean, had caused so many Argives and Spartans to fall in a single day. Again, if I saw any man pluming himself on gold because he had eight rings and four cups, I laughed heartily at him too, for the whole of Pangaeum, mines and all was the size of a grain of millet. (*Icar.* 17)

From the air things look quite different. Nobody owns too vast a tract of land since in the scheme of the cosmos such things are no larger than "an Epicurean atom." All of these things are marginalized by their scope within the vast cosmos. The social distinctions manifest in the control of certain territories are essentially meaningless when examined from the heavenly realm.

Cicero's *Republic* also tells that territories on the earth are not what they seem when examined from a cosmic perspective. Scipio is told to consider how small a section of the vast earth the Romans actually inhabit (*Rep.* 6.19–20). Beyond this consideration, he is instructed to bear in mind the small amount of time that one has to live upon the earth, and the floods and conflagrations that prevent knowledge transfer from various ages (*Rep.* 6.21–23). The cosmic perspective relativizes both space and time.

Heavenly visions and journeys are not at all uncommon in Israelite and Judean tradition.[163] Isaiah is taken up into heaven into the heavenly

---

163. See Aune, *Revelation* 1.276–78.

throne room.[164] John, the author of Revelation, also is taken up into heaven.[165] Micaiah has a vision of the heavenly throne room, as does Ezekiel.[166] Israelite and early Jewish tradition maintains that from a heavenly or cosmic perspective the earth's territory is limited.[167] When prophets and other figures do ascend into heaven or see visions of heaven, it is usually to receive some kind of information about the events that will unfold either at the end of the present age or when people die. Either way, these visions usually contrast the temporary nature of life on earth with the endlessness of life after death or the consummation of the present age. This contrast of the relative insignificance of life on earth with the much fuller significance of life after one's earthly existence is common to Greek, Roman and Jewish sources of the period.

Eschatology and a New Cosmos

There are ancient Greek, Roman and Israelite traditions that all stated that the world as it was currently configured would end and be replaced by a new world. The idea of the devolution of the ages is found among the earliest preserved Greek writings. Hesiod chronicles the period from the original golden age through silver and bronze ages, a heroic age and the present iron age (*Op.* 110–200). The characteristics of the iron age include rapid aging and all kinds of human evils. Good people are not rewarded and evil people are not punished. The culmination of these evils in the iron age is that "bitter sorrows will be left for mortal men, and there will be no hope against evil" (*Op.* 200–201).

These same ages appear in Daniel 2.[168] There the king of Babylon dreams of a statue whose head is gold, its chest and arms silver, its stomach and thighs bronze, the rest of its legs iron, and its feet iron and clay mixed (2:32). The statue was struck and broken to pieces by a stone "cut out, not by human hands" (3:34). The dream is then interpreted as referring to successive kingdoms. The Babylonian kingdom itself represents the golden head. When the four kingdoms represented by these metals are finally destroyed, "the God of heaven will set up a kingdom that shall never be

---

164. Isaiah 6.
165. Rev 4:1–2.
166. 2 Chr 18:18; Ezek 1:1–4.
167. So, for example, Isa 45:10; Wis 11:22; *Apoc. Zeph.* 2:5.
168. See Glasson, *Greek Influence*, 2–3.

destroyed," and it "shall crush all these kingdoms and bring them to an end, and it shall stand forever" (2:44).

In both *Works and Days* and Daniel time is devolving. The iron age represents the last stage in a period of decline which represents the gradual disordering of the previously ordered cosmos. In Hesiod's work, humanity lives in the iron age and there is no hope for a better future for the earth's current inhabitants. In Daniel, God will step in and reestablish an ordered cosmos with his kingdom. This new cosmos, however, will not be subject to the defeat and disordering of the present and forthcoming world kingdoms.

The Stoics and Epicureans were among the ancient peoples who held that the world was either growing old or was impermanent and would grow old. Lucretius, for example, follows Hesiod's line of thinking about the ease of life in the golden age and the difficulty of life in the present age. So, he argues, farming and tending the vine are much more difficult and much less fruitful enterprises in the present age.

> So therefore the walls of the mighty heavens in like manner shall be stormed all around, and shall collapse into crumbling ruin. Even now indeed the power of life is broken, and the earth exhausted scarce produces tiny creatures, she who once produced all kinds and gave birth to the huge bodies of wild beasts . . . Now the ancient ploughman shaking his head sighs many a time, that the labours of his hands have all come to nothing, and comparing present times with times past often praises the fortunes of his father, and grumbles how the old world full of piety supported life with great ease on a narrow domain; since the man's portion of land was formerly much smaller than it is now. Sadly also the cultivator of the degenerate and shrivelled vine rails at the progress of time and wearies heaven; not comprehending that all things gradually decay, and go to the tomb outworn by the ancient lapse of years (*De rerum natura* 1.1149–1174)

Signs of the end of the current cosmos abound. The earth does not produce the same illustrious creatures that it did in earlier times. The diminished physical stature of people in the present age is found in both Pliny and 4 Ezra.[169] The pillars of the heavens themselves threaten to break. Even though the boundaries of the *oikoumenē* have expanded, providing food is a much more difficult undertaking in the iron age.

---

169. See Pliny *Nat.* 7.16.73 and *4 Ezra* 5:51. In both of these texts the declining physical stature of humanity is related to the aging of the cosmos.

The Stoics believed cyclical conflagrations burned the cosmos after which a new cosmos was created. So, Cicero writes in his *De Natura Deorum*:

> As a consequence of this, so our school believes, though it used to be said that Panaetius questioned the doctrine, there will ultimately occur a conflagration of the whole world . . . thus nothing will remain but fire, by which . . . once again a new world may be created and the ordered universe be restored as before. (*Nat. d.* 2.118)

Pliny the Younger suggests that in the aftermath of the eruption of Mount Vesuvius many of those trying to escape the hot dust and ash in Misenum thought that the end of the world was upon them.[170] From the variety and number of references to the aging cosmos whose end is threatened, Downing concludes that "we have to take seriously the implication that the senescence of the age was in fact a commonplace idea, one that could readily be referred to in passing, on the assumption that it was part of many people's vocabulary of ideas."[171]

There are numerous early Jewish texts that address the end of the cosmos or the end of the present age. *Second Baruch* 85:10 reads, "The youth of this world has passed away, and the power of creation is already exhausted, and the coming of the times is very near and has passed by."[172] *Second Baruch* 73–74 represents the return of the golden age in which crops will again shoot out on their own and illness and all kinds of evils will be removed from human existence.[173] *Fourth Ezra* 8:51–55 asserts that humanity will live without evil and sorrow in the coming age. "The root of evil is sealed up from you, illness is banished from you, and death is hidden; hell has fled and corruption has been forgotten; sorrows have passed away, and in the end the treasure of immortality is made manifest" (*4 Ezra* 8:53–54). Not only are the evils that humans commit against one another

---

170. Pliny *Ep.* 6.20.15.

171. Downing, "Common Strands in Pagan, Jewish and Christian," 201. See also Downing, "Cosmic Eschatology in the First Century," 99–109.

172. All translations of *2 Baruch* are taken from Klijn in *OTP*.

173. The curse given to Adam to till the ground in Genesis 3 reflects this same kind of schema. Adam is no longer able to live as those of the golden age, but he must work the earth in order to bring forth its fruit for himself and his family. Eve's pain during childbirth should also be seen as a condition of the loss of the golden age. *Second Baruch* 73–74 clearly suggest that painless childbirth and ease of labor in farming are conditions to mark the return of the golden age. See Aune and Stewart, "From the Idealized Past."

in the present age to disappear, illness and even death will not mark the forthcoming age.

Cosmological descriptions sometimes relativized portrayals of the earth's space, as eschatology sometimes relativized the present age, including notions of a temporary cosmos to be replaced by a new one either through the mixing of the various elements of the cosmos (so Stoicism) or the creation of a new kingdom and order by God. In both cases, the earth as it exists will be radically altered, eliminating social evils and the difficult nature of human life. The end of the age promises a new or renewed cosmos in which humans are able to live a life of ease at peace with one another.

Case Study: Caesar's *Gallic War*

What does all of this mean for interpreting an ancient text that is not primarily "geographical?" The case of the *Gallic War* is instructive here.[174] The text begins with the famous phrase, "All of Gaul is divided into three parts" (*Bell. gall.* 1.1). Before Caesar, Gaul as a whole did not exist. "Before the Roman conquest, these regions displayed no geographical, linguistic or political unity. The application of the Latin "Gallia" to label this heterogeneous whole by tribes and cultures is an anachronism . . ."[175] Despite his original distinction of the three races of Gauls, Caesar eventually contrasts the Gauls as a whole with the Germans (*Bell. gall.* 6.11–28). Caesar presents the Germans, with the exception of the Ubii, as distant from Rome geographically and culturally (*Bell. gall.* 4.1–4). The Suebi, the German tribe most remote from the Romans, are "by far the most warlike among the Germans" (*Bell. gall.* 4.1). Caesar presents the Gauls asking for Roman help to ward off the invading Germans (*Bell. gall.* 1.31). He reminds the Aedui of the things that he had done for them in the course of the war: "the success and distinction to which he had brought them, with the result that they had not only returned to their ancient position, but, to all appearance, had surpassed the dignity and influence of all previous ages" (*Bell. gall.* 7.54). Caesar at one and the same time creates the "Gauls"[176] and

---

174. See the discussion in Evans, "Forma Orbis," 74.

175. Bochum, "Gallia," 763. Translation is my own.

176. Evans, "Forma Orbis," 68, "The division of ethnic categories within this geographically bounded zone is self-contradictory—the Celtae, Aquitani and Belgae generally coalesce to become the *Galli*. Caesar is never able to articulate any cultural or

presents himself as the savior of this oppressed people.[177] "What Caesar's text makes clear is that the Gallic war makes not only the *Gallic War*, but also the Gallic people, the Gallic territory, Gaul itself... It creates a nation so that it can conquer it, then divides it up into administrative zones."[178] The *Gallic War*, while not a "geographical" text per se, is heavily indebted to the personalized type of ancient geography at the same time that it continues to encode it for future authors.

Conclusion

Greeks, Romans, and Jews largely concerned themselves with geographical traditions related to human geography. The known world expanded rapidly during the Greek and Roman periods, and these two civilizations came into contact with numerous other peoples of whom they had previously been unaware. Most Greek and Roman geographical traditions were attempts to explain the differences between peoples and why such differences existed. By and large, they located the reason for these differences in climatic and other geographic circumstances.

The geographic material surveyed in this chapter is found across many different literary genres. Rhetoricians, geographers, novelists, historians, ethnographers, dramatists, comedians, and others all used stock geographic stereotypes in order to portray characters in their tales. So close was the relationship between geography and biography that to tell the history of a city one used the *bios* genre. The stereotypical elements of geography found their way into all types of literature and are assumed in early Jewish literature with only a few modifications in many cases.

Finally, the Greeks, Romans and Jews existed in a world that was divided according to divine will and human prerogative. Every people had an assigned place, and to overstep the bounds of one's place might result in catastrophe for a people. Some peoples, however, by virtue of their favorable location, and the constitution that came with the location, were most

---

racial markers to support his programmatic division of these three groups . . . this is in part due to Caesar's efforts to represent a coherent ethnic group which can fill the neat cartographic boundaries, which he has created."

177. Ibid., 72, "the creation of an ancient and original Gallic nationhood allows Caesar to act as the saviour and protector of this entity. Gallic borders and German transgressions are emphasized throughout, and this works to develop the idea that there is a real threat to a commendable and protectable national identity."

178. Ibid., 73–74.

capable to rule the others by bestowing upon them "civilization." This civilization usually involved the kind of cultivation that was most easily practiced in the Mediterranean basin. There, in the temperate climate of the *oikoumenē*, the most favored nations of the gods, whether Greek, Roman or Israelite, existed. These people had the greatest elements of each human constitution and were, therefore, most able to govern the other peoples of the world. Their geography made them rulers. This characterization of space, however, could be challenged from the cosmic perspective of God or the gods, and humans were sometimes allowed access to such a perspective.

Greek, Roman and Jewish geographical materials encode certain types of power relations. These power relations are presented as "inherent" in the land or in divine will. This manner of speaking about space offers a portrait of space that is arranged ideally in only one way. Describing space this way offers the opportunity to portray one's own culture as normative in spatial terms. For the ancient Greeks, Romans and Jews, they were "favored" because they lived in a favorable land. Other peoples, living in lands less hospitable for cultivation, lived different types of lives, deviating from the "civilized" lifestyle of those occupying the temperate zone. Modern spatial theory has done much to unravel the power relationships encoded in certain ways of describing place. Chapter four will examine more local descriptions of space in ancient literature in light of this modern theory. Finally, chapter five will seek to bring all of this material to bear on the Gospel of Mark. Mark contrasts the space that the Jewish leadership controls with a new space that Jesus creates. Power relationships are embedded within each type of space, and these will be examined and explicated in order to understand better the claims that Mark makes about the space of the kingdom of God.

CHAPTER 4

Categories for Understanding Ancient Space

Introduction

IN CHAPTER THREE, THE investigation of ancient perception of space focused on the inhabited world, its size, scope, boundaries, and the people by whom it was inhabited. Regional and ethnic stereotypes of the peoples of the *oikoumenē* dominated the discussion. In this chapter, more local distinctions take precedence. Topographical and architectural stereotypes are the focus of the present chapter. Many of the generalized stereotypes discussed in chapter two are repeated at a more local level. Those located at various central points (i.e. cities, cultivated areas) distinguished themselves from those living outside of such areas by means of topographic stereotypes that are familiar to us from the geographic stereotypes employed by Greeks and Romans to discuss other "marginal" people at the edges of the earth.

As chapter two demonstrated, the social production of space encodes power relationships within itself. These relationships are then presented as "part of the landscape." Spatial practices are usually construed in such a way as to support the status quo, enabling those with power to maintain it. The Greek and Roman presentation of the world with each of their respective civilizations at its center marginalizes those who come from outside these central places. This chapter will demonstrate that these stereotypical ways of presenting space extend to other types of space as well. Among the majority of preserved written sources, cities were the most honorable places in which to live. Cities are "centers" of various territories by reference to which the surrounding areas are defined. Wilderness areas and mountains, on the other hand, are characterized by negotiation of identity and sometimes by uncivilized behaviors. Such places, inasmuch as they do not follow the conventions of socialized (that is, city) life, offered the possibility for new or changed social configuration. Examples of such changing social configurations are found in Israel's desert wanderings and the reinterpretations of them in the Second Temple period. These interpretations frequently involve the rejection of the current social configurations in centers of civilization (most frequently Jerusalem and its temple leadership in early Jewish literature). Travel involves leaving the safety of civilized regions to pass through dangerous people and places such as frontiers, wilderness areas and mountains. People also could serve as centers, whether through their own travel or through pilgrims and disciples coming to them for teaching and healing. As geographic centers, people often represented challenges to other types of fixed centers. This chapter will treat, then, central sites, such as cities and villages and some of the buildings contained within them, boundary territories, travel, the concept of exile [particularly in early Judaism], and people as geographic centers.

CENTRAL SITES: CITIES AND VILLAGES[1]

Cities in antiquity were dependant upon the villages that surrounded them for food and other material goods. Cities exercised an extractive economic effect on the villages. What was produced by the villages was largely consumed in the cities. Villages could be called "daughters" of cities.[2] Typically the elite resided in the city, with those who served the elite also located there. The peasantry lived in the villages outside the city, but many of the elites who had residences in the city also had large countryside estates.[3] Crops were grown in the fields that surrounded the villages, and most of the goods for cities originated in the villages and their environs (at least inasmuch as the raw materials were extracted from outside the cities).[4] In a detailed study of the cities of the Decapolis, Steven Moors has

---

1. On the following, see Stewart, "City in Mark."

2. So, for example, Judg 1:27. See Rohrbaugh, "Preindustrial City." Much of the information for, as well as the title of, Rohrbaugh's article is derived from Sjoberg, *Preindustrial City*. See also Rohrbaugh, "City in the Second Testament."

3. Malina, *New Jerusalem in the Revelation of John*, 32–33.

4. On the relationship between cities and the countryside see Osborne, *Classical Landscape*.

shown that villages did not contain ruling councils (βουλαί) themselves but were administered by officials (βουλευταί) of the cities under whose control they were placed.[5]

Perhaps ten percent of the population in antiquity lived in cities.[6] The vast majority of the population lived in the villages surrounding these cities. While the countryside was of utmost significance in terms of the production of food and as the area in which the vast majority of ancients lived, Osborne notes that this element of production is underrepresented in Greek source material. "On the one hand, the productive countryside was of fundamental importance. On the other, the arts and literature of Classical Greece largely ignore it."[7] Generally speaking when the inhabitants of the countryside are mentioned it is as caricature of people "ignorant of politics" and who "are unsociable."[8] Put another way, since almost every preserved description of ancient cities originates within a city, they tend to be overwhelmingly positive in their evaluation and estimation of cities and entirely lacking in their description of actual living conditions in the countryside.[9]

Defining the City: Key Variables of Civilization and Honor[10]

The term city (πόλις) was not always used in a technical sense by Greek authors in antiquity. The same author could refer to a place as a village (κώμη) in one instance and a city (πόλις) in another.[11] At other times, "polis" could refer to the entirety of a Greek city-state. Osborne suggests "city" should be used in reference to "the independent political unit of town and territory."[12] Noting that the Greeks could use the term "polis" to indicate either this totality or the urban unit itself, he opts to use the word

---

5. Moors, "Decapolis."

6. Rohrbaugh, "Preindustrial City," 111. See also Osborne, *Classical Landscape*, 13–26.

7. Osborne, *Classical Landscape*, 16.

8. Ibid., 21.

9. Pezzoli-Olgiati, "Images of Cities."

10. On defining ancient cities and their various functions, see Stewart, "City in Mark."

11. See Rohrbaugh, "Preindustrial City," 108.

12. Osborne, *Classical Landscape*, 11.

"town . . . to refer to the largest settlement" of a polis.[13] His distinction is useful in that it highlights the ambiguity of the term polis as urban unit or city-state in the Greek world.

Pausanias describes Panopeus as a city, but questions whether this description is accurate since it contains "no government offices, no gymnasium, no theatre, no market-place, no water descending to a fountain" (*Descr.* 10.4.1).[14] This type of rhetoric indicates that honor was embodied in the public buildings of a city. Only those cities with all of these structures truly deserve the title of polis. Strabo also defines cities in a manner that claims a certain honor status for them. In his discussion of the Celtiberian territory, he dismisses those who claim that there are over a thousand cities there.

> In fact, even those who assert that there are more than one thousand cities in Iberia seem to me to be led to do so by calling big villages cities; for in the first place, the country is naturally not capable, on account of the poverty of its soil or else on account of the remoteness or wildness of it, of containing many cities, and secondly, the modes of life and the activities of the inhabitants (apart from those who live on the seaboard of Our Sea) do not suggest anything of the kind; for those who live in villages are wild (and such are most of the Iberians), and even the cities themselves cannot easily tame their inhabitants when these are outnumbered by the folk that live in the forests for the purpose of working mischief on their neighbours. (*Geogr.* 3.4.13)

Strabo's understanding of the city, then, relies on the idea of people living together in a certain type of social arrangement. This arrangement is evaluated by its cultural similarity to Rome. Cultivation of the soil and adherence to Roman social customs mark "big villages" as cities. Strabo designates only those Celtiberians who live on the shores of "our sea" as city dwellers because their proximity to Roman social configurations exercises a "civilizing" influence upon them. When people behave in ways that are "wild," their social configurations cannot rightly be called cities. To label something a city, then, is to credit it with a certain honor status.

---

13. Ibid.

14. All translations of Pausanias' *Descr.*, unless otherwise stated, are taken from Jones' translation in the LCL. See the discussion in Rohrbaugh, "Preindustrial City," 108–9.

Honor could also be accrued to individuals living within the city. One's city of origin is often a mark of honor.[15] People were commonly known by their city of origin.[16] For this reason, Paul can appeal to his birthplace Tarsus as a "not insignificant city" in Acts 21:39 to claim a high honor status. He is granted permission by the tribune to speak to the crowd because of his honor status (21:40). Luke's description of Paul in Acts locates Paul among the retainers of city elites.[17] This description accords Paul a high honor rating in terms of his urban life. Acts 21:39 portrays Tarsus, Paul's city of origin, as a city worthy of honor.[18] Further Luke locates Paul in virtually every major city of the eastern Mediterranean world.[19] Within these cities, Paul is found in houses of important people (i.e. 28:7) and other significant spaces (i.e.. synagogues, agoras, the Areopagus, and before city councils).[20] Neyrey concludes, therefore, that "Luke portrays Paul as a typical male of considerable social status: he regularly appears in public space; he frequently performs traditional elite male tasks such as arguing, debating and speaking boldly in public."[21] The city was the major place in which honor could be accrued, and the more honorable places within these cities were restricted to elites.

What is important to note for our study is that cities in the ancient world, generally speaking, were parasitic of the territories around them. They took food and raw materials from the surrounding countryside and contributed little directly in return.[22] The cities themselves were centers of religious activity (in that temples were generally located within their confines) and of administrative and legal activity.[23] Cities, however, were also places of honor.[24] They competed for honors with one another. To live in a city was to occupy a position of honor. Cities were also administrative units. Those who divided the land were residents of cities (even if

15. See the discussion in Malina and Neyrey, *Portraits of Paul*, 24–26.
16. Ibid., 24–26.
17. See Neyrey, "Luke's Social Location ."
18. Ibid., 267.
19. Ibid., 268–74.
20. Ibid., 274–76.
21. Ibid., 275–76.
22. See the collection of essays in Rich and Wallace-Hadrill, *City and Country*.
23. Malina, *New Jerusalem*, 35–37. See also Stewart, "City in Mark."
24. On the competition among cities of the eastern Roman Empire for imperial honors see Friesen, *Twice Neokoros*.

they had their own villas outside the city). Villages were governed by the councils of the neighboring polis. One should recall Strabo's discussion of the Artabrians, whom the Romans conquered. As part of their strategy for subduing these people, they "reduced most of their cities to mere villages, though they improved some of their cities by adding colonies thereto" (*Geogr.* 3.3.5). The reduction in the number of cities, as well as the expansion of the few cities that remained should be understood as part of an administrative policy that reduced the number of territories in which power was centralized. Clearly, Roman rule in this instance emanated from the cities out into the villages.

Buildings: Public and Private Space in the City and Villages

Recent thinking about the issues of public and private space in the Greek and Roman worlds has changed somewhat from the previously held general consensus. Many of the scholars who had done work in this area contrasted the public arena as the space of males and the private arena as the space of females. It is now commonplace to distinguish Roman attitudes toward women's participation in meals, for example, from those of the classical Greeks.[25] More recent work, however, has sought to provide further nuance to this presentation.

Among the more insightful recent works on the subject is Riggsby's study on public and private in Roman culture.[26] Riggsby addresses the issue of public and private in the Roman world by discussing the role of the cubiculum within the household. Many parts of the Roman house were "public" in the sense that they did not require special invitation in order for someone to enter into them. This fact might be particularly true for the atrium of a house in which the morning *salutatio* occurred.[27] The cubiculum, however, was a private area in the house. Its space served as a place to sleep, to have sex, to conduct business, and to hang art. It was also the area in which murder and suicide was most common (according to literary sources).[28] In discussing what this room of the house might suggest about Roman notions of private space, Riggsby makes two very important

25. See Cornelius Nepos *Preface* 6–7.
26. Riggsby, "'Public' and 'Private' in Roman Culture."
27. See Laurence, "Space and Text," 13–14. On the public and private areas of Roman houses see Vitruvius *Arch.* 6.5.1.
28. Riggsby, "'Public' and 'Private,'" 36–43.

observations. The first is that the cubiculum is a space in which secrecy could be assumed because there was very little surveillance.²⁹ "What surveillance there was was conducted by persons who were invited and (ordinarily) known to be sympathetic—spouse, other family, close friends."³⁰ Private areas are characterized by a lack of surveillance from one's enemies or competitors. This understanding is very similar to that developed by Jerome Neyrey in his study of public and private space in Acts. There he distinguishes two meanings of the idea of private space. On the one hand, private space exists in the home and is related to the activities of males as heads of households.³¹ On the other hand, "private" can refer to interaction between males in contexts outside the home when such interaction concerns non-political (that is, non-public) matters.³² Since public space is related to the political arena, it is inappropriate to conduct the affairs of Rome in the cubiculum since it is private space.³³ To do so would be considered a threat to the prevailing public order. The things that have to do with the welfare of the public are to be conducted only in public.

The second element of private space noted by Riggsby is that it is a place where social customs might be relaxed a bit. This relaxation can occur not only because the space is private, but because it is out of the public view. Romans did have a norm of privacy, but is was not so much a right as a mandate: 'If you are going to behave that way, you must do it in a certain restricted area.'"³⁴ The Roman strategy regarding privacy "acts to produce consent to the status quo," co-opting "the deviant behavior by assigning it restricted places, times, or occasions."³⁵ Any behavior that is potentially antisocial must be done out of sight of the public world.

In the Roman world, as in the Greek world, public space was privileged over private space.³⁶ By their allotment of certain activities to public

29. Ibid., 43–46.

30. Ibid., 46.

31. Neyrey, "'Teaching You in Public.'"

32. Ibid., 81.

33. Riggsby, "'Public' and 'Private,'" 48. See Pliny, *Pan.* 51.5 and 83.1; also Cicero, *Scaur.* 26.

34. Ibid., 50.

35. Ibid., 51. It is important to remember that these two categories are always in relational opposition to one another. Whatever space is not public is private.

36. Ibid., 52 notes that in ancient Athens the right to privacy within one's household was part of the democratic ideal. The Romans, on the other hand, did not necessarily value this private sphere due to their anti-democratic stance.

space and others to private space the Romans "provided an ideal map for the behavior of the Roman aristocrat."[37] Public and private space, then, were primarily important distinctions for aristocrats. Only the larger houses of aristocrats (and possibly their wealthiest clients) would have been sufficient to provide these private areas such as the cubiculum. Riggsby, however, suggests that the issue of control over private space and encouragement of activity in public space is due to another factor of Roman politics. "The primary tension in Roman politics was not between mass and élite, but among segments of the élite. Aristocrats worried whether one of their fellows would get too far ahead in the competition for honor."[38] Private space, on this reading, then, is that space in which there is no competition for honor.[39] It is a space characterized by the presence of sympathetic persons who do not challenge one another's honor,[40] whereas public space was the space of the community's business, but also a space for honor to be contested and won or lost.[41]

Houses

Houses are considered private buildings in the Greek world. The private nature of the Greek house is demonstrable through the Classical and Hellenistic periods. After the Roman expansion into Greek territories, however, Greek houses began to resemble Roman houses in a variety of ways.[42] Classical and Hellenistic houses were structured around a court onto which all rooms of the house opened. Further, they had generally only one door to the outside world. Greek houses in the Roman period,

---

37. Ibid., 53.
38. Ibid., 52.
39. This understanding is compatible with that of Neyrey, "'Teaching You in Public.'"
40. Exceptions to this general principle are the cases of murder and adultery, particularly of the *paterfamilias* in his own *cubiculum*. See Riggsby, "'Public' and 'Private,'" 37–41. Perhaps it is for this reason that *parricide* is traditionally represented in the *cubiculum*. It is an especially egregious offense in such a place. See, for example, Cicero, *Cat.* 1.10.
41. For a similar understanding of private and public space see Pomeroy, *Families in Classical and Hellenistic Greece*. She suggests that the "traditional dichotomy public/private used to describe Greek life is misleading. A tripartite division is more accurate: public, domestic/public, and domestic/private" (18–19).
42. On the following, see Nevett, "Continuity and Change in Greek Households." She argues that these alterations to Greek houses in the Roman period suggest a freer status for women to come and go from the house and more open interaction between people within the house and visitors.

however, generally were altered to provide a second door to the outside and oftentimes structured so that all rooms did not open onto the main court. Greek houses are marked by separation between men's and women's spaces.[43] In them, none of the public behavior of honor challenges should normally occur. Such honor challenges happened normally only outside the home since the family had an honor rating that applied equally to each of them. Honor challenges between family members would only serve to lower the honor rating of the entire family. The family's corporate honor rating would prevent them from displaying public antagonistic behavior toward one another in the household. It is because of this corporate honor that parents must keep tight reins on their children lest they should shame the family.[44] So, while one might let one's guard down to some extent in the home, there were still precautions to be taken regarding the family's appearance to outsiders.[45]

Roman houses are slightly different in this regard in that they are far more "public." Vitruvius notes that public rooms of the house include "vestibules, courtyards, peristyles and other apartments of similar styles" (*Arch.* 6.5.1). People are allowed to enter these rooms even when they are not invited. The private areas of a house, into which "no one can come uninvited" include "bedrooms, dining-rooms, baths and other apartments which have similar purposes" (*Arch.* 6.5.1). Roman villas are built in order to allow access to people outside the family into the household in order to praise the owner of the house. For this reason, Vitruvius notes that "magnificent vestibules and alcoves and halls are not necessary to persons of a common fortune, because they pay their respects by visiting others, and are not visited by others" (*Arch.* 6.5.1). In this public space in the house, one would expect the requisite public behavior. Thus, upon entering one's house as a client, it is necessary to offer praise to the homeowner.[46] To do

---

43. So, for example, Vitruvius *Arch.* 7.4.5. These spaces can shift during certain periods of the day and are not necessarily always women's or men's spaces. See Antonaccio, "Architecture and Behavior." Lysias's *On the Murder of Eratosthenes* presents a comical case in which these spaces become inverted and the upheaval in social order the situation creates.

44. On this point see Pilch, "'Beat His Ribs while He is Young.'"

45. See Neyrey, "'Teaching You in Public,'" 81–83.

46. Vitruvius *Arch.* 6.5.2 says that "advocates and professors of rhetoric should be housed in sufficient space to accommodate their audiences. For persons of high rank who hold office and magistracies, and whose duty it is to serve the state, we must provide princely vestibules, lofty halls and very spacious peristyles . . . further, libraries and basilicas

otherwise would challenge the honor of the homeowner and initiate a public honor challenge in front of the other witnesses. As demonstrated above, however, in the private areas of the Roman household, the normal ideas of private space would apply. They are not an area for honor challenges in general.

Synagogues

The status of synagogues in the first century is the subject of an ongoing debate among biblical scholars. Some scholars believe that synagogues, by the first third of the first century CE were specific buildings set apart, not only for reading and studying scripture, but also for lodging, dining, a repository for funds, and various other community functions.[47] Other scholars, however, argue that the term synagogue does not refer to a specific building, but rather refers to its more general meaning of "gathering" in the first third of the first century CE.[48]

The ongoing debate about whether there were specific synagogue buildings in the early first century CE, however, is not crucial to this study. It is not important to answer the historical question of whether there were synagogue buildings in Galilee in the first third of the first century, since the present study is interested in Mark's description of synagogues. Since literary texts create their own conceptions of space, the same should be assumed for the Gospel of Mark. While it would be convenient to know how this literary space relates to actual physical and architectural space, in some cases it is not possible.[49]

Synagogues might be considered private or public in nature. Synagogues were public insofar as they dealt with matters pertaining to the ordering of society. They fulfill "political" functions and should be

arranged in a similar fashion with the magnificence of public structures, because, in such places, public deliberations and private trials and judgments are often transacted."

47. Levine, *Ancient Synagogues Revealed*, 3–11. These suggestions for the functions of synagogue buildings come largely from the Theodotus inscription. The inscription itself clearly marks a point before which a synagogue building had been established. Kee, "Defining the First-Century Synagogue," 11–26, argues that there is no longer widespread agreement on the dating of the Theodotus inscription. See Kloppenborg, "The Theodotus Synagogue Inscription," 236–82, for a counter-argument; he argues convincingly for a first-century date for the Theodotus inscription.

48. Kee, "Defining the First-Century CE Synagogue," 7–10.

49. On the scholarly debate and the issues involved see Heather MacKay, "Ancient Synagogues."

considered public institutions. Runesson discusses the developments of the synagogue, particularly in Palestine, from the return from exile onward. His conclusion as to the nature of these gatherings is the preferred understanding for this study. "Spatially, the public nature of the assembly places should be considered. It matters less if the assemblies were held at the city gate or, as later, in a public building. Nevertheless, the city gate must be defined as the spatial forerunner of the later buildings."[50]

In describing synagogues this way, Runesson argues that all of the main elements that are associated with the later activities in synagogue buildings are already present in the Persian period. These activities, according to him, include the public reading of local laws and of the Torah, teaching, and liturgical elements (such as blessings and prayers).[51] These synagogues are characterized by their association with the Jerusalem authorities who, during the Persian period, "controlled the law and its interpretation."[52] These public assemblies "are open to anyone" and deal "with matters concerning people living in the area in question."[53] Horsley understands the leadership of the synagogue to be the local governing officials in Galilee during the first century.[54] Since the discussion of cities above has indicated that villages were under the administrative control of city officials, it is presumably city elites who control the synagogues, whether directly or through local clients. Inasmuch as they operated in the realm of political religion, synagogues constituted public space.[55]

Where synagogues resemble voluntary associations, they are best considered public, non-domestic space.[56] "These small communities ate meals together, observed Sabbaths and festivals, organized the collection of Temple tax dues, taught their children, arranged for the transmission of the first-fruits, heard civil law cases and so on."[57] Runesson calls this type of synagogue a "semi-public" synagogue, and he argues that it arose

---

50. Runesson, *Origins of the Synagogue*, 398.
51. Ibid., 395–98.
52. Ibid., 397.
53. Ibid., 64.
54. Horsley, *Galilee*, 227–33.
55. On the idea of political religion, see ibid., 227–28; Malina, *Christian Origins and Cultural Anthropology*, 84–87; and Malina, "'Religion' in the World of Paul."
56. See Richardson, "Early Synagogues as Collegia."
57. Ibid., 103.

"towards the end of the third century BCE."[58] They arose during a "period of political stability under the Ptolemies" leading to "a loosened attitude of the Jerusalem authorities to the control of the interpretation of the law."[59] These types of synagogues are "denominational" or "sectarian."[60] Runesson says that the school of Ben Sira is the only explicit mention that we have of such a semi-public synagogue, but he imagines similar institutions for such groups as the Qumran community and the Jesus movement.[61]

What is perhaps the most significant element of Runesson's study is that he clearly establishes in Palestine the development of the public institution prior to that of the semi-public one. This position coheres well with our understanding of the synagogue as a public institution in the literature of the early Jesus movements. Mark envisions the synagogue as this type of public institution rather than a semi-public one.[62] As for Runesson's semi-public understanding of sectarian synagogues, the understanding of public and private developed above would place these within a private, non-household context.[63] One should assume that the groups located in them would have been sympathetic hearers and would not have vied for honor among one another.[64]

Temples

Temples were a fairly common feature of ancient landscapes. They were first and foremost locations for worshipping the gods. In some cases, gods/God could be conceived as living in them. These edifices served many other functions in antiquity, serving as places to offer sacrifices, dining halls, residences for priests, hostels, centers of learning and places to go for healing, among other things. Temples, by virtue of their landholdings, could acquire substantial wealth. Many ancient temples served "more or

---

58. Runesson, *Origins of the Synagogue*, 398.
59. Ibid.
60. Ibid.
61. Ibid., 398–400.
62. See chapter 5 below.
63. See the discussion in Neyrey, "'Teaching You in Public,'" 88–89.
64. Runesson, *Origins of the Synagogue*, 64 says of the semi-private synagogues that "they are controlled by membership requirements and open to members only, perhaps also allowing sympathising non-members."

less the same function as banks and credit unions today."⁶⁵ Temples, therefore, could have a stimulating effect on their local economies, but more often served as places of hoarded wealth.⁶⁶ Temple priests also "served as custodians of the legal traditions in the various regions" during the Persian period in various parts of their empire.⁶⁷ While it is safe to say that the primary functions of temples everywhere in the ancient world were "religious," it is important to keep in mind that temples were part of political religion in the ancient world.⁶⁸

The idea of a single temple for a specific ethnos is distinct to ancient Judea. All other cultures of the ANE and the Mediterranean world had multiple temples or cultic sites.⁶⁹ Throughout Israel's history there were major efforts to defend the idea of the centrality of the Jerusalem temple.⁷⁰ The Deuteronomistic traditions contain many references to "high places" that were alternate centers of religious devotion. Deuteronomy 12 is the primary description of the centralized cult in the Jerusalem temple. The temple can only be built after the destruction of all the native places of worship (Deut 12:2–3). The place that God chooses is the place of Israelite worship, consisting of sacrifices and various offerings and eating (Deut 12:5–7). One of the more prominent examples of this concept of centralized cult in Jerusalem is found in 1 Kings 3. Solomon offered sacrifice at Gibeon before the building of the temple (1 Kgs 3:3). After having received the great wisdom that he requested from God, Solomon "came to Jerusalem where he stood before the ark of the covenant of the Lord" (1 Kgs 3:15). In his newfound wisdom, Solomon offers sacrifices before the ark of the covenant that is located in Jerusalem. The position of the Deuteronomistic school is that the site of the Jerusalem temple is sacred because God chose the site.

---

65. Blenkinsopp, "Temple and Society," 23.

66. For a discussion of Greek temples and their similar functions see Burkert, "Meaning and Function of the Temple." On the temple as place of hoarded wealth, see Hanson and Oakman, *Palestine in the Time of Jesus*, 137–43.

67. Blenkinsopp, "Temple and Society," 24.

68. Malina, *New Testament World*, 82–83. Also Malina, "'Religion' in the World of Paul."

69. Bohak, "Theopolis."

70. Hjelm, "Cult Centralization."

There are numerous arguments in the Second Temple period as to why the Jews had only one temple.[71] For Philo, it was because there was only one God and, thus, only one temple (*Spec. Leg.* 1.67). For the sibyl, the temple and the city of Jerusalem were located in the middle of the earth (*Syb. Or.* 5.249–50, 433).[72] As there is only one central site of the earth, so there is only one temple. Bohak argues that another reason to consider Jerusalem as an authoritative center for early Jews is that their revolts always wound up focusing on control of the city and/or its temple.[73] In this conception, the temple represents a fixed sacred space. Fixed sacred space focuses on a central place and "is characterized by redundant aspects of stability, permanence and continuity."[74] It is fixed sacred space because God dwells in the temple (Deut 12:5; 2 Sam 7:13).[75]

There were, however, people who rejected or contested the centrality of Jerusalem and its temple. Perhaps foremost among such people are the founders of the Samaritan temple and the temples at Elephantine and Leontopolis. Both of these temples were founded by high priests from Jerusalem who were alienated from their place at the Jerusalem temple.[76] Bohak also argues that the emergence of sects in early Judaism resulted from disputes over the temple elites' role in defining purity and even in the legitimacy of the ruling priesthood.[77] Bohak suggests that the view that God should have one temple "turned the Temple into a battle-ground, so to speak, for various groups and leaders who were convinced that they, and they alone, knew how God should be worshipped there."[78]

The temple, then, as a central site was politically significant. Bohak's analysis of the temple allows a glimpse into the battle for its control. Since controlling the temple in many ways meant having access to the Roman government's patronage and having the ability to define issues like purity, control of it was both important and contested.[79] The contestation of the

71. On what follows see Bohak, "Theopolis."
72. See Chester, "Sibyl and the Temple."
73. Bohak, "Theopolis," 4–10.
74. Neyrey, "Spaces and Places," 62. See Smith, *Map is Not Territory*, 104–28.
75. There is on ongoing tension in the Old Testament as to whether God dwelt in the temple. First Kings 8:27–30 decidedly rejects this possibility.
76. Bohak, "Theopolis," 10–11.
77. Ibid., 12–16.
78. Ibid., 15.
79. That there was an ideological struggle among several groups for control of the

temple, however, involved mainly the priestly elite. Most people were not privy to the inner politics of the temple or to the power that the temple represented.

Cities and villages, then, and the buildings contained within them, marked civilized areas from non-civilized areas. The spatial practice in these civilized areas, the way in which humans interacted with each other, the presence of religious institutions and the cultivation of the soil all distinguished these territories from those that surrounded them. Within these territories, distinctions were made among elites and peasants. Control over public spaces such as the temple and synagogues equated to being able to establish the norm of "civilized" behavior in first century Judea and the areas over which elite Judeans were able to exercise their influence. The elites and their retainers populated the cities, while peasants generally lived outside the cities and worked the land.

Borders, Frontiers, and Borderlands

Borders were especially vulnerable places in antiquity as they are in the modern world. In the ancient world, borders were areas rather than strictly maintained lines. Control over these areas involved controlling major architectural (cities, fortresses, and the like) and topographical (river crossings, mountain passes) features rather than the entire area.[80] These sites are frequently places for negotiation of identities. Those who live in border regions often differ substantially from those who are located closer to the political, religious, or economic centers of civilization discussed above. Frequently there is pressure exerted from the elite of these centers toward those on the borders to conform to the same patterns of expected behaviors as are customary in these centers.[81]

Second Temple is by now well-established. There is nearly unanimous consent that the Qumran group had a privileged place within the temple's establishment only to be removed at some point. There are numerous indications (cited below in the literature concerning exile) that many groups contested or rejected the legitimacy of the Second Temple entirely. See Nickelsburg, "Enoch, Levi, and Peter."

80. Rogerson, "Frontiers and Borders in the Old Testament." Also Isaac, "Meaning of the Terms Limes and Limetanai."

81. This element of negotiated identity in border regions is seen clearly in the Greek and Roman treatment of the borders of the earth. The people who live in these regions are considered uncivilized as a result of the fact that their behavior does not conform to that of the Greeks and Romans who encounter them.

Only recently have anthropologists studying border regions moved away from a traditional model of center and periphery in which the center dominates the periphery.[82] In this model, social change occurs from the center outward and change gradually transforms the peripheral or boundary areas of a society.[83] This way of understanding center and periphery developed out of a colonialist understanding of peripheral territories. Lightfoot and Martinez identify three stages of research within anthropology and archaeology on frontiers and boundaries. The first stage is "based largely on a colonialist perspective of core-periphery relationships involving territorial advancement, boundary maintenance, and relatively homogeneous colonial populations."[84] A second stage followed in which archaeologists and anthropologists began to take note of this colonialist perspective in a critical way. Rather than considering frontiers as places "that largely inhibit and constrain intercultural relationships" these studies treated frontiers "as interaction zones where encounters take place between peoples from diverse homelands."[85] In this view frontiers are the outer limits of a society's space and borders "equal the social, political, and economic factors guiding interactions between these societies."[86]

The most recent stage in the study of borderlands and frontiers take the second perspective a bit further. From this perspective, frontiers are seen as "possible zones of cultural interfaces in which cross-cutting, segmentary groups can be defined and recombined at different spatial and temporal scales of analysis."[87] Examining frontiers from this perspective allows one to take note of many features that have not been seen clearly by archaeologists and anthropologists before. In this analysis, frontier zones create cultural change through the "interethnic interactions between diverse peoples; the development of new material and cultural innovations; and the construction, negotiation, and manipulation of identi-

---

82. See especially Lightfoot and Martinez, "Frontiers and Boundaries." Also Alvarez, Jr., "Mexican-US Border." Newman, "Boundaries."

83. This center-periphery model is usually a creation of the people at the "center" who define the "periphery." The Greek and Roman idea of civilizing people by changing their behavior to conform to Greek and Roman social practices is a good example of this concept. See the discussion in chapter 3 above.

84. Lightfoot and Martinez, "Frontiers and Boundaries," 472.

85. Ibid., 473.

86. Ibid., 474.

87. Ibid.

ties."[88] Frontiers, then, primarily are loci for construction of identities. Frontier groups should not be seen as homogeneous, and they might react to pressure from various centers in numerous ways including "adoption, manipulation, or creation of new cultural constructs."[89] Frontier groups, particularly those that have been colonized by an outside group, may resist (actively or passively) or accept (and attempt to manipulate to their own advantage) the new colonial situation. It is common, however, for a variety of reactions to be found within the same frontier people once the artificial idea of a homogeneous response among all people of a certain area is removed from the equation.

People who reside in borderlands frequently have more in common with other people in that borderland than they do with people in distant administrative centers.[90] This fact is especially the case in the ancient world where borders were frequently not as clearly established as they are in the modern world. Ancient borders are best considered not as a "formal boundary line dividing up two territories" but rather as "a (frequently contested) claim to the various points of access between one community and another . . . that control communication, trade and movement between states or communities."[91]

Weitzman reads the Samson story as a story concerning the ability of the center to control the periphery. The peripheral area, in this case, is the borderland with Philistia. Weitzman points to 2 Kgs 8:20–22 as evidence that Judah had trouble controlling the populations along the Philistine border.[92] He reads the Samson story as an attempt on the part of the Judean government "to delegitimize Philistine claims to this region and stigmatize border-crossing."[93] As such the story "is an attempt to construct a border . . . to redefine the shephelah as social space, clarifying the allegiances of the population living there, and impose Judahite hegemony."[94] The story progresses from Samson's negation of the Philistines' claim to the countryside through the destruction of the Philistines' crops (Judg 15:4–5),

---

88. Ibid.

89. Ibid., 486.

90. See Weitzman, "Samson Story as Border Fiction," 160–63.

91. Ibid., 159. On the nature of borders in antiquity, see also Rogerson, "Frontiers and Borders in the Old Testament"; and Carney, *Shape of the Past*, 116.

92. Weitzman, "Samson Story as Border Fiction," 162.

93. Ibid., 163.

94. Ibid.

of their city (Judg 16:1–3) and finally of their temple (Judg 16:29–30). "Each act of violence reaches deeper and deeper into the Philistines' settled existence, from fields to gates to temple, progressively undoing the civic and religious order they have imposed on the countryside."[95] In negating the claim of the Philistines to the territory of the shephelah, the story of Samson essentially inverts normal stories of colonization in the ancient world. Rather than providing a justification for colonizing a new territory, this story rejects their claim to the territory "by inverting the sort of story used to legitimize that control."[96]

Boundaries, then, were (and are) primarily sites for negotiation of identities. This fact is due in large part to the absence of "normal" patterns of behavior, as they are defined by centers of civilization, in boundary territories. They were frequently objects of war inasmuch as access to boundary lands could guarantee communications and the movement of peoples and goods. Susan Cole has shown how sanctuaries of Artemis were frequently placed in contested areas, particularly those related to roads, seaports, and mountain passes.[97] Artemis was believed to guard these critical junctures for the people who built the temples in her honor.[98] Even where her shrines are located in cities, they are frequently found in the agora or at the city gates rather than on the acropolis.[99] Artemis is a goddess who resides in those places where encounters between various peoples are likely to occur. She is the goddess of the boundary lands. The temples dedicated to her in these lands are an attempt to assert control over these contested areas. "Rituals of Artemis protected boundary lands, tied boundary lands to the center, and prepared communities for military crisis in vulnerable places."[100] It was these locations of import for commercial and military activity, such as mountain passes, roads, and harbors that Artemis governed. This conception of the deity fits well with the idea that it is not the lines on the sand themselves, but rather the special locations of human activity that marked the borders of ancient lands.

95. Ibid., 170.

96. Ibid., 173. On the use of stories, and particularly riddles and their solutions as stock elements of asserting control over a colonized space, see Dougherty, *Poetics of Colonization*.

97. Cole, "Landscapes of Artemis."

98. Ibid., 472–76.

99. Ibid., 474.

100. Ibid., 481.

As noted above, people who live in borderlands are considered marginal by those in the center. The Greeks and Romans considered those people who lived at the edges of the earth to be marginal inasmuch as they did not cultivate the soil and behave socially in the same way as the Greeks and Romans themselves. Similarly, people who occupied the desert/wilderness and mountain areas were geographically marginal. There is an opportunity that arises with this geographic marginality as well. The negotiation of identities that occurs in borderlands occurs because those who reside in borderlands are not bound by the same societal conventions as those dwelling in centers of civilization. Critique of this "civilized" life and alternative social formations may be found in the marginal geographic territories of borderlands.

Mountains[101]

Mountains represented a number of different things to the Greeks and Romans. In early Greek mythology they were places where gods lived, where one might experience a theophany and common sites for religious shrines and temples. Beyond these things, however, mountains also represented a source of wildness and danger to the Greeks and Romans. They were the haunts of bandits and uncivilized peoples who represented a threat to the peoples who cultivated the plains around the mountains. Mountains, as boundary lands, are places in which identities are negotiated and people come into contact with various other peoples.

According to Hesiod, mountains are born out of the earth (*Theog.* 129–30). They are part of the natural landscape that may be manipulated by humanity, but are not created by humans.[102] Langdon notes that mountains were not typically considered divine things in Greek religions. He suggests that, unlike the civilizations of the ANE, Greek religions "lacked the animism and mysticism needed for conferring this kind of

---

101. Both Butxon, "Imaginary Greek Moutains," and Langdon, "Mountains in Greek Religion," note that the Greeks had no precise parameters for defining a mountain in terms of height. The use of the term ὄρος described many features of the landscape that would most certainly be considered hills to most observers. Langdon suggests that the use of the term ὄρος expressed more the prominence of a hill or rise in elevation relative to its particular surroundings than its actual height (462).

102. Williams, *Landscape in the Argonautica*, 79–81. See Buxton, *Imaginary Greece*, 80–82.

independent divine status on heights."[103] Mountains, therefore, were not themselves the objects of Greek worship.

Mountains represented the arena of the gods and of divine-human interaction.[104] Mount Olympus was home to the gods of the Greek world. Mount Sinai was the site of God's encounter with Moses and the Israelites and the location of the giving of the covenant in Hebrew tradition. Temples were frequently located on mountains, sometimes carved into the mountain itself, so that "there seems to be an idea that the gods needed to live where they could gaze down upon the world."[105]

Besides being a location for the gods and for divine-human interaction, mountains represent a threat because of the lawlessness and ferocity of their inhabitants.[106]

> Inhabitants of a region which is mountainous (χώρην ὀριενήν), rugged, high, and watered, where the changes of the seasons exhibit sharp contrasts, are likely to be of big physique, with a nature well adapted for endurance (ταλαίπωρον) and courage (ἀνδρεῖον), and such possess not a little wildness (ἄγριον) and ferocity" (θηριῶδες). (Hippocrates *Airs, Waters, Places* 24.43)

This wildness and ferocity are the same features that are often associated with those living at the edge of the *oikoumenē*. These characteristics are a threat to civilized people. Again Strabo's reference to the Artabrians should be recalled. They lived in a situation of ongoing warfare that Strabo attributed to the lawlessness of the mountain dwellers.

> It was the mountaineers who began this lawlessness, as was likely to be the case; for, since they occupied sorry land and possessed but little property, they coveted what belonged to the others. And the latter, in defending themselves against the mountaineers, were necessarily rendered powerless over their private estates, so that they, too, began to engage in war instead of farming; and the result

---

103. Langdon, "Mountains in Greek Religion," 464. With few possible exceptions, (Mount Helikon, Lukabettos and Parparos) he argues that the evidence for such worship of mountains is tenuous. Also Buxton, "Imaginary Greek Mountains," 5–6.

104. See especially Langdon, "Mountains in Greek Religion"; Hanson, "Transformed on the Mountain"; Cole, "Landscapes of Artemis"; and Herodotus *Hist.* 1.131.

105. Williams, *Landscapes in the Argonautica*, 79.

106. It is worth noting here that the Cyclops live in a mountainous region according to Homer (*Od.* 9.315). Herodotus relates that mountains are "full of wild animals" (*Hist.* 1.110).

was that the country, neglected because it was barren of planted products, became the home only of brigands. (*Geogr.* 3.3.5)

The mountaineers wanted the things that belonged to those who cultivated the soil, but they were unable to procure those things for themselves since they occupied "sorry land." Mountain dwelling peoples, then, developed a reputation for lawless and aggressive behavior because of their inability to provide for themselves.[107]

This idea of a lawless group of mountain dwellers underlies the account of Aelius Aristides regarding the first human communities. Aristides attributes the dawn of human settlement to Athena, noting that "it is she who persuaded men to give up their solitary mountain life and to assemble and dwell together in the compass of a single, common settlement" (*Or.* 37.13). Mountain life was represented by the lack of human fellowship, and therefore, the lack of orderly behavior that accompanies human community. Arrian attributes this same function to Philip of Macedon, the father of Alexander (*Anab.* 7.9.2). Alexander describes his father as the one who took over the Macedonians "when you were helpless vagabonds, mostly clothed in skins, feeding a few animals on the mountains . . ." After becoming the leader of so destitute a people, Philip "gave you cloaks to wear instead of skins, he brought you down from the mountains to the plains . . . He made you city dwellers and established the order that comes from good laws and customs."[108] The contrast between the lawlessness of the mountains and the order of city life on the plains is again highlighted. There are numerous examples of this type of contrast in Greek and Roman literature.[109]

While the literary presentation of mountains as sites of experience with divine beings and as the haunts of wild and savage peoples pervades Greek and Latin literature, Buxton notes that the image of mountains in Greek myth exaggerates the contrast between mountains and plains. In Greek mythology, mountains are places that "are visited, only to be left again."[110] In actual use, however, mountains were common places for

---

107. Sometimes such people could be lawless without necessarily being violent. Herodotus *Hist.* 1.203 describes the people of Caucasus as violating most norms of civilized behavior, most notably having sex out in the open like wild animals.

108. All translations of Arrian's *Anabasis*, unless otherwise indicated, are taken from Brunt's translation in the LCL.

109. Buxton, "Imaginary Greek Mountains," 6–10.

110. Ibid., 15.

shepherding, for hunting, for collection of wood, and especially common sites for sanctuaries of the gods. Mythology highlighted the distinction between mountains and civilized areas, so that in myth "to behave outside the norm, or outside oneself, is to belong on the *oros*, and in a way to belong to it."[111] The mountains are described in Greek (and Roman) literature as a place where the normal social customs that guide human behavior did not apply.

Wilderness

The discussion of borders and frontier lands provides a clearer position from which to view the quintessential borderland of Israelite history. The wilderness was significant in both political and theological terms for the ancient Israelites. As discussed in chapter three above, the wilderness concept also played an important role in the Greek and Roman descriptions of the world and its inhabitants. It set the limits of the *oikoumenē* beyond which human existence was not possible. Other deserts and wilderness areas, however, were found within the *oikoumenē*. These territories are boundary areas in which we should expect to find the types of interaction among people of different *ethnoi* that characterize such areas.

The wilderness in antiquity is that area in the inhabited world and along its edges that is not marked by human activity. It is, however, defined by human activity insofar as it is distinguished from the human settlements that surround or are adjacent to it.[112] It is marked by the lack of spatial practices that designate "civilization." Wilderness is that part of the *oikoumenē* that is uninhabited or uninhabitable.[113] It might include harsh desert regions or regions too cold for habitation. It could include mountainous regions in which it was difficult or impossible to grow food. The wilderness was that area that humans did not cultivate and in which they did not live.

---

111. Ibid., 9.

112. On this conception of the wilderness, see the discussion in chapter two above. See also the discussion of wilderness among ancient geographers in chapter three above.

113. See, for example, Jer 2:6; also Smith, *Map is Not Territory*, 109.

Uninhabited areas

Uninhabited areas within the *oikoumenē* might have been so for any variety of reasons. The zone theory of the *oikoumenē* visualized uninhabited zones to the northernmost and southernmost parts of the *oikoumenē*. The northernmost part was uninhabitable because of the cold, while the southernmost part was uninhabited because of the heat. Geographers in antiquity believed these areas to have been perpetually uninhabited due to their inhospitable climates. Those areas that are permanently uninhabited are essentially uninhabitable in the minds of the ancients. No one lives there because life there is not possible. This is the distinction here proposed between uninhabited areas and deserts.[114] Deserts were nearer to human settlements, and they were sometimes traversed and sometimes even settled for short or long periods of time. This sense of the term wilderness is the one most frequently used in the ANE. "In the majority of occurrences, 'wilderness' carries negative overtones, referring to parched, inhospitable, and dangerous places."[115]

Desert/Wilderness[116]

Like uninhabited areas, deserts, too, were not routinely considered homes to people in antiquity. They were those uninhabited areas that surrounded inhabited places such as cities, villages, fields and other areas in which people normally lived their everyday lives. There are two major ways of understanding the desert in Israelite tradition. The first is as a place of danger, where demons dwell (Isa 34:9–15). It is a place where humans cannot live (Deut 32:10) and that is not arable (Jer 2:2). It is also, however, a place in which the Israelites are led by Moses into a new type of social configuration, where they are totally dependent upon God's action in order to sustain them (Exod 16:1–12; Exod 17:1–7). It is the place of

---

114. The Greeks did not distinguish linguistically between these two terms. See, for example, Herodotus *Hist.* 2.32. See also *Hist.* 4.18. There, in the same sentence, Herodotus informs us of one desert which is inhabited by cannibals and another which is so severe as not to be inhabitable.

115. Talmon, "Wilderness," 946–49.

116. Whether or not to draw distinctions between these two terms is an open question. Here I have followed the suggestion of Meier, *Marginal Jew*, 2.43–46. For a position that advocates a clearer distinction, see Hareuveni, *Desert and Shepherd*. Hareuveni distinguishes between ערבה (wilderness) and מדבר (desert).

the giving of the Law (Exod 19:16–25). Despite its harsh conditions, there were Israelites who chose to live in deserts, that is, away from the centers of cultivation and the ordered life of a city or village.

In the Israelite tradition the desert obviously holds a tremendous symbolic value. The social significance of the desert begins with the wanderings of the Israelites during the Exodus. The desert is a multivalent symbol in the Pentateuch. In the first instance, it is the place to which the Israelites flee from the bonds of slavery. It is characterized by the giving of the covenant, the provision of food and water (Exod 16–17), and the promise of the conquest of the land. It is also, however, characterized by general discontent (Exod 14:11), challenges to Moses' leadership, and distrust of God's provisions for the people (Exod 16:1–3; 17:1–3). The time spent in the wilderness is even increased in order to allow time for the oldest generation (those above twenty years old) to die off as a punishment for their continued complaints against God (Num 14:27–33).

The inhabitants of Qumran chose to leave a life in the city and live in the desert away from the normal social conditions of Jerusalem.[117] There are numerous proposals put forward concerning their relationship with the Jerusalem temple's priesthood, but it is clear that they rejected the leadership there for some reason.[118] This group went out to the desert in order to live a lifestyle that was defined in every respect by holiness, most probably influenced by the ideas contained in Isaiah 40:3.[119] There the prophet calls upon the Israelites "In the wilderness prepare the way of the Lord, make straight in the desert a highway for our God." The Qumran community apparently took this passage literally and left the "civilized" world of Jerusalem for a life in the area of God's prior redemption of Israel, the desert. They were not able to mingle with the people that they considered profane in the city of Jerusalem or in its surrounding villages.

Other examples of people going to live in desert areas include the "desert fathers." These cenobitic monks lived in caves in the deserts near the villages of upper Egypt. They lived in close proximity to villages, but they did not share the lifestyle of the village people. Contact with villagers was commonplace, so that these monks should not be imagined as living entirely apart from society. They merely lived outside the normal conven-

117. See the discussion in VanderKam, "Judean Desert and the Community."

118. VanderKam, *Dead Sea Scrolls Today*, 71–119; and VanderKam, "Identity and History of the Community."

119. See VanderKam, "Judean Desert," 161, 170–71.

tions of society, and to do so they had to separate themselves physically from the lives they led before venturing into the desert.[120]

In some instances the desert could provide a positive contrast to city life. Philo's *Decal.* 2, for instance, relates that God gave the law in the wilderness because of the wickedness and corruption of city life. Again in his description of the Theraputae, he notes that after selling their belongings, they leave the city of their origin but not to enter another city. "For every city, even the best governed, is full of turmoils and disturbances innumerable which no one could endure who has ever been even once under the guidance of wisdom" (*Contempl. Life* 19). Rather than life in the city "they pass their days outside the walls in pursuing solitude in gardens (κῆποι) or lonely bits of country (μοναγρίαις ἐρημίαν; *Contempl. Life* 20). The desert provides a contrast to the life of the city in which the normal affairs of human community might interrupt one's search for wisdom or, worse, might entice one to all kinds of wickedness.

The desert could function as a place of refuge for people seeking to avoid hostility. David, for example, fled into the desert in order to avoid Saul's murderous intentions toward him (1 Sam 19:8–24:1). First Samuel 24:1 locates David in the wilderness of En-gedi. Elijah also fled from Jezebel (1 Kgs 19:1–18). Elijah's trek takes him to Mount Horeb (Sinai) in imitation of Moses' encounter with God there.[121] Besides being a place in which people might choose to dwell in order to separate themselves from the larger society for purity reasons, the desert could be a place into which one could flee in order to escape persecution.

Several other key texts draw upon the image of the desert. Hosea 2 uses the imagery of the wilderness as a site of covenant renewal.[122] As mentioned above in the brief discussion of the Qumran community, Isaiah 40 was an especially important text in the development of the social significance of the desert. It was there that the way of the Lord was to be prepared. VanderKam reads this text against the backdrop of the return of the exiles from captivity. The text "pictures the return of the Lord to Jerusalem after the Babylonian exile as a triumphant procession over a highway through the wilderness."[123] He suggests that the Qumran com-

---

120. Goehring, *Ascetics, Society, and the Desert.*
121. VanderKam, "Judean Desert," 161.
122. Ibid.; see also Ezek 9:10–13.
123. Ibid.

munity chose their place of habitation in the desert north of the Dead Sea on the basis of this passage from Isaiah.[124] The Israelites had come out of the desert into the land, but now a new excursus into the desert was necessary to "prepare the way of the Lord." The desert operated as a kind of a staging area for this preparation.

Two examples from Josephus are significant to the discussion here. Josephus narrates stories about an Egyptian prophet (*Ant.* 20.8.6//*B.J.* 2.13.5). He relates that "deceivers and impostors, under the pretence of divine inspiration fostering revolutionary changes" had "persuaded the multitude to act like madmen, and led them out to the desert under the belief that God would there give them tokens of deliverance" (*B.J.* 2.13.4).[125] Josephus introduces the story of the Egyptian prophet (in the *B.J.* he is termed ψευδοπροφήτης) by stressing that it is even worse than what had preceded it. This prophet "collected a following of about thirty thousand dupes, and led them by a circuitous route from the desert to the Mount of Olives" (*B.J.* 2.13.5). His plan was to take Jerusalem by force once he and his followers had overthrown the Roman garrison. The outcome was the destruction of all but a few of the Egyptian's followers. The second example concerns Theudas, who also led his followers into the desert (*Ant.* 20.5.1). He promised his followers that, once in the desert, "at his command the river [that is, the Jordan] would be parted and would provide them an easy passage."[126] Clearly this evokes the tradition of the original conquest of the land by Joshua and his forces. It also likely appeals to the parting of the Reed Sea for the Israelites in their flight from Egypt. Both of these stories are motivated by the idea of a new exodus that will enable the Jews to throw off Roman rule in favor of God's rule.[127]

Therefore, though the desert was not a normal place of habitation, it could be variously peopled by migrations, flight from danger or those who sought to separate themselves from the evils or impurities of the society in which they lived. The social significance of the desert in the Hebrew Bible made it a viable option for this type of retreat from society. The prophetic (and eschatological) significance of the desert as a place of preparation for

---

124. Ibid., 170–71.

125 All translations of Josephus' *Jewish War*, unless otherwise stated, are taken from Thackeray's translation in the LCL.

126. All translations of Josephus' Jewish Antiquities, unless otherwise stated, are taken from Feldman's translation in the LCL.

127. See Evans, "Aspects of the Exile and Restoration."

God's appearance took on an increased significance with some early Jewish groups, like the Qumran community. The desert was, therefore, a place of developing social significance well into the second temple period.

As borderlands, deserts and mountains are places in which normal patterns of social behavior do not necessarily apply. The lack of control of these places by human settlements encourages the negotiation of identity within them. The spatial practice of persons in civilized centers does not apply in these borderlands. Spatial practices in these areas vary from those found in the centers of civilization. Wildness in these areas can imply either a heightened sense of observation of civilization or total lawlessness.[128] In the cases related by Josephus of the Egyptian prophet and Theudas, both elements come into play. For these men, their movement into the desert represents a heightened response to God's forthcoming activity in the desert, while to those in the center, it represents lawlessness and the breakdown of the order of society. Borderlands, however, always represent places for the negotiation of identity, which frequently involve alternative spatial practices.

Travel

Though travel increased in the Hellenistic and Roman worlds, travel over significant distances was still a relatively rare activity restricted, for the most part, to government officials and traders. Travel for official government business was one of the main reasons for travel from the earliest periods in antiquity.[129] Besides trade and government business, warfare was also a major reason for travel in antiquity. Travel, as noted in chapter three, could also occur for the purpose of seeing the wonders of the world. Other reasons for travel included education, medical treatment and pilgrimage.[130] Travel was primarily a passage from one civilized territory to another through wilderness areas and boundary territories. Travel is pre-

---

128. In the former case, the Persians who worship Zeus on the mountain should be considered, along with the Israelites in the desert during the Exodus, and the Qumran community. In the latter case, the examples cited above of wild and indecent behavior in these types of territories demonstrates the lawless element.

129. Casson, *Travel in the Ancient World*.

130. Casson suggests that the two largest groups of travelers in the Greek world would have been traders and those who were going to one of the many religious festivals. See *Travel in the Ancient World*, 76. On people traveling to seek medical treatment, see ibid., 82–83.

Categories for Understanding Ancient Space

dominantly considered a hardship in ancient accounts of both travel by sea and land, frequently representing encounters with "savage" people who are not bound by the conventions of civilized society.

Travel by Sea

Travel by sea was a precarious undertaking in the ancient world. Many dangers lurked in the ocean. Storms and the shipwrecks were commonplace occurrences in antiquity, perhaps even more in the minds of the ancients than in reality.[131] Pirates were a constant threat in sea travel as well. Increased sea travel also meant a greater likelihood of naval attack from other countries. The sea, because of its pirates and the threat of foreign nations crossing its waters to attack, was understood as a constant threat to the civilized order of the Greek and Roman worlds. Seneca writes:

> As it is now, domestic evils are not enough for me; I have to suffer also ills from abroad. No country is so distantly remote that it cannot export some of its own ills. For all I know even now some ruler of a great nation (hitherto unknown to me), puffed up by the indulgence of fortune, is not restricting his armies within his own country but is outfitting fleets and moving against people who have never even heard of him. How do I know but that this wind or that is bringing war to me? A great measure of peace would be granted to humans if the seas were closed. (*Nat.* 5.18.12)

Peoples from other *oikoumenai* might be able to traverse the seas with favorable winds and come and conquer Rome. As it is, sea travel brings the ills of every country to Rome. Ability to travel on the seas, for Seneca, is an overwhelmingly negative thing. Sea travel brings peoples together that were meant to be kept apart. This conception of sea travel is why Seneca longs for the peace that closed seas would bring to Rome.

The sea journey par excellence of the Greek (and subsequently Roman) world was Odysseus' *Odyssey*. His return home from the Trojan War lasted some twenty years and included many harrowing events and the loss of his entire crew. Odysseus was forced to undergo this extended journey because of Poseidon's anger that Odysseus killed the Cyclops (*Od.*

---

131. Robbins, "By Land and By Sea," 230, puts the matter succinctly: "At some point, almost every good sea voyage account portrays a storm that threatens or actually ends in a shipwreck."

1.65–79). The journeys of Odysseus cast a long shadow over the description of seafaring that followed in ancient literature.[132]

Given that the seafaring of Odysseus is full of trials and hardship, it should hardly be surprising that much of the ancient literature on seafaring describes it in negative terms. Besides shipwrecks that lead to death at sea, numerous tales of shipwrecks resulted in ancient mariners becoming stranded on barbarian shores, either to be killed or to undergo harrowing adventures.[133] Shipwreck and death at sea were a common way for the gods to punish evildoers.[134] So, for instance, Ovid proscribes traveling with those who do not maintain their word (*Her.* 7.57–58). Andocides explains his innocence on charges of impiety in the following way.

> The prosecution has also found grounds for attacking me in the fact that I am a merchant who owns ships. We are asked to believe that the only object of the gods in saving me from the dangers of the sea was, apparently, to let Cephisius put an end to me when I reached Athens. No, gentlemen. I for one cannot believe that if the gods considered me guilty of an offence against them, they would have been disposed to spare me when they had me in a situation of utmost peril—for when is a man in greater peril than on a winter sea-passage? Are we to suppose that the gods had my person at their mercy on just such a voyage, that they had my life and my goods in their power, and that in spite of it they kept me safe? Why, could they not have caused even my corpse to be denied due burial? Furthermore, it was war-time; the sea was infested with triremes and pirates, who took many a traveller prisoner, and after robbing him of his all, sent him to end his days in slavery. And there were foreign shores on which many a traveller had been wrecked, to be put to death after meeting with shameful indignities and maltreatment. (*On the Mysteries* 137–138)[135]

Andocides discusses several elements that make shipwreck worse than other kinds of death. There is the constant possibility that one will sink in the sea and not be afforded a proper burial. Enslavement by pirates or vari-

---

132. See MacDonald, *Homeric Epics and the Gospel of Mark*; and idem, *Does the New Testament Imitate Homer?* For the influence of Homer upon Apollonius' *Argonautica*, see Fantuzzi, "'Homeric' Formularity," and Rengakos, "Apollonius Rhodius."

133. See Robbins, "By Land and By Sea," 215–34.

134. On this point, see Ladouceur, "Hellenistic Preconceptions of Shipwreck."

135. All translations of Andocides, unless otherwise stated, are taken from Maidment's translation, in *Minor Attic Orators* 1 in the LCL. This text is cited by Ladouceur, "Hellenistic Preconceptions of Shipwreck," 438. See his discussion on 436–69.

ous parties in wars was always a possibility. Finally, landing on the shores of a barbarian people might involve "shameful indignities and maltreatment" prior to death.[136]

Sea travel and trade had expanded considerably during the Hellenistic and Roman periods. Indeed, the Romans were, in some instances, known as masters of the sea.[137] Once they had established naval control of the seas by destroying or commandeering the fleets of their enemies, "Rome's chief task on the water was anti-piracy control, communications, transports."[138] The efforts at anti-piracy, however, were never quite successful. Even so powerful a figure as Julius Caesar was once taken by pirates and ransomed for 50 talents.[139]

Though sea travel was significant in the Hellenistic and Roman periods, most of the literary accounts largely consist of negative examples. There was clearly a sense among the ancients that seafaring involved the possibility of losing one's life. This idea was combined with the general sense that the gods could use the seas as a means of exacting revenge upon people who wronged them.[140] Merchants who frequented the seas were held in low esteem.[141] They were considered to be of shady character compared to the land owning elite.

Early followers of Jesus were no strangers to travel by sea.[142] Paul recounts some of his harrowing travails in 2 Cor 11:25–27. He tells of three shipwrecks (including a day and night adrift at sea), several journeys that included "danger from rivers, danger from bandits, danger from my own people, danger from Gentiles, danger in the city, danger in the wilderness, danger at sea, danger from false brothers and sisters . . ." (2 Cor 11:26). Paul, as other early Christian traditions record, traveled frequent-

---

136. See also Seneca, *Nat.* 5.18.7–8.

137. This description is primarily due to their overwhelming success in naval warfare. See Meijer, *History of Seafaring*, 167–85. Also Casson, *Ships and Seamanship*, 141–47.

138. Casson, *Ships and Seamanship*, 141.

139. On his capture by Cilician pirates, see Suetonius, *Jul.* 4.2; and Plutarch, *Caes.* 1.2–2.4.

140. See Ladouceur, "Hellenistic Preconceptions." Obviously the idea of the gods using the sea as an arena of retribution is at least as old as the *Odyssey*.

141. The case of Andocides, among others, demonstrates this fact. On negative stereotypes concerning merchants in the ancient world, see Kraybill, *Imperial Cult and Commerce*.

142. See Robbins, "By Land and By Sea," 226–28.

ly.¹⁴³ Paul's seafaring was especially well-known. He and his companions regularly sailed in Acts.¹⁴⁴ His difficulties encountered on the sea highlight many of the stock examples of troubles at sea (Acts 27–28). The winds are against Paul and his companions (27:4, 7), forcing them to travel beyond the normal sailing season (27:9–10). This fateful decision causes them to be at sea during a storm that shipwrecks them (27:13–20). Normally one might expect the loss of life in a shipwreck, but Paul assures them that this will not be the case (27:22). The crew and prisoners, including Paul, survive the shipwreck and encounter "natives" (βάρβαροι; 28:2). The usual condition of encountering barbarian peoples might be, as Andocides says, indignities followed by death. Rather than this harsh treatment, however, Paul is treated "hospitably" (φιλοφρόνως; Acts 28:7).¹⁴⁵ The native people interpret the shipwreck as a means of justice by the gods (or God in this case) when a viper bites Paul, a sure token that he is guilty of murder (28:4). Paul not only survives but is totally immune to the effects of the viper (28:6). Ladouceur suggests that it is in Acts 28:11–13 that Paul's innocence is truly demonstrated. He sails under the sign of the Dioscouri, those twin brothers whose functions included the execution of justice, and is blessed with a south wind. To the

> ancient reader who would come to the text with preconceptions of shipwreck, pollution, and divine retribution, the fact that Paul, who had three times given evidence of his innocence in the courtroom, not only survived the shipwreck at Malta, but also sailed safely . . . under the protection of the guardians of truth and punishers of purjurers [sic], would certainly be evidence of that innocence.¹⁴⁶

While sea travel was a fact of life in Hellenistic and Roman times, piracy, storms, and the ever-present notion of justice coming to meet evildoers at sea helped to produce a literary tradition of the sea as a place of danger.¹⁴⁷ This tradition was relatively widespread, and most sea travel

---

143. See especially Acts 9 and 13–28.

144. For example, Paul and Barnabas in Acts 13:4; Paul and his companions in 13:13; the famous "we passages" of 16:10–18; 20:5–16; and 27:1—28:16. There are several other examples found throughout Acts. On the "we passages" see Robbins, "By Land and By Sea."

145. Robbins, ibid., 229, notes that the idea of a friendly reception upon initial embarkation on foreign shores is part of the literary convention of seafaring tales.

146. Ladouceur, "Hellenistic Preconceptions," 446.

147. In one case, it is even known that students were taught to write "storms at sea" as part of their schooling. See the text in Dionysus of Halicarnassus, *Rhet.* 10.17. See the

were restricted to a relatively small number of people in the Hellenistic and Roman worlds. Early Christians were familiar with the idea that the sea was a place of danger, and tales of shipwreck found in Acts and other early Christian literature suggest that they adopted the same views as the Greeks and Romans concerning such travel. Since trade by sea and government travel was fairly restricted in terms of the number of people who participated, it is probably safe to assume that the traditions concerning the dangers of sea travel held some force in the popular imagination.[148]

Land

Travel by land was also difficult in the ancient world. In his discussion of travel by roads in the Greek world, Casson says that the preserved sources "do not often mention highwaymen, but these were no doubt as much of a plague as pirates."[149] Even if cities had police forces, these "were for keeping order within the town walls; the open country to all intents and purposes was a no-mans' land."[150] Since there was no system of credit, whatever monies would be needed for journeys had to be carried. For this reason, "Greek bandits could be pretty sure that their efforts would be rewarded."[151]

The Roman road system made travel somewhat easier, to be sure, but it was still an undertaking fraught with danger for most travelers.[152] For the most part, government officials, traders and soldiers did most of the traveling; "we must always remember that these roads were built first and foremost for the army."[153] Transport by land, especially among traders

---

discussion in MacDonald, "Shipwrecks of Odysseus and Paul." It is possible that these tales represent a common fact about Hellenistic and Roman sea travel. Most such travel was not done on the open sea. By far the majority of travel by sea took place along coastlines. See Casson, *Ships and Seafaring*, 127–40. The idea of shipwreck usually involved some period of time when the ship reached the open sea, and the sight of the coastline was lost.

148. It is difficult to tell, given the paucity of sources, how widespread such beliefs may have been among the Israelites and early Jews. Jonah attests to the idea that the sea could be used by divine agents as a place of judgment.

149. Casson, *Travel in the Ancient World*, 73.

150. Ibid.

151. Ibid., 74.

152. On the Roman road system in general see ibid., 163–75. Casson notes that the Romans learned road construction from the Etruscans.

153. Ibid., 168.

was still far less common than that by sea because it "was prohibitively expensive."[154] It also frequently took much longer than travel by sea. Pack animals and horses were a feature of the Greek and Roman periods, and carriages were available to the wealthy.[155] Even travel by horse or other animal, however, was extremely difficult in these periods. "Riding a horse in ancient times, particularly for long distances, was a wearisome business" since the Greeks and Romans "limited its usefulness by riding without stirrups or a proper saddle but also by leaving it unshod."[156] The roads were mainly, then, used for official government purposes.[157] In fact, the roads may not have been used for travel all that extensively in some parts of the empire. Indeed, Laurence suggests that the building of roads, "bridges, towns, forts and so on," might be related to altering "the geography of an area to create a new Roman landscape."[158] The laying of roads, then, Romanized the landscape in the same way that the adoption of the toga Romanized foreign peoples.

Like piracy, banditry is a common phenomenon in ancient novelistic literature.[159] Frequently the hero or heroine of a novel is taken by bandits and sometimes forced to participate in their evil plots. The roads are full of bandits looking for opportunity to overcome travelers. When Aristomenes is attempting to flee the inn where he had witnessed his companion's brutal slaying, he calls upon the innkeeper to open the gate. The innkeeper, however, replies, "What? don't you know that the roads are infested with robbers?" (Apuleius, *Metam.* 1.15).[160] The Parable of the Good Samaritan (Luke 10:25–37) assumes that travel could be an especially dangerous undertaking.[161] Bandits on the road were a common enough feature to become a stock part of stories related to travel by roadways. Certain pro-

154. Ibid., 129.
155. Ibid., 176–80.
156. Ibid., 181.

157. Ibid., 130. Government purposes still accounted for the vast majority of all travel, perhaps matched only by traders.

158. Laurence, "Afterword: Travel and Empire," 169.

159. Banditry, particularly in isolated areas away from the city was a widely recognized feature of the Roman world. See MacMullen, *Roman Social Relations*, 1–4. On the role of social banditry in first-century Galilee and Judea, see K. C. Hanson, "Jesus and the Social Bandits"; and Horsley and J. S. Hanson, *Bandits, Prophets, Messiahs*, 48–87.

160. All translations from Apuleius's *Metamorphoses*, unless otherwise stated, are taken from Hanson's translation in the LCL.

161. On this parable see especially Oakman, "Was Jesus a Peasant?"

fessions, notably the military, government and medicine, involved much more frequent travel than should be assumed for the population of antiquity generally.

The final section of Casson's book on travel is about ancient tourists.[162] These tourists were exceedingly rare in number because of the difficulties, dangers, and expense that came with travel in the Hellenistic and Roman worlds. Tourists visited temples, shrines, and sometimes public buildings in the cities they visited.[163] Casson's preeminent example of such a tourist is Pausanias. Granted that there were some travelers who traveled apparently to see sights, such a phenomenon should be considered quite rare, and impossible for the vast majority of the people who populated the Hellenistic and Roman worlds. Extended travel was a relatively restricted phenomenon even in the Roman world, though "most people would have known others who had gone on journeys or had met travellers in the their locality."[164] The preserved literary accounts of travel by land, like those of travel by sea, stress the danger and hardship inherent in travel.

Travel, whether, by land or sea involved leaving those areas designated for normal social activity and entering territories in which one could not expect such behavior. On the sea and in open territory such as borderlands, mountainous territories and deserts, threats lurked constantly. Travelers could be easily overcome by pirates and bandits. Travel between major cities involved leaving the areas of settled living and venturing through the territories of uncivilized people.

Because of inefficient policing, the Greeks and Romans were unable to replicate their spatial practices on the sea and over the lands that lay some distance from cities. The fact that travel increased during the Hellenistic and Roman periods but is continually presented negatively in texts from these periods, illustrates the way that texts are able to create their own space. In these textual traditions, despite the advances in travel efficiency (and probably safety) especially during the Roman period, spaces outside of the cities and their immediate environs are not considered safe. There is no cultivation of crops in these places, no normal social modes of intercourse. There is only "non-civilization." Non-civilization can only mean one thing in ancient geography: dangerous otherness.

162. Casson, *Travel in the Ancient World*, 229–329.
163. On the selection of locations to visit by later Christian pilgrims see Leyerle, "Landscape as Cartography," 119–41.
164. Laurence, "Afterword," 169.

Exile

Another type of travel in antiquity was not made under voluntary circumstances but under the compulsion of military or political powers. Not infrequently, individuals and groups were exiled in antiquity. Individuals critical of the government were often forced to leave their homelands.[165] These exiles were often philosophers who spoke out against certain policies or practices of the Roman government. They could be banished for a limited time and from a limited area, or they could be eternally banished from Rome and its territories. Lucian relates that since "all men seem to prize their own country . . . lawgivers everywhere, as one may note, have prescribed exile as the severest penalty (χαλεπωτάτην ἐπιβεβληκότας τὴν φυγὴν τιμωρίαν; *My Native Land* 12).[166] Given the severity with which lawbreakers were sometimes treated in the ancient world, one might quibble with his characterization of exile as the most severe penalty of all, but clearly banishment could cause severe hardship for individuals and groups.

Forced population shifts were a fact of life in antiquity.[167] Wars, famines and natural disasters often forced people to live in an area in which they were not indigenous. These populations shifts did not necessarily involve every member of an ethnos, but they involved enough members (particularly among the political and religious leadership of groups) that the landscape was altered as new peoples were moved into areas while indigenous peoples were moved out. While exile was not uncommon for many peoples in the ancient world, attention here is specifically focused on the Israelite traditions concerning exile as most directly relevant to the present study.

Myth of the Empty Land

The idea that the land of Israel lay empty and dormant during the Babylonian exile, explicitly expressed in 2 Chronicles, is related to a specific ideological and theological understanding of both the land and the com-

---

165. Cicero, Ovid, Dio Chrysostom, and Diogenes of Sinope are among the more famous exiles of antiquity.

166 All translations of Lucian's *My Native Land*, unless otherwise stated, are from Harmon's translation in the LCL.

167. Usually they came as a result of war; see, for example, Herodotus *Hist.* 1.164.

munity that rebuilt the temple upon their return to the land. Portraying a land devoid of human inhabitants enables the author of the Chronicles to claim that the returnees were restoring the land rather than usurping land already occupied by other people. The returnees have a legitimate claim to the land since it was theirs to begin with and unoccupied in the intervening period.

There is another important reason in the logic of the Chronicler why the land must remain empty and fallow during the period of the exile. The land itself, like the people, must do its penance in order to be purged of its evil and be restored to right relationship with God.[168] The land had to remain empty until it "had made up for its sabbaths. All the days that it lay desolate it kept sabbath, to fulfill seventy years" (2 Chr 36:21). Unlike the accounts of the exile in 2 Kings,[169] the Chronicler paints a picture of an abandoned Palestine. Carroll suggests that by presenting an empty land, the Chronicler creates an opportunity for a return to a purified land. "The land by becoming empty of people *paid off* the guilt/debts incurred by the pollution, by means of keeping the sabbath for seventy years."[170] Since the debt incurred by the pollution of the people is paid the return to the land marks "the beginning of the second temple period and it is based on the idea of a land purified from pollution and empty of people."[171] The logic of purification in the account found in 2 Chronicles relies heavily on the deportation of all who "escaped from the sword" (2 Chr 36:20).

The 2 Chronicles text is clearly influenced by the text of Jeremiah.[172] The seventy-year length of the exile is a datum provided by Jeremiah and borrowed by the Chronicler.[173] But in Chronicles, "'seventy years' is not a chronological datum which may be explained by various calculations, but a historical and theological concept: a time limit for the duration of the

---

168. On the following, see especially Carroll, "Myth of the Empty Land"; see Lev 26:34–35.

169. Second Kings 25:12, 22 narrates that the "poorest of the land" remained in Judea "to be vinedressers and tillers of the soil."

170. Carroll, "Myth of the Empty Land," 80.

171. Ibid., 80.

172. Indeed, 2 Chr 36:21 says that the inhabitants of Jerusalem are exiled until the time of Persia "to fulfill the word of the Lord by the mouth of Jeremiah."

173. See Jer 25:11–12 and 29:10. Japhet, *I & II Chronicles*, 1075–76, suggests that the Chronicler accepts the concept of a limited exile from the tradition of Lev 26:43 and combines it with the traditions concerning the exile found in Jeremiah.

land's desolation, established by a divine word through his prophet."[174] Jeremiah 36:29 prophesies that the king of Babylon "will cut off from it [the land] human beings and animals." This text seems to contradict Jer 40:7 where the "poorest of the land" are left behind.[175] While only the Chronicler (and perhaps Jer 36:29) present the land as completely devoid of people, Carroll thinks that all three of these traditions—2 Kings, 2 Chronicles, and Jeremiah—present "a kind of territorial *tabula rasa*" in which "the poorest who eked out a livelihood working the land presumably did not count."[176]

The presentation of the land as devoid of people during the exile allows the returnees from Babylon to claim the land for themselves. The people who remained have no right to claim the land as their own in the story of Ezra.

> Whatever the origins of these people (cf. Ezra 4:2) they are not permitted to identify themselves with the community gathered together around the altar and the partially rebuilt sanctuary. Their identity is strictly other than that of those who had lived in Babylonia, and in relation to the cult of YHWH they are non-persons.[177]

These people "occupy space but that space is purely geophysical, it is not part of the symbolic geography whose ideology underwrites so much of the Hebrew Bible."[178] The reason for their being non-persons in the symbolic geography of exile and return is that only those people who had gone into exile "shared the land's sabbath rests (repayments), the others had not."[179] When viewed from the perspective of critical spatiality, then, the symbolic maps of texts like Jeremiah, 2 Kings, and 2 Chronicles present a land devoid of inhabitants during the period of exile.[180] Those who returned to the land returned according to conditions spelled out in the

---

174. Ibid., 1076.
175. This view of the exilic situation is shared with 2 Kings.
176. Carroll, "Myth of the Empty Land," 80.
177. Ibid., 81.
178. Ibid., 83–84.
179. Ibid., 85.
180. That the land was physically occupied by some of the invading army and some non-deported Israelites is historical fact, but mental maps do not necessarily reflect such historical facts. In thinking about the presentation of the land in these texts, then, the historical situation is not symbolically relevant.

biblical texts themselves.[181] Only those people who had gone into exile, repented of their iniquity, and atoned for it, are fit to be returned to the land. The people who remain, the non-persons in the symbolic geography of exile and return, obviously were not subject to the pattern of exile, atonement, and restoration.[182]

The Babylonian exile, of course, is not the only time the Israelites were forced from the land. The migration to Egypt (Genesis 42–46) also represents a forced removal from the land. In this instance, however, it is famine that forces the withdrawal from the land. What starts as a seemingly temporary move because of famine, however, ends up as four-hundred year enslavement in the service of Egyptian Pharaohs. When God finally liberates the people through a series of plagues that force the Egyptians to allow the Israelites to leave, problems arise on their return to the promised land. The promised land is occupied by other peoples. These peoples have a claim to the land by virtue of their living on it and working its soil. Since the land has been promised to the Israelites, however, the book of Joshua relates the Israelites' conquest of the land and destruction of the people who occupy it.

While the biblical texts are clear that the Israelites,[183] with God at their head, destroyed most of the inhabitants of the land, there are later interpretations that explain the conquest of the land in other terms. These stories allow for the inhabitants of the land to leave voluntarily. In some of these later traditions, those who do leave the land promised to the Israelites are resettled in other lands set apart for them by God.[184] So, for example, *Lev. Rab.* 17.6 relates the story of Joshua offering three choices to the Canaanites: flight, peace or fight.[185] Other early Jewish texts also present alternative versions of the conquest of the land. Philo, in his *Hypoth.* 6.6, suggests that the original inhabitants of the land of Judea voluntarily surrendered their lands to the Israelites in view of their divine claim to the land.

---

181. So, for example, Ezra 1:1–4 and 2 Chr 36:21–23.

182. See Weinfeld, *Promise of the Land*, 183–88.

183. So, for example, Joshua 6 (on the conquest of Jericho); Josh 8:1–29 (on the conquest of Ai); other conquests are described in Joshua 10–11. Further Israelite conquests are describes in Judges 1.

184. On what follows, see Blenkinsopp, "Bible, Archaeology and Politics."

185. Ibid., 173. The *Leviticus Rabbah* text is quoted in Weinfeld, *Promise of the Land*, 211.

> Or shall we suppose that they were unwarlike and feeble, quite few in numbers and destitute of warlike equipment, but won the respect of their opponents who voluntarily surrendered their land to them and that as a direct consequence they shortly afterwards built their temple and established everything else needed for religion and worship?[186]

Philo's point is that the Israelites never would have been able to defeat the inhabitants of the land in direct military confrontation. There are other, non-Jewish accounts of the arrival of the Israelites into the land as well. Strabo, for instance, relates that the land was empty because no one else wanted to live in such a rocky, barren place. According to Strabo, Moses was an Egyptian priest who "held a part of lower Aegypt" (*Geogr.* 16.35). Because of his opposition to Egyptian, Libyan and Greek images of God, Moses decided to leave Egypt.[187] Strabo relates the Israelite "conquest" of the land in this way.

> Now Moses, saying things of this kind, persuaded not a few thoughtful men and led them away to this place where the settlement of Jerusalem now is; and he easily took possession of the place, since it was not a place that would be looked on with envy, nor yet one for which anyone would make a serious fight; for it is rocky, and, although it is well supplied with water, its surrounding country is barren and waterless (λυπρὰν καὶ ἄνυδρον), and the part of the territory within a radius of sixty stadia is also rocky beneath the surface. At the same time Moses, instead of using arms, put forward as defence his sacrifices and his Divine Being, being resolved to seek a seat of worship for Him and promising to deliver to the people a kind of worship and a kind of ritual which would not oppress those who adopted them either with expenses or with divine obsessions or with other absurd troubles. Now Moses enjoyed fair repute with these people, and organised no ordinary kind of government, since the peoples all round, one and all, came over to him, because of his dealings with them and of the prospects he held out to them. (*Geogr.* 16.36)

---

186. All translations of Philo's *Hypothetica*, unless otherwise stated, are taken from Colson's translation in the LCL. A similar tradition is found in *Mekhilta Pisha* 18. For a discussion of these passages, see Blenkinsopp, "Bible, Archaeology and Politics," 173–75.

187. Strabo attributes a pantheistic position to Moses inasmuch as he presents Moses' opposition to idols as a rejection of making images of God who "is this one thing alone that encompasses us all and encompasses land and sea—the thing which we call heaven, or universe, or the nature of all that exists" (*Geogr.* 16.35).

Strabo presents an account that involves the pacification of the original inhabitants of the land. Rather than violent overthrow or voluntary exile, the inhabitants of the land recognize the superiority of Moses' governance and agree to live under it. Because of its rugged terrain, however, Judea is not a particularly suitable place to live. It is this rugged condition of the place that makes it devoid of much human settlement in the first place.[188]

These varying traditions concerning the conquest of the land of Israel have led Blenkinsopp to the conclusion that "the story in circulation in the Hellenistic period about the *original* occupation of an empty Palestine is a retrojection from the time of the 'return to Zion', therefore a reflection of the ideology of the dominant immigrant group during the early decades of Persian rule."[189] The reason for such developments lies in the attempt to present the returnees from exile as the true inhabitants of the land. Not only are there no legitimate claimants to the land among those who stayed behind during the exile, but also, because the land had always been empty, there were *never* any people other than the Israelites with a legitimate claim to the land.[190] The immigrants that returned during the Persian rule, then, as direct descendants of those Israelites that originally occupied the land, are the only ones who have a rightful claim to the land.

During the Persian period the returning immigrant groups made numerous mythic claims to be the original, and therefore legitimate, inhabitants of the land of Judea. They did so by creating various versions of the "myth of the empty land." There were either no people in Judah during the exile, or the people that did remain were symbolically nonexistent in the eyes of the returnees. Against this understanding of the situation, however, there were several groups who did not agree that the descendants of the Ezra/Nehemiah return were legitimate claimants to the land and temple. For these groups, the exile continued after the return of the Ezra/Nehemiah groups.

---

188. Hecataeus of Miletus and Apollonius of Molon had described the territory as a desert wasteland in which no one lived before the Israelites occupied it. See the discussion in Blenkinsopp, "Bible, Archaeology and Politics," 174–75.

189. Ibid., 176.

190. Of course, the traditional biblical account also assumes that, because of God's initiative, those who lived in the land of Judah were not legitimate occupants of the land.

Continued Exile

As clear as the texts of Ezra and Nehemiah are about the return to the land, there are other early Jewish texts that call this return into question.[191] These texts present exile as a continuing situation in the life of Israelite and early Jewish communities. There are numerous texts that fall into this category, and this idea is especially prevalent in apocalyptic literature.[192] There are essentially two ways in which the exile was thought to continue in the second temple period. The first is that the exile never ended, while the second recognizes a return from exile, but it does not consider such a return to have been a complete.

Several writings from the Second Temple period fall under the first heading. Numerous groups, for many different reasons, did not understand the exile to have ended with the return of the groups led by Ezra and Nehemiah and the construction of the Second Temple. The Dead Sea Scrolls preserve the idea that the Second Temple does not represent the return from exile, which is still awaited by the group at Qumran. Abegg suggests that the "Qumran Sect expected to remain in exile until the time of God's judgment on the nations."[193] He bases this opinion, in part, upon 1QM 1:2–3. There the Qumran community is referred to as "exiled of the desert" and "the exiled sons of light" who will "return from the desert of the peoples to camp in the desert of Jerusalem."[194] The exile, according to this understanding, ends only with the final battle between the sons of light and the sons of darkness and the establishment of the rule of the sons of light. The Babylonian exile forms the backdrop for this presentation in that the Qumran community experiences itself in exile from Jerusalem and its temple. The exilic imagery became "the framework for their un-

---

191. There are numerous recent studies that discuss this idea of continued exile in the literature of Second Temple Judaism. Among the more significant of these studies are Knibb, "Exile in the Damascus Document," and "Exile in the Literature of the Intertestamental Period"; Soll, "Misfortune and Exile in Tobit"; Campbell, "Essene-Qumran Origins in the Exile"; Chilton, "Salvific Exile in the Isaiah Targum"; Weitzman, "Allusion, Artifice, and Exile"; Scott, "Exile and the Self-Understanding of Diaspora Jews"; Abegg, "Exile in the Dead Sea Scrolls"; Porton, "Idea of Exile in Early Rabbinic Midrash."

192. See VanderKam, "Exile in Jewish Apocalyptic," 94–104.

193. Abegg, "Exile and the Dead Sea Scrolls," 123.

194. 1QM 1.3. All translation from the DSS, unless otherwise indicated, are taken from Martínez, *Dead Sea Scrolls Translated*.

derstanding of God's future dealings with Israel."[195] Significantly, in some texts from Qumran, the community entered into their exile voluntarily in order to prepare for God's coming.[196] The Rule of the Community (1QS) 8:12b-14 reads in part, "When men such as these come to be in Israel . . . they shall separate from the session of perverse men to go into the wilderness, there to prepare the way of truth."[197] The justification for such separation was found in Isa 40:3.[198]

The idea that the exile would not end until the eschatological age is already found in the biblical text of Daniel.[199] Daniel 9 interprets Jeremiah's seventy years of exile "to mean that the exile was to last for seventy weeks of years, i.e. for four hundred years and ninety years."[200] The Animal Apocalypse in *1 Enoch* 85–90 follows Daniel in that it accepts the end of the exile only with the inauguration of the messianic age. "What we have here, in fact, exactly as in Dan 9, is an understanding of the exile and post-exilic periods as a unified era which is only to be ended when God comes to the earth to establish the Messianic age."[201] The idea that the end of the exile would only come with the establishment of the messianic age was widespread in other literature of the Second Temple period as well.[202]

There are other traditions that recognize the return to the land but see it as an incomplete return. The Testament of Moses tells of the return of "some parts of the tribes" who "will arise and come to their appointed place, and they will strongly build its walls."[203] The text retains its awareness that not all of the Israelites returned to rebuild Jerusalem. These parts of the two tribes that do return, however, will be "sorrowful and sighing because they will not be able to offer sacrifices to the Lord of their fathers" (*T. Mos.* 4:8). The other ten tribes "will grow and spread out among the

195. Abegg, "Exile and the Dead Sea Scrolls," 118.

196. Ibid., 122.

197. Quoted in ibid.

198. There is another tradition within the DSS that relates the end of the exile to the period of the foundation of the Qumran community. See ibid., 120–21; and Knibb, "Exile in the Intertestamental Literature," 262–63.

199. Knibb, "Exile in the Intertestamental Literature," 255.

200. Ibid., 254.

201. Ibid., 256.

202. So *4 Ezra*, *2 Baruch*, and the "Apocalypse of Weeks" (*1 Enoch* 93:1–10; 91:11–17).

203. *Testament of Moses* 4:7; translation is by Priest in *OTP* 1.919–34.

nations during the time of their captivity" (*T. Mos.* 4:9). The text recognizes the situation of continued exile for the ten northern tribes, as well as some of those from the two southern tribes. The return from exile, however, is not a complete reestablishment of the cult in that those who do return find themselves unable to offer sacrifices to the Lord. This is almost certainly a rejection of the Second Temple, though it is unclear whether the rejection is of the Temple itself or of the specific leadership of it.[204] The *Testament of Levi* preserves a similar tradition about the inefficacy of the Second Temple. The priesthood that will be established upon the return to the land will be ungodly. These priests will become "idolators, adulterers, money lovers, arrogant, lawless, voluptuaries, pederasts, those who practice bestiality."[205] It is only with the creation of a "new, eschatological priesthood" that the situation will be reversed.[206] The Animal Apocalypse (*1 Enoch* 85–90) and *Jub.* 1:7–18 also represent traditions that acknowledge the return from exile, but see it as part of a pattern that will be only altered with the advent of the eschaton.[207]

Two traditions concerning continuation of the exile were widespread in the literature of Second Temple Judaism. Some texts make no mention of the Second Temple at all and insist that the only return from exile will be with the inauguration of the messianic age. For others, the return and rebuilding of the Second Temple represent a return, albeit an incomplete and ineffectual one. These readings of the return from exile contrast sharply with the portrait painted by the texts of Ezra, Nehemiah, and the Chronicles. For the authors of those texts, the rebuilding of the Second Temple represented the return to a true worship of Yahweh complete with the sacrifices compelled by the covenant. The early Christians largely fell into the former ways of thinking, though there are some early Christian texts that seem to acknowledge the centrality of Jerusalem even before a coming restoration.[208]

---

204. See the note of Priest in *OTP* 1.929. VanderKam, "Exile in Jewish Apocalyptic," 93–94, maintains that it is possible that the two tribes who "will not be able to offer sacrifices" are those who are not the part of the tribes who return from exile. If this is the case, the reading of the text obviously changes. On this reading, there is a definite return and an endorsement of that return and the worship in the reestablished temple.

205. *Testament of Levi* 17:11. Translation is by Kee in *OTP* 1.775–828.

206. VanderKam, "Exile in Jewish Apocalyptic," 102.

207. Ibid., 94–104.

208. See chapter five below.

Some Israelites, both within and outside Palestine continued to understand their situation as one of exile well into the second temple period. For those inside the land, like the Qumran community, exile seems to refer to a position dislocated from the operations of the temple. For those outside the land, exile refers more literally to the condition of living outside of the land promised to their ancestors by God. The literary evidence that remains suggests that all of the groups who believed themselves to exist in an exilic situation also believed that that situation would eventually end, whether through the intervention of military or heavenly power.

Around the idea of the exile continuing into the second temple period, a negotiation of identities emerges. Some of the communities that did not have access to the center of Jerusalem nevertheless supported it as center through taxes or donations, by making pilgrimages, and by writing it as center in the literature they produced. Many Diaspora communities would fall under this heading. On the other hand, there were numerous groups who subverted that centrality and authority (at least as it was then constituted) by moving into the desert or refusing to acknowledge the leadership of the second temple. The varied reactions to Jerusalem, and particularly to the second temple, as a center highlight the issues at stake in the anthropological understanding of boundary territories and the issues of core and periphery. As is obvious, influence did not flow only from the center to the periphery, and various reactions by different groups of early Jews give direct evidence that people living in boundary territories do not respond to centers in homogeneous fashion.

People as Geographic Centers

People were sometimes considered geographic centers.[209] The Roman emperor was the symbolic center of the empire wherever he went even outside of Rome. Delegations were sent to him, and administrative decisions were made by him. If one wanted to seek counsel, it was necessary to go the emperor himself rather than send a delegation to Rome when the emperor was away. A visiting emperor might grant special privileges to cities or individual citizens.[210] In commenting upon the effect of the change from the Republic to a monarchy, Laurence suggests that people no longer needed

---

209. On kings as geographic and symbolic centers in Homeric Greece and the ancient Near East, see Launderville, *Piety and Politics*, 99–145.

210. See Millar, *Emperor in the Roman World*, 28–40.

to come to Rome necessarily to have a hearing because "the emperor travelled, encountered petitioners, and made decisions outside of Rome. This mobility of the court and centre of government had a knock-on effect: information had to find its way to the mobile emperor."[211]

Other types of people, such as philosophers and teachers, also served as geographic centers. People came to them in order to learn and perhaps to adopt the lifestyle of the philosopher to whom they wished to attach themselves. Philosophers and teachers were sought for advice and favors in the same manner as the emperor. In some instances, the philosopher might displace the emperor as the symbolic center of the empire. These philosophers, while they drew students to themselves, also traveled. Their travel made them geographic centers in the same manner as Odysseus (who saw everything) and the Roman emperors.

The Emperor as Geographic Center

Besides being the place to which all goods came, Rome also was the home of the emperor. People came to Rome to interact with the emperor about the business of the empire. When Augustus was made *pontifex maximus*, "such a concourse poured in from the whole of Italy to my election as has never been recorded at Rome before that time" (*Res Gestae* 10.2).[212] Strabo relates many episodes of envoys sent to the emperor to inquire into one matter or another. So, for example, the Aedui come to Rome to seek "friendship" with the Romans (*Geogr.* 4.2.3). Artemidorus of Ephesus also went to Rome to entreat the emperor concerning the restoration of funds to a local shrine (*Geogr.* 14.1.26). When he was sailing from Gyaros, Strabo's ship takes an envoy to Rome to entreat the emperor (*Geogr.* 10.5.3). Strabo also recounts the journey of three Indian envoys to Caesar who were going to Rome to try to become "friends" of Rome (*Geogr.* 15.1.73). The emperor himself, therefore, was often a geographic place to which people would come.

When the emperor was away from Rome, however, he, not the city, was the geographic locale of power. "Both Rome and the emperor were centres of attraction for goods and people, and much of the time they coincided geographically. However, there were occasions when Rome was

---

211. Laurence, "Afterword," 173.

212. All translations of this text, unless otherwise stated, are taken from the translation of Brunt and Moore.

not the centre of power."²¹³ The idea of a moving imperial center developed during Augustus' travels. "On these travels, a feature developed that was to be characteristic of monarchy: The center of the empire moved with the ruler . . . Wherever he went, that site became the center of politics and the only place where major political decisions could be made."²¹⁴ Rather than going to Rome, people would come to him from every part of the empire wherever he might be.²¹⁵ The emperor, then, functioned as the geographic center of the empire, whenever he traveled from Rome.

Philosophers

Philosophers were geographic centers in two senses. Either people traveled to them, often from great distances, to study and adopt their lifestyles, or they themselves traveled throughout much of the *oikoumenē* in order to seek wisdom, which they then taught to others. Since people regularly came to study with philosophers, a few illustrations will suffice here to make the point. Diogenes Laertius' discussion of the origins of philosophy in the Prologue to his *Lives* discusses the two major schools at the beginning of philosophy. The first was founded by Thales in Ionia, and the other by Pherecydes in Italy (*Lives* 1.13). The most famous philosophers of Greece came to these two locations to study under these men and their disciples. Pythagoras was known for drawing large crowds, and in one instance drew a crowd of over two thousand at Rome. They were so inspired by his teachings that they refused to return home and instead built a school at the site where they could further partake of Pythagoras' wisdom (Iamblichus *On the Pythagorean Life* 6.30). There were other schools, to be sure, that drew adherents (famous, infamous and anonymous).²¹⁶ As with all elements of "higher" education in Greece, one had to travel in order to find the best teachers. The exceptions to this rule were sons of emperors

---

213. Clarke, *Between Geography and History*, 220.

214. Eck, *Age of Augustus*, 105. Nevertheless, the idea of the Roman emperor as a geographic center of politics never displaced Rome's centrality. "In spite of this Rome remained the actual center of power; it would never have crossed Augustus' mind to shift it elsewhere permanently" (106).

215. Millar, *Emperor in the Roman World*, 38: "But what is perhaps more striking and ultimately more important about imperial journeys is the volume of evidence indicating that embassies, and to a lesser extent individual petitioners, came to him not just from the general region where he was but from all over the empire."

216. See Diogenes Laertius *Lives* 1.17, 19–21.

and other people of high status and wealth who could afford to bring teachers to their own houses.

It is not uncommon in the biographies (and other stories) about philosophers for them to travel abroad in order to learn from significant figures of wisdom in other parts of the ancient world.[217] Apollonius of Tyana traveled the entire known world (Philostratus *Vit. Apoll.*).[218] Elsner has recently argued that the motif of the traveling philosopher plays a different role in Philostratus's *Life of Apollonius of Tyana*.[219] Like Odysseus in his travels, the knowledge that Apollonius receives from travel represents not only a "collection of facts or information" but "a collection of places and personal experiences."[220] Apollonius travels extensively within the known Roman world in addition to traveling to the easternmost, southernmost and westernmost boundaries (India, Ethiopia and Spain). The now standard view of Apollonius' travels is that they are "a trope of Second Sophistic rhetoric."[221] As Graham Anderson describes them, they "reflect the canonic sites of 'rhetorical' geography; Arabia, Babylon, India, Asia Minor, Athens, Sparta, Rome, Gades, Libya, Egypt."[222] Elsner examines two types of travel in regard to Apollonius: pilgrimage and the traveler's tale. Rather than being a normal pilgrim, who travels out of piety or out of curiosity regarding miraculous sites, however, when Apollonius visits these sites "he corrects the rites and lectures the priests."[223] So Philostratus presents Apollonius "not as a suppliant but as a master, not as a client but as an expert."[224] Furthermore, Apollonius himself becomes an object of pilgrimage.[225] After Apollonius escaped from Domitian (*Vit. Apoll.* 8.5), all of Greece (as well as those scattered abroad from Athens) comes to see him at Olympia.

---

217. Thales, for example, left his Milesian home and traveled to Egypt in order to learn from the priests there (Diogenes Laertius *Lives* 1.27).

218. The single exception is Scythia. Philostratus rejects the idea that Apollonius traveled there because of a sexual slander made against him in that territory (*Vit. Apoll.* 1.13).

219. Elsner, "Hagiographic Geography."

220. Ibid., 22.

221. Ibid., 23.

222. Anderson, *Philostratus*, 129; see also 199–226.

223. Elsner, "Hagiographic Geography," 27.

224. Ibid.

225. Ibid.

> A rumour as sudden as insistent now ran through the Hellenic world that the sage was alive, and had arrived at Olympia. At first the rumour seemed unreliable . . . But when the rumour of his arrival was confirmed, they all flocked to see him from the whole of Greece, and never did any such crowd flock to any Olympic festival as then, all full of enthusiasm and expectation. People came straight from Elis and Sparta, and from Corinth away at the limits of the isthmus; and the Athenians too, although they were outside the Peloponnese; nor were they behind the cities which are at the gates of Pisa, for it was especially the most celebrated of the Athenians that hurried to the temple, together with the young men who flocked to Athens from all over the earth (ἐξ ἁπάσης τῆς γῆς). Moreover there were people from Megara just then standing in Olympia, as well as many from Boeotia, and from Argos, and all the leading people of Phocis and Thessaly. (*Vit. Apoll.* 8.15)[226]

People come to see Apollonius from all over Greece as well as from Italy (*Vit. Apoll.* 8.15). The people who gathered together to witness Apollonius' amazing return think him divine. In the description of these visitors to Apollonius, "Philostratus turns Apollonius from a pilgrim into an object of pilgrimage."[227]

The other type of travel that Elsner discusses is the travelers' tale. These types of tale have been discussed in much detail in chapter three above. Philostratus uses the customary ethnographic descriptions of the strangeness of foreign lands that we have seen in other authors. Philostratus, however, does many of these tales one better. Apollonius visits every region of the world (again with the exception of Scythia). In describing these extensive travels, "the very range of ethnographic topoi experienced by the sage suggests the depth and universality of wisdom which he has mastered and with which he is equipped to teach."[228] In relating these tales, Philostratus presents a symbolic portrait of Apollonius' travels "whereby the whole earth as far as its boundaries is in the orbit of his holy man's personal experience and knowledge."[229] It is this universal wisdom gained from his travels to the peripheral regions of the world that allows him to

---

226. All translations of Philostratus' *Life of Apollonius*, unless otherwise stated, are taken from Conybeare's translation in the LCL. See the discussion in Elsner, "Hagiographic Geography," 27–28.
227. Elsner, "Hagiographic Geography," 27.
228. Ibid., 29.
229. Ibid., 30–31.

return to the center of the world and confront the tyrant Domitian.²³⁰ Apollonius had been to Rome once before during Nero's reign, but he did not meet Nero, who was in Greece at the time (*Vit. Apoll.* 4.47). Apollonius, however, did meet with two other emperors, neither of whom are considered tyrants by Philostratus. He meets Vespasian outside of Rome, in Alexandria (*Vit. Apoll.* 5.27–8), and Titus in Antioch (*Vit. Apoll.* 6.29–32), "in both cases where they are about to enter the imperial purple but before either is sole ruler of the empire."²³¹ He instructs both of them on the nature of governing. The encounter with Domitian, then, is the only one that takes place in Rome and with an emperor who has already assumed his office. Apollonius overcomes the emperor with the superior knowledge gained throughout his travels abroad. "The spiritual victory in Rome, at the centre of the empire, is the sage's claim to sacred conquest of the empire as a whole."²³² Apollonius, then, is presented in terms of his travels as the most widely traveled of all sages. His universal wisdom gives him the key to a philosophical/religious conquest of the empire. By virtue of this wisdom he displaces the emperor as the symbolic center of the empire, and people come to him from everywhere rather than going to the emperor.

In contrast to temples, philosophers as holy men (like Apollonius and Pythagoras) represent fluid sacred space.²³³ Malina describes groups formed around philosophers and holy men as strong group/low grid.²³⁴ These groups are characterized by a fluid understanding of sacred space. "Sacred space is located in the group, not in some impersonal space like the temple."²³⁵ Such groups develop discourses that become "the mobile, portable, exportable focus of sacred place."²³⁶ Jonathan Z. Smith comes to the same conclusion about holy men in the Hellenistic and early Roman periods.

> Rather than a city wall, the new enclave protecting man against external, hostile powers will be a human group, a religious association or secret society. Rather than a return to chaos or the

---

230. Ibid., 33.
231. Ibid., 34.
232. Ibid.
233. See Neyrey, "Whence and Whither," 62–63.
234. Malina, *Christian Origins and Cultural Anthropology*, 37–44.
235. Ibid., 38.
236. Ibid.

threat of decreation (sic), the enemy will be described as other men or demons, the threat as evil or death. Rather than a sacred place, the new center and chief means of access to divinity will be a divine man, a magician, who will function, by and large, as an entrepreneur without fixed office and will be, by and large, related to those "protean deities" of relatively unfixed form whose major characteristic is their sudden and dramatic autophanies.[237]

Normal fixed centers such as temples do not have priority in view of the philosopher or holy man (categories that were increasingly blended in the Roman world). People are the centers of authority and, in some cases, mediators of the gods. In the case of Apollonius, his confrontation with Domitian is a clear indication that, for Philostratus, it is the holy man rather than the emperor who mediates the divine. The emperor only participates in this process inasmuch as he is a philosopher.

Conclusion

The space of cities was significant for defining identities. The walls of a city were a physical boundary created in order to limit admittance into the territory controlled by the elites of the city. In centers of civilization such as cities and their villages, strictly defined social patterns distinguish people from others outside of these centers. Alternative ways of living, found in wilderness territories, represent threats to the Roman order. Borderlands and frontiers are also spaces in which the negotiation of identities occurs, allowing for the formation of new social movements with their own spatial practices. Travel over land and sea brings contact with these peoples who do not share the Roman way of life. Travel is generally looked upon negatively by the literary traditions we have examined. It is described as difficult and often dangerous. It is especially significant to note that at least one Roman author thought that the closing of all sea lanes was the very thing that might secure a permanent peace for the Roman empire. Part of the reason that the Roman empire thrived in the first place was its exploration by sea, its ability in naval warfare (particularly against the Carthaginians) and its sea-based trade. Forced travel in the form of population shifts and exiles were part of the spatial landscape of antiquity.

The various understandings of the return from exile among early Jews exemplifies negotiation of identity in terms of spatial practice. For the re-

237. Smtih, *Map is Not Territory*, 187.

turnees under Ezra and Nehemiah, a new center emerges at the site of the old center. Other groups, however, challenge this center and find alternative spaces in which to craft other patterns of socialization. Finally, there is the territory delimited by the body of a person as a geographic center. The emperor, for example, relativized even the space of Rome when he traveled since his physical body represented the locus of Rome's power. Similarly, philosophers and teachers might come to represent geographic centers as people traveled to study under them or to partake in their wisdom.

The Gospel of Mark demonstrates a conflict between a fixed type of sacred space found in the spatial practice of the temple and synagogue and a fluid sacred space constructed around Jesus. Jesus views the world from the cosmic perspective, which qualifies the spatial designations of the earth. Further, Jesus moves easily in boundary territories and on the sea, but he encounters difficulty in civilization centers, particularly in the cities of Jerusalem and Capernaum. Jesus' spatial practice, and that of his disciples, offers an alternative to the spatial practice of the temple and synagogue.

CHAPTER 5

The Spatial Presentation of Mark's Gospel

Space in the Gospel of Mark

THE LACK OF CORRESPONDENCE between Mark's description of the land and the actual physical layout of ancient Palestine has occasioned extensive discussion among scholars.[1] There have basically been two major schools of thought with regard to Markan geography: that Mark is not at all familiar with the geography of ancient Palestine (writing from Rome or some other place remote from the area about which he writes) but nevertheless tries to "get it right," or that Mark uses the spaces presented in his text as a mythical or theological backdrop to the story of Jesus' ministry and is not at all concerned with "real, on the ground" geography. This study adopts a view that is somewhat in the middle of these two options. While it seems unlikely that Mark was completely familiar with the geography of Palestine, his description of the territories through which Jesus travels is very much in line with Greek and Roman geographical traditions.

Mark is not scientific geography, even by ancient standards, but the description of the spaces found within the text are similar to those of human geography discussed above in chapter three. This geographical tradition deals largely in topographic and geographic stereotypes. Certain geographic and topographic areas are designated by particular types of spatial practices. These stereotypes developed over a long period in Greek and Roman historiography and geography. Mark, for the most part, simply assumes these traditions, but in some key ways, he inverts them in order to suggest a new type of space centered around the person of Jesus

---

1. See the discussion in chapter one above.

in opposition to the civilized spaces of cities and the architectural spaces of synagogues and the temple.

Mark's Gospel, like all texts, creates its own "representational space."[2] Representational spaces "have their source in history," but do not necessarily repeat the understanding of space found within their historical cultures.[3] These spaces may support or challenge the representations of space found in society. The Gospel of Mark challenges a representation of space of first century CE Palestinian Judaism based around the temple and synagogue in several significant ways.[4] For Mark, these institutions represent a *spatial practice* that is organized around purity rules concerning food consumption, illness, and Sabbath observance. Mark's Jesus rejects this spatial practice through consistent violation of these purity rules throughout the Gospel. Jesus also rejects the spatial practice of the Romans (Mark 5:1–20; 15:1–5). Jesus creates his own spatial practice which replicates itself in the work assigned to the disciples.

Civilized Centers in Mark

As noted in chapters three and four, Greeks, Romans, and early Jews measure the civility of other societies based on their conformity to spatial practices of their own societies. For the Romans, cultivation of crops and the adoption of togas become the mark of being Roman. The Gospel of Mark represents a challenge to the civilized spaces of cities with their architectural spaces of temples, synagogues and even houses. These are not spaces of an ordered society which brings the peace promised by the Romans or the structure and blessings promised in the Torah. Mark challenges both Roman and early Jewish ways of thinking about space, rejecting these "civilized" centers and providing alternative loci for the formation of Jesus' movement.

Jesus and Roman Space

In addition to being Jewish space, Galilee and Judea were Roman territories in the first century CE. Jesus' direct encounter with the "Romans"

---

2. See chapter two above.

3. Lefebvre, *Production of Space*, 41.

4. For an argument that the temple and synagogue are linked in Mark's spatial representation, see below.

is limited, apart from his trial and crucifixion, to the story of the Gerasene demoniac (5:1–20). There Jesus encounters, and defeats, the Roman legion. This story follows upon the episode in which Jesus calms the storm in the sea. Like his exorcism of the unclean spirit in the synagogue (Mark 1:21–28), Jesus' stilling of the storm causes amazement inasmuch as it commands obedience from the wind and waves (4:41). Stilling storms was a task performed by Roman and Greek rulers as well.[5] Jesus' mastery over the sea distinguishes him from normal human beings who are subject to nature. After demonstrating his mastery over the sea, he next encounters the Gerasene demoniac.

The Latin word *legion* occurs in Mark 5:9. Commentators on Mark 5:1–20 have made much of this fact when interpreting this passage. The well-known article by Hollenbach takes the political dimension of the story very seriously.[6] Hollenbach notes that the demoniac's possessed status "permitted him to do in a socially acceptable manner what he could not do as sane, namely, express his total hostility to the Romans; he did this by identifying the Roman legions with demons."[7] He suggests that the exorcism of the demon, in this case, "brought the man's and the neighborhood's hatred of the Romans out into the open, where the result could be disaster for the community."[8] Part of the function of the accusation of demon possession was to promote social stability.[9] Ostracizing someone who openly criticized Roman rule and labeling them "demon possessed" could effectively mitigate the seriousness of their criticism. Removing them from the community was a way of protecting the larger community from hostility from the Romans. Hollenbach suggests that when the demon is cast out, those of the community do not have this same type of protection. It is for this reason that they ask Jesus to leave, since he has jeopardized their safety.[10]

Kotansky argues that the story of the stilling of the storm taken together with the account of the Gerasene demoniac is best read against the Greco-Roman traditions of sailing through the Straits of Gibraltar at

---

5. See Collins, "Rulers, Divine Men," 207–27.
6. Hollenbach, "Jesus, Demoniacs, and Public Authorities," 567–88.
7. Ibid., 581.
8. Ibid.
9. Ibid., 571–77, 584.
10. Ibid., 581.

the edge of the world.[11] He first notes that the "other side" in Mark 4:35 has as its antecedent the sea in Mark 3:7.[12] This sea is not identified in 3:7 as the Sea of Galilee. Kotansky argues that this sea should be read as the Mediterranean rather than the Sea of Galilee.[13] The trip, then, becomes a voyage to the "Other Side," that is, to the edges of the *oikoumenē*. "Accordingly, all the sea-crossings of both miracle catenae, at least in the mythic imagination, are to be construed as true sea-voyages; their destinations, when recorded, will not tally well with known geographies of the circum-Galilean region."[14] Kotansky notes that the context of Jesus' landing fits better within the context of a westward journey on the Mediterranean. Sailing past the edges of the earth to the west in Greek mythology, one would arrive at the land of the dead, that is, the house of Hades.[15] This context, the realm of the dead, is the one into which Jesus lands in Mark 5:2. Kotansky's argument relies heavily on the textual variants in Mark 5:1. He supposes that the textual problem indicates that the text was not originally set in a circum-Galilean locale, but rather at Gadeira, the symbolic end of the earth to the west.[16] While Kotansky's argument as a whole contains certain problems,[17] the idea that Mark's text (or its pre-Markan source) alludes to the traditions of seafarers arriving in strange and distant lands seems likely.[18] There are many common elements between the stories of sea travel discussed in chapter four and this Markan unit. The disciples and Jesus are threatened with shipwreck and death (4:37–38) and land on a distant shore in which the "natives" behave in uncivilized fashion—liv-

11. Kotansky, "Jesus and Heracles in Cádiz," 160–229.

12. Ibid., 165.

13. Ibid., 168–70.

14. Ibid., 171.

15. See the discussion in chapter three above. Also ibid., 173–76; Kotansky notes many elements of the sea-crossing and Jesus's arrival that hint at themes of death and dying in the narrative.

16. Ibid., 185–92.

17. For several criticisms see Aune, "Jesus and the Romans in Galilee," 230–51.

18. Kotansky, "Jesus and Heracles," 183: "The particular phrase, 'they came into the land of x,' carries with it a ring of a far and distant place. We have already met up with it in the epic narratives describing the lands of the Laestrygonians and the Phaeacians, and, in the apocryphal acts, the land of the cannibal Myrmidons. The notion of an entrance into a faraway country signifies the wayfarers have disembarked onto the mysterious shores of fable and not into the familiar territory of history. The expression calls to mind distant and unfamiliar places not belonging to the known geographies of the hero's frame of reference—for Odysseus, his island home of Ithaca; for Jesus, his Galilean homeland."

ing among the tombs and in the mountains (5:2–5). This wild figure, ironically, is the only one to show Jesus hospitality, treating him with the reverence due to him (5:6—where he "does obeisance" to Jesus). The "civilized" people of the region, upon seeing evidence of the exorcism, ask Jesus to leave their "borders" (ὁρίων, 5:17).

Aune criticizes several elements of Kotansky's interpretation of this text. First, he notes that it is possible that the mental map that a reader brings to a text may or may not have any relation to the kind of scientific geography of the modern world, allowing for the possibility that Kotansky's identifications of sites could, in fact, be correct.[19] He challenges Kotansky's identification of the sea as the Mediterranean, though, rather than the Sea of Galilee.[20] Aune notes that there is "not even a hint in the Synoptic tradition that Jesus was ever active on the Mediterranean coast."[21] Aune also argues against Kotansky's claim that the textual variants "are all later attempts to historicize an embarrassing mythical geography."[22] He also notes that Gadeira, while it does represent the limits of the *oikoumenē* to Greek and Latin authors, never itself represents the land of the dead.[23] Aune concludes that the story represents a more political than mythic point. The demon called legion "representing an entire Roman army, wants to stay in the land it occupies (5:10). This 'legion' of demons is driven into the sea (perhaps symbolic for the underworld), reflecting the Jewish desire to drive the Romans out of the land."[24]

Aune and Hollenbach are surely correct to read this text against the background of the Roman occupation of the land.[25] Jesus' casting out of the demon "legion" is best understood as a reaction to Roman rule. Jesus is able to control, by himself, an entire Roman legion. Jesus controls the space that the Romans occupy as well. The cleansed demoniac no longer oper-

19. Aune, "Jesus and the Romans," 230–33.

20. Ibid., 236–44.

21. Ibid., 239. Aune suggests that the material in Mark that locates Jesus in the regions of Tyre and Sidon could be several miles inland from the coast. More significantly, while Jesus is in these territories, there is no mention of any visit to the sea or coastal areas.

22. Ibid., 245; Aune prefers the reading "Gerasenes" since it is contained in both Mark and Luke.

23. Ibid., 248–49.

24. Ibid., 250; Aune also notes that the "Roman tenth legion Fretensis, stationed in Syria from 6 BCE on, and in Judaea following the first Jewish revolt, had the image of a boar on its standards and seals."

25. See also Theissen, *Gospels in Context*, 109–12.

ates according to Roman spatial practice (that is, by exhibiting obedience to the dictates of Legion), but operates according to Jesus' spatial practice in spreading Jesus' message (Mark 5:20). Jesus "cleanses" by exorcism the space of the Gentiles in his first action in Gentile territory. This cleansing is the same activity as his first action both in Galilee (in the synagogue) and in Jerusalem.[26] For Mark, demon possession characterizes the space controlled by Romans. The breakdown of civilization is in effect here. This demon is located in a boundary territory (that is, among the tombs in the mountains),[27] but its identification with the Roman legion calls into question the civilizing effect of the *pax Romana*. Roman rule brings disorder and death (hence the location of "legion" among the tombs). The text also calls into question the placement of the Romans at the center of the *oikoumenē*. In this instance, they occupy only the fringes, and are expelled from there into the sea (representing death here). It is the kingdom of God, rather than the *pax Romana*, that brings order to this fringe area.

Elite Space: Mark and the City

Several scholars have noted an anti-Jerusalem bias in the Gospel of Mark.[28] Mark, moreover, does not mention the major cities of Galilee. Nowhere, in fact, does the Jesus tradition contain such references.[29] While it may not be terribly surprising that the sayings material (in Q, for instance) would not preserve references to Jesus' traveling into cities, it is surprising that a narrative Gospel like Mark would make no mention of these cities. Sepphoris, with its proximity to Nazareth, and Tiberias, lying close to Capernaum, are perhaps the most striking omissions. The supposed anti-Jerusalem bias combined with the lack of activity in these cities might be more suggestive of an anti-city bias in Mark.[30]

---

26. Jesus cleanses Galilee in his first action there, the Decapolis in his first action there, the area around Tyre in his first action there, and finally Jerusalem in his first action there. This pattern was already noted by Kelber, *Kingdom in Mark*.

27. As argued in chapter four, the same characteristics that characterize the edges of the *oikoumenē* in the ancient world also characterize boundary territories such as mountains and borderlands. In this sense, many of the characteristics noted by Kotansky as applicable to the westernmost edge of the *oikoumenē* would also be part and parcel of a mountainous coast of the Sea of Galilee.

28. See chapter one above. Also Donahue, *Are You the Christ?*

29. See Batey, *Jesus and the Forgotten City*.

30. One of the major weaknesses of much of Markan scholarship on the issue of space

There is one other named city in the Gospel of Mark—Capernaum. The fact that Capernaum is a village rather than a city is of no consequence in terms of Mark's portrayal of Galilean geography. Mark understands Capernaum as a city, and he describes it in the same terms as Jerusalem for the most part. Rather than compare Galilee and Jerusalem, a territory to a city, it is best to proceed by comparing Capernaum to Jerusalem, a city to a city in Mark's mind, to see how Mark treats each of these spaces. These cities are both presented negatively in Mark's Gospel as they are places in which a spatial practice is operative that is opposed to the new one that Jesus introduces in the Gospel.

Jerusalem and Capernaum: Cities in Mark[31]

Mark obviously knew of Jesus' crucifixion outside the city of Jerusalem. In order for him to have been killed outside of Jerusalem there necessarily would have been some interaction between him and Jerusalem leaders (whether Jewish or Roman or both).[32] There is very little in Mark to suggest, however, that Jesus spent much time in the city. When he does go to the city to meet his impending death, he does not stay within the city at night. He stays outside the city in Bethany (so Mark 11:11–12). Jesus' first foray into Jerusalem is exceedingly brief, as he surveys the temple and leaves the city (11:11). The only time Jesus really spends in the city are those times when he teaches in the temple (primarily 11:27—12:44), cleanses the temple (11:15–19), eats the Passover meal itself (14:17–25), and returns after his arrest. As in his first foray into "Roman" territory, Jesus' first action in Jerusalem is a cleansing (Mark 11:15).

The most negative aspect of Mark's portrayal of Jerusalem in the Gospel involves Jesus' prediction of its coming destruction.[33] Malina reads Mark 13 as belonging to the genre of "final discourse."[34] This genre preserves the last words of a dying person in order to convey information

---

has been the opposition of Galilee and Jerusalem as if they were parallel entities. Jerusalem is a city located within the territory of Judea while Galilee is itself a territory encompassing several cities.

31. On the negative portrayal of Jerusalem in Mark's Gospel, see chapter one above.

32. Since only the Romans would have had the necessary authority to crucify Jesus, it is obvious that Jesus' accusers had access to Pilate at some point in the process.

33. See Malina, "Exegetical Eschatology," 49–59.

34. Ibid., 54–55.

about what is about to occur. The chapter begins with the prediction of the temple's destruction (13:1–3). The scene shifts from outside the temple (13:1) to opposite the temple, on the Mount of Olives (13:4). From this vantage point, a borderland, Jesus discusses the coming total breakdown of civilized society (13:8–9, 12). This disorder on earth is matched by a disorder in the heavens (13:24–25). When this breakdown occurs, "those in Judea must flee to the mountains" (13:14). It is in this borderland, outside the now chaotic and strife-laden centers of civilization, that the followers of Jesus are to flee. The city provides no safe refuge in the time of trial.

Jerusalem is clearly negatively portrayed in the Gospel. Two things should be noted, however, that alter the arguments of Lohmeyer, Lightfoot, Marxsen, and Kelber. There is no corresponding negative portrayal of the rest of Judea. Indeed, there is not a "southern" (i.e. Judean) versus "northern" (i.e. Galilean) dynamic at work here. The spatial practice of the temple/synagogues dominates both of these spaces making one hardly distinguishable from the other on the level of spatiality according to Mark. The second item that needs to be taken into account is Mark's overall presentation of cities. Except for Jerusalem and Capernaum, Jesus does not enter cities in Mark. They are spaces of the elite, and Jesus is not among these elite.

Capernaum was clearly a village in terms of it size and number of inhabitants.[35] Mark, however, describes it as a city (πόλις) in 1:33. Not long after this description, Jesus tells his disciples that they will be moving on to the surrounding towns (κωμοπόλεις) in order for Jesus to preach there (1:38). This term, κωμοπόλεις, is a curious mixture of the Greek words for village and city. What is, in fact, meant by the term is difficult to say with any precision. Since Mark does not have Jesus enter into any Galilean cities, perhaps this is a way of referring to villages. Since Mark, however, already labeled Capernaum a city, one could reasonably question whether Mark knew the difference in reference to Galilean geography.[36]

Mark, however, refers to Capernaum as a city because it is an administrative center in Mark's mental map. The city exercises a "civilizing" function by its control over the surrounding territories. What is key for Mark, is that cities are sites in which spatial practice is controlled and those

---

35. See Rohrbaugh, "Preindustrial City," 108.

36. There is little doubt that the author of Mark would have known the difference between a city and a village in whatever place he lived, but whether he recognized that Capernaum was, in fact, a village rather than a city is not clear.

who would operate outside of the normal pattern of behavior are subject to surveillance.[37] Jesus is constantly watched not only by onlookers, but by his opponents in these spaces. That fact, indeed, is what constitutes a city for Mark. It is because of this surveillance that when Jesus' reputation grows, he is not able to enter a city (Mark 1:45). As in Jerusalem and in the territory of *legion*, Jesus' first action in the city of Capernaum is a cleansing. This time the location is in the synagogue and the cleansing is of an unclean spirit. Structurally, through the presence of the synagogue and its leadership, who are related to the leadership of the temple in Mark's Gospel, Capernaum and Jerusalem are similar entities.

Other Cities in Mark

Since cities are places where Jesus is under surveillance by his opponents, there are instances in the Gospel in which Jesus avoids cities. Caesarea Philippi is mentioned in Mark (Mark 8:27–38), but Mark clearly locates Jesus in the villages surrounding the city rather than within the city itself. The Decapolis is also mentioned in Mark (particularly in 5:20), though Jesus does not enter the cities themselves. Mark describes Jesus' journey to the "region of Tyre" (τὰ ὅρια Τύρου; 7:24), but he does not enter the city in the narrative. Upon leaving the region of Tyre, he goes "by way of Sidon" (διὰ Σιδῶνος; 7:31) to the Sea of Galilee. This particular geographical reference has been the subject of no small amount of conjecture since Sidon is north of Tyre while the Sea of Galilee is southwest of it.[38] Mark, however, does not locate Jesus within the boundaries of the city.[39]

Jesus, from Nazareth, and his first four disciples, from Capernaum, all come from villages. As non-elite persons, Jesus and his followers would likely not have had easy access to enter cities. Freyne sees another possibility for Jesus' avoidance of Galilean cities, particularly of Sepphoris and Tiberias. "His avoidance of the main Herodian centres in Galilee is best explained, therefore, in light of a conscious decision not to become directly embroiled in a confrontation with Herodian power."[40] That city officials, however, presided over village life as well, makes this possibility

37. See Stewart, "Mark and the City," 212–18.
38. On the difficulty with this passage and the textual problems contained in it see Mussies, "Jesus and 'Sidon.'"
39. Ibid., 266–69.
40. Freyne, *Galilee, Jesus and the Gospels*, 140.

seem less likely. Avoidance of cities in this instance would merely have delayed the inevitable, as can be seen by the Herodians' confrontation with Jesus (Mark 3:6).

Other instances of the term *polis* in Mark's Gospel do not shed much more light on the question of the omission of these cities. Mark uses the term several more times throughout his Gospel. Mark 1:45 seems to suggest that at some point early in his ministry that Jesus could enter a city. After Jesus heals the leper, the healed leper proclaimed it freely, despite Jesus' directive not to do so (Mark 1:43–5), after which Jesus is unable to enter a *polis* freely. A similar incident occurs after Jesus exorcises the demon from the Gerasene demoniac. There swineherds report Jesus' exorcism and the subsequent destruction of the swine "in the city and in the country" (εἰς τὴν πόλιν καί εἰς τοὺς ἀγρούς; Mark 5:14). The "city/country" pair is a familiar one from the discussion of city and countryside in chapter four. The net effect of the swineherds' words is that the people of the region ask Jesus to leave their region (5:17).[41] The analysis of surveillance by Jesus' opponents above, however, offers an indication of the trouble here. Jesus' healings might provoke hostility from the Jewish and/or Roman leaders in the same way that John's preaching had done (6:14–29). If opponents were nearly constantly watching Jesus, then his presence might bring danger. Mark 13:9–13 certainly envisions such danger as a part of the disciples' future.

Jesus, like John, draws crowds from cities. Jesus drew an audience from nearly every named place in the Gospel. That he specifically drew city crowds is expressed in Mark 6:33. There the people of the cities have seen Jesus and his disciples retreat to a deserted place, and they come "from all the cities" (ἀπὸ πασῶν τῶν πόλεων). Jesus, like John, draws crowds away from settled areas into borderlands. These territories, again, are places in which identities might be negotiated. Such spaces represent the possibility for creation of new spatial practices. New spatial practices, those that do not replicate the spatial practices of the temple/synagogue, the Romans or the city elites, represent a threat to the centers of "civilization." Jesus' activity at the topographic margins (in the wilderness, on the mountain, on the sea, among the tombs) represents this threat vividly. What is significant for the purposes of this study is that people come to

---

41. Again we may note here that Jesus, though in proximity to the city, does not enter the city proper, but only its regions (τῶν ὁρίων; 5:17).

Jesus from centers of civilization, that is, the cities and form a new community around Jesus in the borderlands.

Architectural Spaces: Synagogue, Temple, Household

The spaces of Mark's cities consist of synagogues, the temple, and houses. There are no other descriptions of the spaces in these cities. All of these architectural structures, moreover, are places in which Jesus' opponents watch him in order to challenge him. The synagogues of Galilee are linked to the temple in Mark's description of space. The connection may go beyond Mark and represent a historical relationship between pre-70 synagogues and the temple. Schmidt argues that these two institutions were linked through the repetition of ritual practices.

> Far, therefore, from developing in opposition to the Temple, already before 70 the synagogal institution is a bearer of the thinking of the Temple . . . it is one of the principal vehicles of the extension to the whole of Jewish society of the ritual prescriptions expressing the categories of the sacred and the profane, of the pure and the impure, as well as the mode of classification proper to the thinking of the Temple. As such, the synagogal institution appears as a manifestation of the extension—in the strongest sense of the term—of the Sanctuary.[42]

Synagogues, in this understanding, reproduce the spatial practice of the temple by upholding its purity rules. The "space" of synagogues and the temple consists not only in their physical space, but in the physical extension of these purity rules to other spaces. These purity rules are spatial practice for the "pure," but also are representations of space for the leadership of these institutions. By application of these purity rules, these spaces reproduce themselves and expand their spatial practices.[43]

In Mark these two institutions are linked through connections of their leadership. The groups that control one are related to the groups that control the other inasmuch as their behavior is the same, and they are unified in their opposition to Jesus. In fact, their opposition to Jesus is geographically aggressive insofar as they come after Jesus in a (his own?)

---

42. See Schimdt, *How the Temple Thinks*, 263. See also Binder, *Into the Temple Courts*, 32: "the synagogues in both Palestine and the diaspora served as subsidiary sacred precincts that extended spatially the sacrality of the Temple shrine and allowed Jews everywhere participation within the central cult."

43. See the discussion on how spaces are replicated in chapter two above.

house (Mark 2:1–12; 3:22–27). By using the authority vested in them in the control of other spaces (i.e. the synagogue and the temple), they attempt to control all space in an attempt to thwart Jesus' activity. The leaders of these two institutions are united in their control of the space that they physically dominate (i.e. the architectural space of the temple and the synagogues) as well as over various spaces which their leaders seek to control.

It is not, of course, the institutions themselves that control space. Mark, rather, presents the leadership of these institutions as attempting to exert control over certain types of spaces. The attempt to conceal power relations inherent in spatial control is part of a strategy for maintaining those power relations without highlighting them.[44] The temple itself is a building that does not "act" in any way. Those in control of the temple act to control space in certain ways. Divisions of the land into "holy" and "non-holy" spaces is itself a social act.[45] The space of the temple is "holy" insofar as the leadership of the temple is able to uphold the distinction in the minds of others.[46] As sacred space, however, the temple is fixed. Patterns of activity are reproduced in the same way each time in order to preserve the holiness of the temple.[47] The activities endorsed by the leadership of the temple and the synagogues are reinforced through surveillance and enforced conformity to the spatial practice of the temple/synagogues by these groups throughout the Gospel.[48] Such surveillance belongs to the element of "control" in the model of territoriality outlined in chapter three.[49]

---

44. See chapter two above. In other words, to declare the temple and the synagogue "sacred" space is to hide the fact that it is the priests, scribes, Pharisees and elders (according to Mark) who create and enforce the spatial practice of these institutions. On the idea that spatial practice requires ritual (and therefore social) maintenance, see Jonathan Z. Smith, *To Take Place*, 96–117. See also the discussion concerning continued exile in chapter four.

45. Here it is useful to recall Johnston's three elements of the creation of a region: 1) it is created by a social act, 2) is self-reproducing, and 3) is not deterministic. See chapter two above.

46. See the discussion on continued exile in chapter four.

47. In this sense Johnston's idea of regions as self-reproducing is significant. See chapter two above.

48. On the notion of surveillance as a means of controlling space see chapter two above.

49. This surveillance by the authorities of the synagogue and the temple will be examined in more detail below.

Mark presents a frontal assault on the status quo of spatial control in his representation of ancient Palestine. Before Jesus arrives on the scene, the leadership of the synagogues and the temple control not only the space of those physical places, but, by virtue of their leadership of those institutions, lay claim to control of all other spaces as well. Mark, however, turns this control of space on its head by asserting that Jesus not only is free to do what he wishes outside of the confines of these institutions, but that he, in fact, is able to control the physical space of these very institutions themselves.

Synagogues

Synagogues are mentioned regularly in the first six chapters of Mark's Gospel. The first mention of a synagogue is found in Mark 1:21–28. Jesus enters the synagogue at Capernaum and teaches (1:21). Jesus' teaching has authority, unlike the teaching of the scribes (1:22). Unexpectedly, a demoniac appears in the narrative (1:23). Jesus casts out the demon and the people are even more impressed by his ability to "teach" (1:27). His teaching compels the obedience of the demon. From this short text, two important things concerning synagogues in Mark become clear. The first of these things is that the scribes are teachers in the synagogues. Jesus' distinction from the scribes only makes sense in the text if scribes normally teach in these places. Mark 12:38–40 makes clear the scribes' role in the leadership of the synagogue. They are those who like "to have the best seats in the synagogues and places of honor at banquets" (12:39).[50] The scribes, moreover, are linked with other groups that represent other places in the Gospel. Perhaps most importantly, they are associates of those who have authority over the temple. At least some scribes present in Galilee come from Jerusalem (3:22).[51] The scribes are linked to the chief priests and

---

50. There are historical problems in identifying the scribes to which Mark refers inasmuch as they did not constitute a single group in Palestine at this period Whether scribes were a part of the historical leadership of the synagogue is not the issue here. Indeed, since it is impossible to identify "scribes" as any single group in ancient Galilee or Judea, it is impossible to say with certainty even to whom Mark refers with the designation "scribe." See the discussion in Meier, *Marginal Jew*, 3.549–60, where he notes, "the scribes *in their capacity as scribes* did not form or belong to any one religious group in Palestinian Judaism at the time of Jesus" (549–50).

51. It should be noted that there are no synagogues in Jerusalem according to Mark's text.

elders in Jesus' first prediction of his death (Mark 8:31–33). In the third prediction of Jesus' death the scribes are again linked to the chief priests (10:33). The scribes join in plotting Jesus' death in 11:18, and they, together with the chief priests and elders test Jesus with a question relating to his authority (11:27). Elsewhere, the scribes are linked to Pharisees (2:16). Mark presents a unified group of scribes who are accomplices of the chief priests and Pharisees in their opposition to Jesus.

The synagogues described in Mark are the public type of synagogues discussed by Runesson.[52] Runesson noted that the synagogues of the Persian period were overseen by Jerusalem authorities that had control over the interpretation of the law. It is the Jerusalem authorities and their associates who control the interpretation of the law within the synagogues. Synagogues are always public institutions in which the contest for honor is constantly present. Jesus and his followers do not form a semi-public synagogue.[53] They instead abandon the synagogue altogether at Mark 6:1–6. Perhaps it is not surprising to find that, upon being rejected by his own village, Jesus does not enter the synagogue again. His honor rating has been diminished within Nazareth (6:4), but also within the institution of the synagogue. So, accordingly, he and his followers leave the synagogue at Nazareth never to enter another in the Gospel.[54] The fact that Jesus and his followers no longer enter synagogues, however, does not mean the end of their dealings with the leaders of the synagogue. Jesus is under near constant surveillance by the leaders of the synagogue and temple throughout the Gospel. The leaders of the synagogue are a constant presence within the Gospel and, in every case, act to oppose Jesus.

That unclean spirits are located in the synagogue is an important element of Mark's presentation of these institutions. As places for the reading of Torah and discussion concerning legal and cultic matters, the synagogues represented a locus of the community's order. Mark's presentation challenges the idea that synagogues establish order for the community,

---

52. See the discussion in chapter four above.

53. On the idea of "semi-public" synagogues along the lines of Greco-Roman voluntary associations see Runesson, *Origins of the Synagogue*, 398–40.

54. There are only two further mentions of the synagogue after Mark 6:1–6. The scribes' position of honor in the synagogue (Mark 12:39) and Mark 13:9 which warns the disciples that the synagogues will be a place of physical violence against them in the future. In both cases, the synagogue is a negative place, in the first instance as a negative example, and in the second as a place of threat to the followers of Jesus. They will not enter into synagogues, but handed over to be beaten in them.

suggesting instead that they display negative elements of peripheral territories. They are not centers of purity, but rather the haunts of, as Mark labels them, "unclean" spirits.

Smith treats "demonic" as a locative category in antiquity.[55] The haunts of demons are on the fringes of society. Speaking of the category "devil worship," Smith notes this category "functions primarily as a locative term which establishes the outer limits or distance much as wild men or monsters are depicted as inhabiting the borders of antique maps."[56] Smith continues this line of thought by asserting that "in archaic traditions, the dwelling place of the demons is in wild, uninhabited places or ruined cities—that is to say, beyond city walls or where walls have been broken or allowed to fall into disrepair."[57] Demons, then, inhabit those places where borders are not maintained. If a city falls into ruins, they might overrun that city. More often than not, however, demons are encountered where humans do not cultivate and maintain social life. It should come as no surprise, therefore, that Mark locates Jesus' encounter with Satan in the wilds (εἰς τὴν ἔρημον; Mark 1:12). Apart from being a locative category, however, "demonic" is also a relational category. Rather than thinking of demons as "substantive categories," they represent "situational or relational categories, mobile boundaries which shift according to the map being employed."[58] Due to the presence of unclean spirits within them (and also to their leadership's opposition to Jesus), Mark presents synagogues as places of the breakdown of civilized order.

If Mark 1:21–28 were the only time that a demon appeared in a synagogue, it might only be a curiosity.[59] In the summary statement about Jesus' "tour" of Galilee, however, casting out demons is characteristic of Jesus' activity in the synagogue. Mark 1:39 makes clear that Jesus goes through "the whole of Galilee preaching in their synagogues and casting out demons" (κηρύσσων εἰς τὰς συναγωγὰς αὐτῶν εἰς ὅλην τὴν Γαλιλαίαν καὶ τὰ δαιμόνια ἐκβάλλων). The association of demons

55. Smith, "Towards Interpreting Demonic Powers," 425–39.

56. Ibid., 427.

57. Smith, "Towards Interpreting Demonic Powers," 427.

58. Ibid., 430.

59. The significance of this tale as the first action of Jesus' public ministry, however, should not be discounted. As Mack, *Myth of Innocence*, 240, notes, "Mark would have the reader see that the synagogue will be the scene of the first battle, and that the synagogue is possessed of people with unclean spirits."

and unclean spirits is made here, although the Greek text is ambiguous about whether these demons are to be located within these synagogues. It seems likely to be the case since this tour follows basically on the heels of the incident in the Capernaum synagogue. Whether these demons are to be located in the synagogue or not, however, is not precisely the issue. If they are located with civilized centers (the only places which would have social organizations like synagogues) the basic point remains the same. Within places of civilization, rather than outside of such places, demons have found homes. As Jesus was tempted by Satan in the wilderness, so now Satan's minions have infiltrated these civilized centers (including synagogues) and confront Jesus there.

There is still another instance of Jesus dealing with aggressive spirits in the synagogue. John Pilch, in a series of articles and books, has demonstrated that people in the ancient world most commonly believed that spirit aggression was the cause of disease and physical malady.[60] Mark 3:1–6 relates the story of Jesus' restoring a man's withered hand in the synagogue on the Sabbath. Since this type of physical malady was commonly attributed to aggressive spirits (unclean spirits in this case), this is yet a further example of an unclean spirit found in the synagogue and of Jesus' driving it out.[61]

Mark presents synagogues at the center of a disorder, not as part of the civilized order of society,[62] overturning the map of the synagogue as a place of order from which decisions regarding "pure" social behavior emanate. Decisions about the law are made within these spaces, but, according to Mark, they result in disorder not only in the spaces outside the synagogue, but within these spaces as well inasmuch as they are besieged by demons. Smith argues that "a given society at a given moment may conceive of

60. See Pilch, *Healing in the New Testament*. On the etiologies of illness in the ancient world see also Avalos, *Health Care and the Rise of Christianity*, 62–66. The connection between unclean spirits and illness in Mark is made in Mark 3:10–11, where Mark says, "he cured many, so that all who had diseases pressed upon him to touch him. Whenever the unclean spirits saw him . . ." Absent any mention of exorcism in this passage, it seems that Mark understands these unclean spirits as emanating from those whom Jesus healed.

61. We might add Mark 6:1–6 to this inventory as well insofar as there are clearly demon-possessed and ill people located in the synagogue there (assuming that Mark 6:5 still occurs within the setting of the synagogue at Nazareth).

62. Smith, "Towards Interpreting Demonic Powers," 430, notes that categories like "demonic" represent "situational or relational categories, mobile boundaries which shift according to the map being employed." Since Mark is, in effect, creating a map, it is no surprise to see the locus of demons shifted in his Gospel.

law and order as a bulwark against the demonic; at another time, it may perceive law and order as a repressive imposition of the demonic."[63] Mark presents two elements of a society disagreeing on precisely this issue. For Jesus and his followers, the synagogues are demon-possessed and oppose Jesus' true understanding of God's mission. In the case of the Jerusalem scribes, representing the interests of both synagogue and temple, it is Jesus who is the problem (3:22–30). He represents impurity and disorder by offering an alternative spatial practice. Since synagogues are located only in Galilee, it is important to note that the disorder that Mark connects to Jerusalem is to be found in its incipient stages in Galilee.

In presenting the synagogue in this way, Mark is challenging the classification of the synagogue as a "pure" and "sacred" place. Mark communicates his rejection of such a classification by locating demons within the synagogues. The scribes, lacking the authority of Jesus to expel demons (so Mark 1:27), are unable to control the space of the synagogue. Since they are unable to control such space, their classification of the space as "sacred" becomes meaningless.

The Temple

The sacrality of the temple is also challenged in Mark's new classification. Jesus' initial action in the temple is parallel to his initial action in the synagogue. In the first instance, he cleanses the synagogue of the unclean spirit, while in the second instance, he "cleanses" the temple.[64] "And he entered the temple and began to drive out (ἐκβάλλειν) those who were selling and those who he were buying in the temple . . ." (11:15). Mark uses the same Greek term, ἐκβάλλω, to describe both Jesus' exorcisms and his action in the temple. After this cleansing, Jesus is also able freely to enter and teach in the temple just as he did in the synagogue (Mark 11:26—12:44). A significant weakness of the many interpretations of Mark that link the cleansing of the temple to Jesus' death is that they make no explanation of Jesus' ongoing presence in the temple.[65] Sanders typifies this approach in his book *Jesus and Judaism*, arguing that Jesus and perhaps some of his disciples overturned a few tables "as a demonstrative action. It would ap-

---

63. Ibid., 429.
64. See Mack, *Myth of Innocence*, 242.
65. Donahue and Harrington, *Gospel of Mark*, 332, can be viewed as representative of this approach.

pear that the action was not substantial enough even to interfere with the daily routine; for if it had been he would surely have been arrested on the spot."[66] While this reading might work as a plausible historical rendering of the event,[67] Mark's text clearly does not leave this possibility since it says that "he would not allow anyone to carry anything through the temple" (11:16).[68] Sanders seems to undermine his own case in one respect, saying that any observers of Jesus' actions would have understood

> almost surely, at least in part, that Jesus was attacking the temple service which was commanded by God. Not just priests would have been offended, but all those who believed that the temple was the place at which Israel and individual Israelites had been commanded to offer sacrifice, to make atonement for their sins.[69]

If any observer would have been offended and the timing of the incident was around the time of the Passover, it is inconceivable under ordinary circumstances that Jesus could have "escaped" the temple after such a provocative action. Jesus, according to this Gospel, has taken control of the space of the temple. Jesus is not threatened in this space because he has authority over it. This authority, though not spelled out as clearly as in Mark 1:21–28, is implicit in that people are physically prevented from carrying anything through the temple (11:16), and the leadership of the temple is unable to carry out the plan to kill Jesus in the wake of this event for fear of the crowd (11:18). As in the synagogues, Jesus' authority is later challenged in the temple (Mark 11:26–33).[70] The temple serves the same major function in Mark as does the synagogue. It is a place of teaching and debate concerning the law. Jesus' teaching authority is greater than the temple leadership in the same way that it was greater than the leadership of the synagogue in Galilee.[71]

---

66. Sanders, *Jesus and Judaism*, 70. It is only fair to say that Sanders's argument is about the historical Jesus and not necessarily about Mark's description of the incident.

67. Though there is a significant number of scholars who deny the historicity of the account; see recently Braun, "Major Episodes in the Biography of Jesus," 201–26.

68. This point is reinforced in the text by the impression that some matter of time passes between Jesus's entering and leaving the temple. He enters during the day (Mark 11:12) and leaves when it is evening (Mark 11:19).

69. Sanders, *Jesus and Judaism*, 70.

70. Mack, *Myth of Innocence*, 242: "Jesus' action in the synagogue precipitated conflict with the scribes and Pharisees over his authority. Jesus' action in the temple will precipitate conflict with the authorities there over his authority."

71. Interestingly, Mark seems to suggest that the function of the temple is as a place of

The Influence and Spatial Control of These Institutions

Recalling that Lefebvre argued that it is necessary for the leaders of a society to have special places at their disposal by which to distinguish certain places and from which to manage and give meaning to other spaces, the temple and the synagogues function in these ways in Mark.[72] The leadership of the synagogues and the temple exercise a spatial control over the land. They do this through purity regulations that became more widely spread during the Herodian period.[73] The purity concerns of the temple are related especially to eating habits in the Gospel. The type of food, in what manner, and with whom it is consumed are essential points in the accusations against Jesus (Mark 2:15–17, 18–22; 7:1–23). A second major point of dispute is the observance of the Sabbath. Clearly the Sabbath has significance for the synagogues. In Mark the Sabbath is the time when we expect to see the community gathered in the synagogue (Mark 1:21; 3:1–2; 6:1–2). Proper observance of the Sabbath, however, concerns not just participation in the communal life of the synagogue, but also refraining from restricted behaviors. When Jesus and his disciples pluck grain on the Sabbath, they violate the purity rules of the Pharisees (2:23–28; also 3:1–6).

Purity concerns stem from the temple for Mark. This is confirmed by Jesus' instruction to the healed leper (Mark 1:44) to show himself to the priest. The text is set in Galilee, but the temple is the place where his purity is to be confirmed.[74] In this instance, at least, Jesus seems to affirm both the purity of the temple and of its sacrificial system. Elsewhere, however, Jesus challenges the purity of the temple. Jesus speaks against the temple (13:2; also the charges against him in 14:58 and 15:29). His "cleansing" of the temple challenges the claim of the temple authorities over the space of Judea and Galilee around the issue of purity. As further evidence of Jesus' rejection of the temple's purity map, one might note "Jesus' negative atti-

---

teaching. There is no indication in the Gospel of its function as a place of sacrifice. Though, of course, Mark 1:44 seems to indicate such a function. In the temple, however, Jesus behaves exactly as he does in the synagogue—casting out unclean elements and debating over the interpretation of the Law and purity rules.

72. See the discussion in chapter two above.

73. See the discussion in Schmidt, *How the Temple Thinks*, 231–33.

74. On the idea of "temple space" and "purity" in Mark see Neyrey, "Idea of Purity in Mark's Gospel."

tude toward temple space" in that he endorses the scribe who says "that love of God and neighbor is 'worth more than all whole burnt offerings.'"⁷⁵

It is not only in relation to purity that the temple leadership exert their authority. They have policing functions within and beyond the territory of Judea. That the scribes, particularly those who "came down from Jerusalem" (3:22), monitored Jesus' activity in Galilee suggests that the temple establishment exerted a kind of policing control over this space as well.⁷⁶ This control over space in Judea ultimately manifests itself in the fact that the chief priests, scribes and elders conspire with Judas to arrest Jesus (14:10–1), send a crowd to arrest Jesus (14:43), try Jesus (14:53–65), hand him over to Pilate (15:1) and incite the crowd to call for Jesus' crucifixion (15:11). Indeed, their major point of contention with Jesus seems to their continued control of space through the central symbol of that control. Jesus is a threat to the temple (Mark 14:58).⁷⁷

The primary means of enforcing the control over space used by the leaders of the synagogue and temple is that of surveillance. The first indication of Jesus' activity being monitored occurs in Mark 1:45. After the leper is healed, he ignores Jesus' command to silence and instead proclaims his story freely "so that Jesus could no longer go into a town openly, but stayed out in the country." At this point in the text, however, it is not clear whom Jesus is trying to avoid. The next pericope, however, clarifies the issue. The scribes closely watch Jesus' activity "at home" (2:4). From this point on in the Gospel, Jesus is under near constant surveillance. The scribes of the Pharisees observe his activity when he dines with Levi (2:16), Pharisees follow him through the grain fields (2:23) and continue to monitor his activity in the synagogue (3:1–6). When Jesus heals the man with the withered hand on the Sabbath in the synagogue, the Pharisees and the Herodians conspire to kill him (3:6). When he returns to the house in Capernaum from his time spent alongside the sea and on the mountain, the scribes from Jerusalem watch him and accuse him of being demon possessed (3:22–30). Information concerning Jesus, one presumes from the surveillance of the "Herodians," reaches Herod as well (3:6;

---

75. Ibid., 109.

76. The argument here is not an historical one. It is only in relation to the way in which Mark describes the space in the Gospel.

77. While Mark indicates that this testimony about Jesus' destroying the temple is false, Mark 13:2 makes clear that Jesus envisioned the coming destruction of the temple. See Neyrey, "Idea of Purity in Mark's Gospel," 109.

6:14–16). Back among the "centers" of civilization after a sea voyage, the Pharisees and some Jerusalem scribes again scrutinize Jesus. The next time Jesus is watched by the Pharisees occurs "in the district of Dalmanutha" (8:10–11).

The surveillance begins again when Jesus enters Judea (10:1–2). When Jesus is in Jerusalem, he is under constant surveillance.[78] The chief priests, elders, and scribes observe Jesus' activity in the temple (11:15–18; 11:27—12:13). The Pharisees and Herodians try to trap Jesus (12:13–14). The Sadducees press Jesus for an answer to their query (12:18–27). Even when they are not physically present, the scribes' presence is felt (12:38). The temple leadership plots to kill Jesus (14:1) and carry out their plan (14:43–15:11). Surveillance is an attempt to control space through intimidation, restriction of movement, and control information. The centers of civilization, such as the city, the synagogue, and the temple, are those in which Jesus' activity is monitored. The spaces in which his activity is not monitored are just as significant. He is not watched by the synagogue or temple leadership alongside or on the sea, on mountains, in the desert or in Gentile territory. It is in the peripheral spaces of Mark's territory, in the borderlands, that Jesus is not under observation by his opponents. It is in those spaces in which Jesus is freer to form the new people of God's kingdom.

The presence of the scribes and Pharisees throughout the Gospel as hostile witnesses to Jesus' activities provides a spatial extension of the control of these groups over the synagogue and temple. Even in the household setting Jesus is confronted with hostile opponents (2:1–12). It is only in deserted places that Jesus is able to escape from the gaze of his opponents. These encounters consistently revolve around the issues of purity and the law. Jesus rejects their classification of space and, in his teaching, begins to communicate a new one. Jesus rejects the fixed sacred space represented by the temple and the synagogues. It is to be replaced by a fluid sacred space centered on the person of Jesus.

---

78. Indeed, Jerusalem is basically presented as consisting of nothing more than the temple, the high priest's house and the praetorium.

The Household as an Alternative?

Several scholars recently have suggested the household as an alternative space to the synagogue in Mark's Gospel.[79] Moxnes asserts that Mark "seems fully integrated in a worldview where household and family are at the center of the world, and where that holds true also of the world of Jesus."[80] The household in Mark, according to Moxnes, is "a social and spatial location for the new, fictive kinship group."[81] In support of the idea that the household is an alternative space for community gathering in Mark, scholars normally marshal three pieces of evidence:

- Jesus heals within the household
- Jesus forms a new family, and
- Jesus gives private instructions to the disciples there.

Perhaps the clearest starting point for those who argue that the household provides an alternative to the synagogue in this Gospel is Mark 1:29–31. Mack calls this discussion of the household and the healing within it Mark's "picture of the way things might be were there no conflict in the world: the master, disciples, at home, a slight bit of fever taken care of quickly, women in attendance, a meal together."[82] Mack's description is similar to that of many other interpreters who view this scene as idyllic in Mark's Gospel.[83] Trainor suggests that "for Mark the Christian household becomes the place of healing, where an alternative model of social equality and freedom is evident."[84] The healing narrative ends with Peter's mother-in-law "serving" (διηκόνει) Jesus and his disciples (1:31).[85]

---

79. See, for example, Elliot, *Home for the Homeless*, 252–54; Moxnes, *Putting Jesus in His Place*, 69–71; Trainor, *Quest for Home*; Malbon, *Narrative Space*, 117–20.

80. Moxnes, *Putting Jesus in His Place*, 69.

81. Ibid. Although Moxnes points to the fact that Jesus himself has a house in Mark's Gospel (2:1, 15; 3:19), John Painter, "When is a House not Home?" argues against taking any of these as references to Jesus's house.

82. Mack, *Myth of Innocence*, 240–41.

83. So, for example, Trainor, *Quest for Home*, 91. "If the synagogue is the place where unclean spirits can roam, the next scene and its domestic setting (1:29–31) provide a dramatic contrast where healing is sought, the resurrection anticipated, and ministry endorsed." Yet see Mark 3:1–5.

84. Trainor, *Quest for Home*, 94.

85. Though this text has been read in a utopian manner concerning the role of women, Krause, "Simon Peter's Mother-in-Law," 42, objects to this view as "a positivistic exaggeration of women's discipleship in the Gospel tradition at the expense of critically

Other healings also occur within the household setting. The paralytic is cured in a household (2:1–12) and the daughter of Jairus is raised (3:35–43). Healing activity, however, does not distinguish the household from the synagogue. Healings also occur within the synagogue (3:1–5). Furthermore, in at least one instance, demon possession is recorded in a household setting (7:24–30; see also Mark 1:34). The distinction between household and synagogue, with the former as a place for healing and the latter as a place of conflict with demons is not upheld in Mark.[86]

A second reason for the argument that the household offers an alternative to the synagogue in Mark is found in the idea of fictive kinship. Mark 3:31–35 is an important text for understanding the household in the Gospel. There Jesus, while in a house, comments that those who do the will of God are his true family (3:35). The true family is contrasted with his biological family "outside" (ἔξω; 3:31–2). Biological family relationships are marginalized in this text. Later Jesus tells his disciples that those outside the circle of Jesus' disciples receive teaching only in parables so that they will not know the secrets of the kingdom of God (Mark 4:11). There is a clear contrast, then, between outsiders and insiders in these two texts. The insiders, unlike Jesus' biological family, do the will of God and receive private instruction. The creation of a fictive kinship network, however, does not necessarily involve the architectural structure of the home. Moxnes has shown that in Q Jesus rejects the patriarchal household, forms a fictive kinship group, but does not relocate them within a reformed household setting.[87] No new or renewed architectural setting is necessary for a fictive kinship association.

The final reason for understanding the household as an alternative to the synagogue is that the household is often the locus of private instruction in this Gospel.[88] Private instruction, however, does not always occur in the home in Mark's Gospel. Such private instruction more frequently occurs outside of the household than within the household. Jesus teaches

examining the context and object of Simon's mother-in-law's service."

86. This is even more the case recalling that illness is caused by aggressive spirits. In the synagogue as well as the house, therefore, Jesus encounters aggressive spirits. Furthermore, it should be noted that demon possession can also be found within the context of the house. The daughter of the Syrophoenician woman is demon-possessed within her own home (7:30).

87. Moxnes, *Putting Jesus in His Place*, 72–107.

88. Elliot, *Home for the Homeless*, 254.

his disciples privately in a household setting at Mark 7:17–23. The final meal of Jesus and his disciples occurs within the private setting of a household (Mark 14:17–25), but moves from there to the Mount of Olives and Gethsemane (14:26–42). The private instruction to the disciples in 4:10–34 is not located specifically within a household setting. There are other instances, also, of private teaching occurring outside the household context (on board the boat, 8:15–21; in the villages of Caesarea Philippi, 8:27–30; down the mountain after the Transfiguration, 9:9–13). The episodes, taken together, show that Mark more frequently locates private teaching to the disciples outside the home rather than within it. It is certainly not clear, then, that Mark makes the home an alternative space to the synagogue. It is proximity to Jesus, rather than a locale within the household, that guarantees one access to private teaching.

A contrast between the synagogue and the household in the Gospel, then, is not upheld throughout Mark's text. In the first place, as seen above, the enemies of Jesus observe his actions within a household setting. The scribes observe Jesus' activity in his house in Capernaum in 2:1–12. The Jerusalem scribes also accuse Jesus of being demon possessed when he is at home (3:20b–30). The scribes of the Pharisees monitor Jesus' dining habits in Levi's home (2:16). The household is not a space free of the surveillance that marks the synagogue and temple spaces. Nor is it free of the controversy regarding purity regulations that these spaces involve (so 2:1–12 and 2:15–17).[89] This type of surveillance within the home would be characteristic of the public space of Roman households, and that is likely the type of house Mark has in mind. It is not the household, then, but the gathering (συνάγω) around Jesus himself, wherever that occurs, that is the locus of the new community.[90]

The fact that Jesus encounters inimical spirits within the household, that he offers private instruction to his disciples outside, as well as within, the house, and that he encounters his human opponents within the household all mitigate against a utopian understanding of the household in opposition to the synagogue. Mark's understanding of the household is not altogether different from his understanding of the synagogue (and

---

89. While Mark 7:1–6 is not expressly located in the house, the question about washing and dining clearly involve household behavior.

90. In this sense, Jesus is like both philosophers and emperors who serve as geographic centers in the literature discussed above in chapter four. For a fuller explication of these similarities, see the section on "Jesus as Geographic Center" below.

the temple). It is a space that ultimately must be abandoned by Jesus' followers (Mark 10:29). Though Mark's Jesus promises a hundredfold return of houses, these things come "with persecutions" (μετὰ διωγμῶν) in the present age (10:30). This treatment is similar to what the followers of Jesus are told to expect in the synagogue (13:9). The household, then, is no utopian sanctuary for the Jesus movement within Mark's Gospel.[91]

Boundary Territories as Spaces for a New Spatial Practice

The social formation of Jesus' new gathering occurs largely in wilderness and borderlands. The Gospel opens in the wilderness with John's preaching. Jesus' disciples are called in the topographical borderland of the mountain. Jesus' Transfiguration occurs on the mountain as well, as does his teaching regarding the future coming of the Son of man. These borderland areas are a place in which identities can be forged and in which divine beings are frequently encountered in Greco-Roman and Jewish literature. The Gospel of Mark follows these topographical traditions, emphasizing the absence of the spatial practice of both the temple/synagogue and the Romans.

John in the Wilderness

The Gospel of Mark mentions the wilderness in several instances, two of which occur in the Gospel's opening scenes. John, the "messenger" (ἄγγελλόν, Mark 1:2) is introduced as "the voice of one crying out in the wilderness" (φωνὴ βοῶντος ἐν τῇ ἐρήμῳ, Mark 1:3). The first half of the quote in 1:2 is taken from Exod 23:20. There is little doubt that the reference to Exodus, coupled with John's baptizing in the wilderness is meant to evoke Exodus imagery.[92] The journeying motif suggests that the Lord (in this case Jesus) is about to lead a new conquest of the land.

Mark follows this quotation with the activity of John. The people of "the whole region of Judea" (πᾶσα ἡ Ἰουδαία χώρα, Mark 1:5) and

---

91. None of this is to deny that the Markan community may have been a (or a series of) house church. It is simply to suggest that Mark does not portray the household as a clear alternative as a locus for Jesus and his followers by painting it as a private haven in opposition to the synagogue.

92. In general, the position of Meier, *Marginal Jew*, 2.44–46 is adopted here, that there is no necessary reason to assume that if geography is used in a symbolic way it therefore has no correlation to actual, physical geography.

"all the inhabitants of Jerusalem" (οἱ Ἱεροσολυμῖται πάντες, 1:5) come out to John from their places of habitation in order to be baptized by him. Scholars have typically read the text of Mark 1:5 as an exaggeration. So, for example, Donahue and Harrington suggest that the use of "all" is characteristic of Mark's "universalizing" tendency.[93] Moloney, similarly, interprets 1:5 to be a rhetorical statement which "is hardly likely, but the author makes his point: John the Baptist made a great impression."[94] Certainly some exaggeration is at work here, but the point of the exaggeration still needs to be addressed.[95] Why would Mark choose to open his Gospel in this fashion?[96]

Lightfoot suggests that Mark has presented the whole region of Judea and all the people of Jerusalem coming to John as a sign of the end of time (or the era). Rather than read the verse "as picturesque exaggeration" he thinks its purpose is to "emphasize that which was only to be expected at the appearance of the herald of the end."[97] Lightfoot compares this text with Josephus' *B.J.* 2.259. Josephus' text describes a number of charlatans (in Josephus' estimation) who attempted to destroy the peace of the city of Jerusalem. He compares these people to the *sicarii* (described in *B.J.* 2.257). Of these charlatans he says that they feigned divine inspiration for the purpose of bringing about revolution. In doing so, "they persuaded the multitude to act like madmen, and led them out into the desert under the belief that God would there give them tokens of deliverance" (σημεῖα ἐλευθερίας, *B.J.* 2.259). Though both Mark and Josephus tell of people from Jerusalem going out of the city and into the desert, the comparison of these two texts seems a bit forced. John the Baptist does not lead people

---

93. Donahue and Harrington, *Gospel of Mark*, 62.

94. Moloney, *Gospel of Mark*, 34.

95. While John may have drawn large crowds at times, there is little reason to believe that all of the Judeans and those in Jerusalem would have come out to him, particularly at one time as the Gospel suggests.

96. Waetjen, *Reordering of Power*, 65, suggests that the reason for John's "extraordinary success" is to be found in the description of John's dress which "corresponds almost literally to the Septuagint translation of 2 Kings 1:8, where it refers to Elijah the Tishbite . . . The narrator is alluding that all the Jews of Judea and Jerusalem went out to John in order to be baptized by him and so 'to prepare the way of the Lord . . .'" While Waetjen is certainly correct that Mark presents John the Baptist as Elijah *redivivus* (see also Mark 9:11–12; the implicit connection is made also in 6:14–16 where Jesus' identity is compared to both John the Baptist and Elijah), it does not really answer why Mark presents all those of the region of Judea and all of the people of Jerusalem coming out to John.

97. Lightfoot, *Locality and Doctrine*, 114.

anywhere in Mark's Gospel, and clearly he is not inciting a revolt (according to Mark). The people leave Judea and Jerusalem to come to John rather than being led out of the city and region.

The discussion of the desert as borderland in chapter four offers an alternative explanation for this text. The usual assumption when one reads the opening verses of Mark's Gospel is that the inhabitants of the region of Judea and those of Jerusalem have returned to their respective home places by the time Jesus arrives to be baptized by John. Nowhere, however, does the text indicate such a mass departure from John. As it stands, when Jesus enters the picture, the reader should presume that all of those people from Jerusalem/Judea are still gathered around John.[98] This concept of a depopulated Judea leaves open the possibility for the formation of a new identity. No longer do these people belong to the Roman empire or to the space of the temple in Jerusalem.[99] They have come out to prepare the way of the Lord (Mark 1:2–3). This reading is similar to that of Ched Myers. He argues that the primary meaning of the wilderness in the opening of Mark's Gospel is that it "represents the 'peripheries.'"[100] He reads the conflation of texts in Mark 1:2–3 as a challenge to the center.

> By inserting this coordinate in place of "Malachi's" temple (representative of the "center") as the site of Yahweh's renewed action, Mark creates a spatial tension between two archetypically opposite symbolic spaces. This wilderness/temple polarity becomes explicit in Mark's wry report—a typical Semitic hyperbole—that "all the country of Judea and all the people of Jerusalem" seek John in the wilderness (1:5). According to the dominant nationalist ideology of salvation history, Jerusalem was considered the hub of the world to which all nations would one day come (see Ps 69:35f., Is 60:10–14). Mark turns this "circulation" on its head: far from embarking on triumphal pilgrimage to Zion, the crowds flee to the margins, for purposes of repentance.[101]

---

98. Marcus, *Way of the Lord*, 42 says that of the assembly of people that come out to John: "the Jewish crowds . . . stand generally for the potential disciples of Jesus."

99. Meier, *A Marginal Jew*, 2.24 makes this very point about John the Baptist. If Meier's historical analysisis correct, that John is the son of a priest, then he clearly leaves a "center of civilization" in order to enter into a borderland where a new identity may be forged—that is, instead of operating as a priest, he operates as a prophet, thereby rejecting the old spatial practice in favor of a new one.

100. Myers, *Binding the Strong Man*, 126.

101. Ibid., 126.

In introducing the Gospel this way, Mark establishes a further link to the period of the Exodus, before the Israelites occupied the land. The people of Jerusalem depopulate the center by their excursion into the wilderness. The social creation of the new people of God occurs, quite naturally according to Israelite tradition, in the wilderness. The symbolic map of Mark begins with a motif of journeying ("preparing the way") and an empty Judea/Jerusalem inasmuch as all of its inhabitants have come out from there to John.[102] They dwell in the wilderness as had their ancestors when God fashioned a people from them at Sinai. Furthermore, the quotation of Isa 40:3 invokes the idea of Israel's return from exile. As discussed in chapter four, numerous scholars recently have noted that, for many early Jewish groups, the exile did not end with the rebuilding of the temple and the return of Ezra. Many early Jewish groups believed that the exile was still ongoing long after the period of Ezra's and Nehemiah's return. Mark, it seems, by invoking the idea of an empty Jerusalem/Judea, is taking the reader into a geographical area outside the land, a geography of exile.[103] Several of these groups had already created new spatial practices in the desert by the time of Jesus.[104]

Previous interpretations of the first several verses of Mark have not paid attention to the fact that in them Mark creates a depopulated Judea/Jerusalem. This depopulated area fits well with Second Temple interpretations of both the conquest of the land and the continuing exile. Mark creates a space into which he can place the significant players. Jesus ultimately takes control of the space that Mark creates through the creation of his new spatial practice, which allows him to "destroy" the temple. Furthermore, a new social grouping of Israelites is created through repentance and baptism. The baptism of John is available apart from the temple. Repentance and baptism replace sacrifice in the temple as a means of "preparing the Lord's way." The space of the wilderness in the opening verses of Mark is a borderland. It is a place for the contestation of identities and the forging of a new identity for the people of God.

---

102. The trek of the people out to John could be seen either as a "reverse exodus" or as following the same path that the exiles themselves took in their forced removal to Babylon.

103. On the idea of continued exile for early Christians, see Wright, *New Testament and the People of God*, esp. 268–72; and idem, *Jesus and the Victory of God*, esp. 126–29, 428–30; also Evans, "Aspects of Exile."

104. In addition to the examples cited in chapter four, see 2 Macc 5:27.

The Spatial Presentation of Mark's Gospel

One final point deserves consideration here. Malbon argues that the negative portrayal of Jerusalem in the Gospel of Mark is very damning since the opening salvo of the Gospel creates the possibility of the city's people participating in John's or Jesus' movement.

> ... at the very beginning of Mark's Gospel, Jerusalem, *all* Jerusalem, is glimpsed in a positive, hopeful light. Jerusalemites witness and are responsive to the preparatory events of the kingdom of God. Thus the opening of the Markan narrative illustrates an awareness of the positive view of Jerusalem that is challenged and denied in the remainder of the text. The critique is stronger because the potential is acknowledged.[105]

The problem with such an analysis is that Jerusalem is never portrayed positively. People come to John from cities, as they will later come to Jesus, but the space and spatial practice of Jerusalem is not redeemable for Mark. It is only in their willingness to abandon the centers of civilization (Jerusalem and its temple) and come to new centers of fluid sacred space that such a possibility for hopefulness emerges.

Jesus and His Movement in the Wilderness

Other mentions of the wilderness in the Gospel of Mark confirm that Mark understands this area as a borderland. The temptation story of Jesus (Mark 1:12–13) portrays the wilderness as a place of complete dependence upon God (in that Jesus is tended to by angels; 1:13).[106] At the same time it is also a place of testing. So Jesus is "tested" (πειραζόμενος) by Satan (Mark 1:13).[107] Mauser makes an important point about Satan's testing of Jesus. "It is mostly overlooked that Mark, in contrast to Matthew (4.11) and Luke (4.13), reports neither Jesus' victory over Satan nor the end of the temptation."[108] Jesus' testing continues throughout the Gospel of Mark.

That he is not victorious over Satan in the encounter in 1:12–13 is seen in the constant struggle between Jesus and the unclean spirits throughout the Gospel. Satan's presence in the desert temptations highlights a more

---

105. Malbon, *Narrative Space*, 45.

106. Mauser, *Christ in the Wilderness*. The connections with Elijah's stay in the Wadi Cherith (1 Kgs 17:4–6) should be noted here.

107. On the theme of testing in the wilderness, see Mauser, *Christ in the Wilderness*, 128–32.

108. Ibid., 100.

negative aspect of the wilderness. "It is the demonic land, the wasteland, the dangerous land."[109] The presence of wild animals (1:13) confirms the wildness of the desert.[110] At the same time, Jesus is not threatened by the wild animals in Mark's wilderness, he is simply "with" them (1:13).[111] A further example of the wildness of borderlands is introduced in Mark 5. The Gerasene demoniac is said to live "among the tombs" (5:3), but also frequents the mountains (5:5). His behavior ("howling and bruising himself with stones", 5:5) and his inability to be restrained by humans identify him as a threat to society (5:2–3). This demoniac resembles the lawless figures in the mountains of the Greek and Roman world discussed in chapter four. Those who dwell on mountains do not behave in socially appropriate ways and are not welcome in centers of civilized living. It is clear, then, that Mark understands borderlands to be, at least in part, areas in which strange and even dangerous people are found.

Other instances of Jesus spending time in wilderness areas in the Gospel, however, reflect a more positive tradition concerning its potential as a place for an alternative spatial practice. It is significant that every prayer of Jesus in the Gospel of Mark is offered in a borderland locale. Mark 1:35 presents Jesus withdrawing to a "deserted place" (ἔρημον τόπον) to pray after performing exorcisms and healings (1:34). Jesus likewise prays on the mountain after dismissing the crowd of five thousand whom he had fed (6:46). The one other instance of Jesus' praying in the Gospel occurs in the garden of Gethsemane (14:32–42).[112] Within this story, the disciples are also encouraged to pray (14:38). As mentioned above, private teaching also occurs in wilderness areas. Teaching and prayer are fundamental elements of the spatial practice of Jesus' movement (so Mark 3:14; 6:6b–13). Furthermore, both of these things are supposed to be part of the spatial practice of the temple/synagogue, but are either ineffectual (1:22, 27) or absent (11:17).

---

109. Smith, *Map is Not Territory*, 109. "It is the place of demons and monsters, the place where the night hag shrieks. It is the land of confusion and chaos, the land that is waste and void as in the beginning . . . The desert or wilderness is a place of strange, demonic, secret powers. It is a sacred land, a holy land in that it is a demonic realm; but it is not a place for ordinary men." See also the insightful discussion in Pedersen, *Israel: Its Life and Culture*, 1.454–57.

110. Compare Isa 34:9–15; also Isa 13:20–22; Jer 50:39–40; and 51:36–40.

111. See Caneday, "Mark's Provocative Use of Scripture."

112. Recall that Philo says that the Theraputae retreated to gardens because they were places of solitude.

Feeding stories also occur in the desert. Jesus' disciples, after returning from their healing and exorcising mission (6:12), retreat to a deserted place (ἔρημον τόπον, 6:31) in order to rest, but the crowds, having seen them, assemble around them. The disciples recognize a problem in that there is nothing to eat in the deserted place (6:35).[113] Jesus feeds the crowds by multiplying five loaves and two fish (6:38–44).[114] A similar feeding story occurs in Mark 8:1–9. Again the location is "in the desert" (ἐπ' ἐρημίας: 8:4). Feeding, as can be seen in the numerous controversy stories surrounding eating, is an important element of social formation and spatial practice. Here Jesus and his disciples institute a new type of feeding in the borderland of the wilderness. It is not coincidental that eating, an area of constant dispute between Jesus and his opponents is practiced differently by Jesus and his followers in a desert region.

Perhaps the clearest example of the formation of a new social identity in a borderland in Mark is the call of the twelve.[115] Jesus withdraws from the crowd "up the mountain and called to him those whom he wanted, and they came to him" (3:13). Here the formation of Jesus' new group involves the appointing of twelve disciples (3:14), surely a number meant to symbolize the restoration of Israel.[116] They are commissioned "to be with him, and to be sent out to proclaim the message, and to have authority to cast out demons" (3:14–15). From the space of this borderland, the new community is formed and commissioned to replicate the spatial practice of Jesus himself.

Creation of identity within Jesus' new movement is further exemplified in the Transfiguration. Only Peter, James, and John are privy to this revelation of Jesus' identity (9:1–9). The mountains are also the place to which the followers of Jesus are to flee when the desolating sacrilege is set up (13:14). The mountain, as borderland, serves as a place of refuge for

---

113. This complaint, and that in 8:4 regarding the desert location and the inaccessibility of food are reminiscent of the complaints of the Israelites in Exod 16:2–3. Compare also the complaints of the Israelites in Philo *Vit. Mos.* 1.35.191–193.

114. The cuisine provided here goes beyond the tradition of bread found in Exodus. Philo *Vit. Mos.* 1.37.209, however, relates that God, not satisfied just to provide bread, provided the Israelites all the foods of an inhabited country (οἰκουμένῃ χώρᾳ) while they were in the desert (ἐρημίᾳ). He mentions specifically quail that come up from the sea as part of their cuisine.

115. It should be noted that the first four disciples are called in a borderland, that is, the seashore (1:16–20) rather than a city or a village.

116. See Meier, *A Marginal Jew*, 3.148–54.

Jesus' followers. This fact might be clearly seen in that there is no surveillance by Jesus' opponents in these wilderness areas. The one exception is the garden of Gethsemane, and then it involves a member of his inner group betraying him. Ordinarily, the wilderness areas are places of safety for Jesus and his followers.

The wilderness and mountains, as borderlands, are loci for identity formation in the Gospel. In the desert, people come to John the Baptist, forsaking centers of civilization in order to be baptized. Crowds are fed miraculously in the desert, recalling the miraculous feeding of the Israelites during their wilderness wanderings and instituting a new spatial practice in contrast to that of the temple and synagogue. Jesus chooses his disciples on a mountain, and the revelation of his identity in the Transfiguration occurs on the mountain. Prayer and private teaching are part of the experience of wilderness areas. Perhaps most importantly, Jesus' way is prepared in the desert, enabling him to exist at peace with wild animals during his temptation. While there are trace threads of the desert as a place of danger, it is mostly a positive place in the Gospel and establishes a space for the formation of the new community of the kingdom of God.

Jesus as Geographic Center

Though borderlands offer different locales for community formation in the Gospel of Mark, Jesus himself becomes the geographic center in the imagined world of Markan geography. People come to him from all places on the Markan map for many different reasons. The formation of his spatial practice occurs largely in borderlands and wilderness areas, apart from where the spatial practices of the "cultured centers" hold sway. In the wilderness, on the mountain and on the sea, Jesus forms a community of his followers by teaching them, feeding them and acting as a center around which they gather. Jesus' spatial practice puts him in direct conflict with the authorities of the temple and synagogue since he offers a purity not mediated by their spatial practices. It also places him in conflict with Rome and its agents (i.e. the Herodians) since it represents a threat to the order of the *pax Romana* through the establishment of a new order, the kingdom of God.

John Elsner recently discussed what he calls "hagiographic geography," which refers to a story that is composed around the travels and geographic centrality of the (or a) major character in the text.[117] Jesus is a traveler and a centripetal force in the Gospel of Mark. People are drawn to him from every quarter of Mark's world. As a "traveling" center, the space of Jesus' company represents fluid sacred space.[118] It is no longer the temple, which is in any event, about to be destroyed (13:1–3) or the synagogue, which represents a place of oppression for Jesus' followers (13:9) in which Jesus' followers will "gather." Rather they "gather" around Jesus.

People came to him . . .

It is now commonplace to discuss the similarities between Jesus and John the Baptist in Mark's Gospel.[119] They preach similar messages: "a baptism of repentance for the forgiveness of sins" (Mark 1:4) and "repent, and believe in the good news" (Mark 1:15), are both executed by political authorities for what they teach, and are both presented as prophets in the line of Israel's prophets. When examined from a spatial perspective, one notices another similarity. As discussed above, people come out from Jerusalem/Judea (and Galilee) to visit John in order to be baptized. They come to hear his message, be baptized and confess their sins. Numerous people throughout the Gospel also come to Jesus to hear his message. Jesus attracts a far wider audience than John. While John's audience comes only from Jerusalem/Judea (indeed Jesus is the lone exception, being from Galilee), Jesus' widest following consists of people "who came to him from every quarter" (1:45) and "a great multitude from Galilee" and "great numbers from Judea, Jerusalem, Idumea, beyond the Jordan, and the region around Tyre and Sidon" (Mark 3:7–8). Obviously, Jesus' audience comes from a much wider area than does John's: "crowds flock to him from all points of the compass."[120] Jesus' location is, in fact, the meeting place for his group. Both John and Jesus represent alternative spatial practices to the temple. John's spatial practice involves purity through baptism rather than sacrifice, while Jesus' involves exorcisms through the Holy Spirit.

More than curious onlookers, however, come to Jesus. At numerous points throughout the Gospel his opponents watch him, challenging

---

117. Elsner, "Hagiographic Geography."

118. On the concept of healers representing fluid sacred space in opposition to the fixed sacred space of temples, see Smith, *Map is Not Territory*, 172–89.

119. So, for example, Malbon, *Narrative Space*, 22–25.

120. Marcus, *Mark 1–8*, 258.

him with questions. Part of the role of the emperor as a traveling center involved receiving embassies that brought questions concerning legal matters. Jesus is often cast in this role in the Gospel of Mark. In Galilee, his authority to forgive sins is questioned (2:1–12), as are his eating practices (2:13–22; 7:1–23), and his Sabbath observance (2:23–28; 3:1–6). In Judea (10:2–12) and Jerusalem (11:27–33; 12:13–17, 18–27, 35–37) the challenges continue. People often approach Jesus hoping for a miraculous healing (1:27–29, 40–45; 2:1–12; 5:1–20, 21–24, 25–34; 6:53–56; 7:24–30, 31–37; 8:22–26). The Pharisees also approach Jesus for a miraculous sign that would establish his authority (8:11–13).

Like Apollonius, Jesus travels widely in the Gospel, and he challenges the spatial practices of the central institutions of the civilized centers that he encounters. Jesus draws numerous types of people to himself, in the same way that emperors and traveling philosophers did in the ancient world. Through the power of the holy spirit that he possesses, Jesus is able to perform miracles and answer his opponents' challenges concerning his spatial practice relative to their interpretations of the law.

. . . and gathered around him

The verb συνάγω (to gather) is significant in the Gospel of Mark, although it is used only five times (2:2; 4:1; 5:21; 6:30; 7:1). The compound form ἐπισυνάγω is used twice (1:33; 13:27). In every instance except one, Jesus is the object of this verb.[121] The verb is related to the noun συναγωγή (synagogue). Since the synagogue is no longer the meeting place for the Jesus movement, the space around Jesus becomes the new meeting place. At the first instance of the compound form of the verb, the "whole city" gathers at the door of the house of Peter's mother-in-law so that Jesus might heal or exorcise their sick and demon possessed. A similar case occurs in Mark 2:2. The crowd is so large it blocks access to the paralytic who needs Jesus' healing. Another crowd "gathers" to hear Jesus' teaching on the seashore (4:1). A great crowd "gathers" again when Jesus returns from the territory of Geresa (5:21). The apostles "gather" around Jesus (6:30) to report the results of their mission. Finally the Pharisees and some scribes from Jerusalem "gather" around Jesus (7:1).

---

121. Mark 13:27 reads, "Then he will send out the angels, and gather his elect from the four winds, from the ends of the earth to the ends of heaven." There Jesus, as the returning Son of man, is the subject of the verb. The followers will be gathered (ἐπισυνάγω) around Jesus.

All of these instances occur in the land of Galilee. There are no "gatherings" around Jesus in Judea. The contrast between Jesus as a gathering place and the synagogue likely has something to do with this fact. The first "gathering" around Jesus occurs immediately following his first entrance into and exit from the synagogue (1:21–29). Jesus represents an alternative gathering place to the synagogue, and since there are no synagogues in Judea (according to Mark's text), there is no contrast with Jesus' space. It is ironic that Pharisees and scribes, those groups that represent the interests of the synagogue, "gather" around Jesus in order to question him about issues relating to the maintenance of purity rules presumably originating in the synagogue and/or temple. The source of the law's correct interpretation, then, is in that space that is the "gathering" around Jesus.

As noted above, this space, because of Jesus' ability to exorcise, is free of demons and the chaos that they engender. The space in which people gather around Jesus is pure space, free of malady and possession. It is characterized by Jesus' holy spirit. Inasmuch as that is the case, it represents a space that is civilizing. It is contrasted with the space of the synagogue/temple and the space of the Romans. After the destruction of these spaces, the Son of man will return and "gather (ἐπισυνάγω) his elect from the four winds, from the ends of the earth to the ends of heaven" (13:27). The community of the kingdom will be gathered after the destruction of the civilized spaces of the world. This cosmic perspective of the forthcoming destruction relativizes the spaces of these civilized centers.

Jesus' gathering space is also characterized by a purity system. This purity system, however, is based on the healings and exorcisms of Jesus. He restores people to wholeness in order that they might become part of his gathering. His gathering is also spatially characterized by its meal practices. They do not fast (2:18–22), they eat with tax collectors (2:15–17), all foods are clean for them (7:19), and they do not behave like Gentile rulers (10:41–45). It is also characterized by a different attitude toward Sabbath observance (2:23–28; 3:1–6). These activities of Jesus' gathering represent a different spatial practice than that of the synagogue.

Another element of Jesus' gathering highlighted in the Gospel is the idea of following Jesus. When Jesus calls his first four disciples, he changes their spatial practice in that they no longer make their living on the sea, but become part of Jesus' wandering lifestyle (1:16–20). Jesus' disciples follow him in the Gospel at several points (6:1; 10:28; 15:45; also 1:16–20). Crowds follow him (2:15, 3:7; 5:24), as do Levi (2:14) and Bartimaeus

(10:52). Others are invited to follow him when he begins his journey on the "way" (8:34), though the rich man rejects Jesus' invitation to follow (10:21–22). Those who follow Jesus also represent members of his gathering. They (presumably) share the spatial practices of his gathering (so 8:34). In doing so, they fail to observe the purity rules of the temple and synagogue, thereby rejecting the spatial practice of these institutions.

He Sends out Disciples and They Return

Mark makes clear the purpose for Jesus' calling twelve disciples. They are called in order that they might "be with him, and to be sent out to proclaim the message, and to have authority to cast out demons" (3:14–15). These activities are the same ones in which Jesus is engaged in the Gospel. Like Jesus proclaiming (κηρύσσων) the good news (1:14), so the disciples proclaim (κηρύσσειν). As Jesus casts out demons (1:25–26, 39), so also do the disciples. Once Mark has made clear the task for which the disciples are called, they are sent out on a mission to perform these activities (6:7–13). They proclaim a message of repentance (6:12), cast out many demons, and anoint and heal many people (6:13). From their proximity to Jesus these disciples are sent out to perform the same functions as him. They return to him and report the accomplishment of their tasks (6:30).

The disciples enlarge the space of Jesus' gathering, performing healings and exorcisms. Exorcism, in particular, extends the reach of the kingdom (9:38–40). John tells Jesus that they stopped someone who cast out demons in Jesus' name because "he was not following us" (9:38). Jesus tells John not to stop him because "whoever is not against us is for us" (9:40). Even this person who casts out demons in Jesus' name furthers the spatial practice of the kingdom.[122] When exorcising, healing and preaching, the disciples function as emissaries of Jesus. They reproduce the spatial practice of Jesus' gathering in the same way that the scribes and Pharisees reproduce the spatial practice of the temple and synagogue.

---

122. John's notice of this person might also indicate that the Jesus movement had its own surveillance network. They, too, kept an eye on various people outside of their group.

Outsiders and Insiders

Yet another element of the Gospel's portrayal of space involves the concept of insiders and outsiders. The idea of outsiders in the Gospel first occurs at 3:31–35. There the family of Jesus are those "outside" while the ones who listen to Jesus are "inside" the house with him. Jesus rejects biological family ties and announces that "those who sat around him" (περὶ αὐτὸν κύκλῳ καθημένους) are his true family (3:34). Jesus concludes his statement by saying that "whoever does the will of God is my brother and sister and mother" (3:35). The contrast between "outsiders" and "insiders" occurs again at 4:11. There Jesus tells his disciples and those with him that they will know "the secret of the kingdom of God, but for those outside, everything comes in parables" (4:11). The "insiders" are privy to private teaching that is unavailable to the "outsiders." The purpose of this contrast is spelled out in the Isaiah quotation that immediately follows. Jesus relates parables to those outside "in order 'they may indeed look, but not perceive, and may indeed listen, but not understand; so that they may not turn again and be forgiven'" (4:12; the quotation is from Isa 6:10).[123] According to Mark 4:11–12, it seems as though the "outsiders" are destined to remain outsiders throughout the Gospel since the purpose of Jesus' parables is to keep them in that position.

There is another element, however, to the inside/outside pattern in the Gospel. This element has to do with physical proximity to Jesus. The Gerasene demoniac, for example, seeing Jesus "from a distance (ἀπὸ μακρόθεν), he ran and bowed before him" (5:6). After he is cleansed of his demon, he asks to "be with him" (5:18). While Jesus refuses, he sends the man "to proclaim" (κηρύσσειν; 5:20),[124] the same task to which the disciples had been appointed earlier (3:14). In this instance, Mark presents a shift from outsider to insider. Mark also indicates that the crowd involved in the second feeding miracle came "from a distance" (ἀπὸ μακρόθεν; 8:3). In these instances, the physical distance between Jesus and people is bridged by the people coming to Jesus.

Elsewhere Mark uses the phrase "from a distance" to indicate the increasing rather the decreasing distance between Jesus and his followers. The reader, having already been prepared for Peter's denial (14:29–31),

---

123. On this history of the interpretation of Isa 6:9–10 in early Jewish and Christian literature, see Evans, *To See and not Perceive*.

124. It is possible that this preaching represents an early effort to expand the space of Jesus' gathering into Gentile territory.

sees a growing distance between Jesus and Peter in the scene of the trial. Peter follows Jesus "from a distance" and remains outside in the courtyard while Jesus is tried before the high priest (14:54). It is in that courtyard, standing "below Jesus," that Peter denies three times that he knows Jesus (14:66–72). That is the last time Peter appears in the narrative as a character. The women "who used to follow" Jesus in Galilee and "other women who had come up with him to Jerusalem" (15:41) look on at Jesus' crucifixion "from a distance" (ἀπὸ μακρόθεν; 15:40). These women "provided (διηκόνουν) for him when he was in Galilee" (15:41), but here they are reduced to observing Jesus' death apart from him. At least in the case of Peter, then, it seems that an insider becomes (temporarily, see Mark 16:7) an outsider. This fact is no doubt due in part to Jesus' prediction that all of the disciples would become deserters when their shepherd was struck (14:27). Still, physical proximity to Jesus and fidelity to the tasks to which one is appointed (i.e. proclaiming) mark the insiders. At the death of Jesus, then, all have become outsiders. No one retains either physical proximity to Jesus or fidelity to appointed tasks. The disciples, however, have already been prepared for a successful reconstitution of Jesus' gathering to come after his death (13:27).

The Gerasene demoniac represents a character whose distance from Jesus is overcome in that he is able to enter into the spatial practice of Jesus' gathering through his proclamation. Peter, on the other hand, represents a figure who moves from the gathering of Jesus to a place of distance from Jesus. Fidelity to Jesus' message is the criterion that distinguishes those on the "outside" from those on the "inside." The secret teaching offered to the disciples in Mark is the element of spatial control from the model of territoriality. The only way to have access to this special teaching, in Mark's narrative, is through physical proximity to Jesus.

He Has Voice Everywhere

A final element of Jesus as a geographic center in Mark's Gospel is the fact that he has voice in every area into which he travels. He is never silenced in the Gospel. To speak publicly is to make an honor claim.[125] "Inferiors did not initiate conversations nor were they accorded a public audience. They had no 'authority' to speak."[126] Only adult, elite males were expected

---

125. See Neyrey, "'Teaching You in Public,'" 99–101; also Rohrbaugh, "Legitimating Sonship."

126. Rohrbaugh, "Legitimating Sonship," 186.

to speak in public situations.¹²⁷ Even as an elite male, Paul is silenced and expelled from the synagogue (Acts 17:2; 19:9).¹²⁸ Jesus, however, is never silenced in Mark's Gospel. He has voice everywhere.

As can be seen in the initial report of Jesus' public ministry, the exorcism in the synagogue, authority (ἐξουσία) is consistently in view in Mark's story of Jesus. Jesus' authority gives him the ability to teach in a manner unlike that of the scribes. As Mack has argued, his teaching is really a deed of power in Mark 1:21–28. "The new teaching is not a matter of instruction (for the content of Jesus' teaching is not given). It is a matter of power."¹²⁹ Jesus speaks freely in the synagogue.

Authority again becomes an issue in Jesus' actions in the temple. The question of Jesus' authority comes up in connection with his behavior in the temple (Mark 11:27–33). The chief priests, elders and scribes are unable to answer Jesus' question to them, so he refuses to answer the question of the origin of his authority.¹³⁰ It is unclear to what these opponents of Jesus refer when they ask "By what authority are you doing these things?" (Mark 11:28).¹³¹ It could refer to Jesus' teaching in the temple (the context immediately following the question) or to the overturning of the tables from the previous day (Mark 11:15–7). What is critical to note is that the authorities, wishing to silence Jesus (by means of death), are unable to do so because Jesus has the ability to speak freely and influence the crowds. They cannot even prevent him from speaking on their own turf.¹³²

It is an ironic twist on this theme when Jesus refuses to speak at his trial before the Jewish authorities and before Pilate. In Mark 14:61 Jesus "was silent (ἐσιώπα) and did not answer." Further, in his hearing before Pilate, Jesus "made no further reply" (οὐκέτι οὐδὲν ἀπεκρίθη,

---

127. Neyrey, "'Teaching You in Public,'" 100.

128. Ibid., 101.

129. Mack, *Myth of Innocence*, 234.

130. It is certainly clear to the reader that Jesus' authority is derived from God. The voice at the baptism has, by this point in the narrative, been confirmed by the same voice at the Transfiguration.

131. On the question of authority and its relation to the question of public voice, see Rohrbaugh, "Legitimating Sonship," 192–95.

132. The fact that Jesus is not arrested immediately after his demonstration in the temple is a narrative device designed to stress that Jesus is able to control the space of his environment. Part of this control is the use of public voice. On the issue of "public voice," see Neyrey, "'Teaching You in Public,'" 99–101.

15:5). Voluntary silence is a strategy of public speaking.[133] Jesus' refusal to speak is not because of his lack of public voice, but rather because of the assertion of his ability not to speak even in the company of the leaders of Jerusalem and Rome.

Jesus' public voice is part of the honor ascribed to him by virtue of his relationship to God which provides his authority. His opponents are unable to control the space of the temple and the synagogue because Jesus has more authority than they do. Mark presents Jesus, then, as a figure who has voice in every space of the Gospel. This public voice is related to the space of Jesus' gathering. He controls the space around his physical person, transforming it into the space of his gathering.[134]

Jesus is a geographic center in Mark. He is the source of the interpretation of the law. He makes legal decisions that form the new community of the kingdom of God. When examined from a spatial perspective, Jesus has authority to inaugurate a new spatial practice (the kingdom of God) because he has access to the cosmic realm of space. He receives the Holy Spirit through the opened heavens, has access to the heavenly realm in the Transfiguration, and he also knows the unfolding story of the coming Son of man. Through his exorcisms, he cleanses the spaces into which he and his followers travel. His followers also perform these functions, thereby extending the space of Jesus' gathering. This extension through the preaching, healing and exorcisms of the disciples also provides a model for the continuation of the community after Jesus' death.

Conclusion: Jesus's Power over Space in Mark

The Gospel of Mark falls very much in line with the human geography of Greek, Roman, and Jewish geographical traditions. There is no attempt to present material "scientifically" in the Gospel. Caricatures and stereotypes play a predominant role in Mark's space. Either a person is one type of person or they are another. There is very little "character development" in the Gospel.

---

133. Maximus of Tyre *Or.* 3 argues that Socrates was silent in his own defense since his jury was not fit to receive his defense and it would do him no good.

134. At his arrest, Jesus says "day after day I was with you in the temple teaching, and you did not arrest me" (14:49). Jesus here indicates the lack of control of the temple space on the part of the chief priests, elders and scribes. Further, Jesus allows himself to be arrested in order to fulfill scripture (14:49). It is not because Jesus has lost control over the physical space of his body.

Rather than presenting civilized centers, such as cities, and their institutions as promoting a positive spatial practice, Mark presents these spaces as characterized by uncleanness, necessitating Jesus' driving out the unclean elements upon entering such spaces. The Romans are unable to provide "peace" to the territory purportedly under their control, but Jesus is able to restore order to such places by cleansing the Gerasene demoniac. It is Jesus who brings order rather than the Romans. The temple and synagogue represent another type of spatial control in the Gospel of Mark. This type of control extends outward from the temple as fixed sacred space in the center of Jewish civilization. It extends itself spatially in two major forms: the application of purity rules outside of these specific places (so, e.g., Mark 7:1–23) and the surveillance of opponents by the leadership of these institutions (so, e.g., Mark 2:1–12 and 3:1–6). Further, Mark suggests that the purity rules of these spaces do not apply to the Jesus and his followers (for example, all foods are clean for them), and portrays Jesus as constantly besting the leaders in challenge and riposte. The household does not offer an alternative to the synagogue in Mark since it, too, is a location in which Jesus encounters aggressive spirits and his opponents. It is also a contested site.

Jesus' movement is founded in the borderland territories of the wilderness/desert, the sea, and the mountain. It is there that people gather around Jesus, have access to healing, practice alternate customs relating to table fellowship, and learn the secret teachings of the kingdom of God. His movement also, however, invades the spaces of the synagogue and temple and that of the Romans. His opponents are unable to control him even on their own turf, since he is able to speak freely and come and go as he pleases.

Jesus, then, creates the new space of the kingdom of God in gathering people around himself and sending them out in order to enlarge the space of that gathering. After the destruction of the centers of civilization (that is, Jerusalem and its temple), Jesus, as the Son of Man, will return and again gather his elect from the four winds and from the ends of the earth to the ends of heaven. This reconstituted gathering will resemble the gathering that began during Jesus' lifetime in the space of Galilee and Judea. The new spatial practice of Jesus and his followers will come to fruition when the centers of the old spatial practice, the temple and, by extension, the synagogue have been destroyed, creating a pure space, free of unclean spirits, in which Jesus and his followers might gather.

CHAPTER 6

Conclusion

THE STUDY OF MARK'S geography has generated numerous scholarly works. Most often it is noted that Mark does not accurately reflect the layout of ancient Palestine. Chapter one surveyed a number of these works that have dealt with Mark and space, dividing them into three major groups.

The first group of these studies, which began with the works of Lohmeyer and Lightfoot, stressed the theological dimensions on Mark's presentation of Galilee and Jerusalem. These studies contrasted a positive portrayal of Galilee with a negative portrayal of Jerusalem in the Gospel of Mark. The basic elements of the argument are that preaching the message of the kingdom only occurs in Galilee, that Jesus only calls followers in Galilee, and that Jerusalem is the place of Jesus' rejection and death.

In response to this supposed contrast, numerous studies appeared questioning whether such a distinction was valid for Mark. On the basis of texts such as Mark 6:1-6, numerous scholars have argued that Mark does not present Galilee positively in every instance in the Gospel, and some have argued further that Mark demonstrates acceptance of the inevitability of Jerusalem as a messianic center.

The third major group of studies conceived of Markan space somewhat more widely, taking into account architectural, topographical, and cosmic space. None of these studies on space in the Gospel of Mark, however, have dealt with issues of the critical theory of space, nor have any paid much attention to the social element of the Gospel's space. The failure to use critical theory on space has left these studies wanting at a number of points. Further, none of the studies surveyed in the first chapter make use of Greek and Roman geographical traditions in any significant way. Attempting to understand Mark's space in the absence of compara-

Conclusion

tive material from ancient Greek, Roman, and Jewish sources compounds many of the shortcomings of these studies on Mark and space.

Chapter two examined modern theories of space and place. Modern theorists are virtually united in understanding that space encodes social practices and power relations. Those who control space exert their control by means of particular spatial practices. Models of critical spatiality, such as that of territoriality, show how social relationships are predominant in the classification, communication, and control of space. Space is seen as a relational category rather than an absolute category, with Christopher Tilley going so far as to assert that "space has no substantial essence in itself, but only has a relational significance, created through relations between peoples and places."[1] Every space is controlled by people, and these people exhibit that control by means of a spatial practice.

Spatial practice is the "way things are done here." It consists of the normal social behavior of the inhabitants of a region. Spaces reproduce themselves through institutions that recreate their spatial practices. When there is general acceptance of and conformity to these spatial practices, the power relationships that are encoded in space are largely unchallenged. Despite the attempt by those who control space to present it as an element of nature that is unchanging, however, space, since it is socially defined, is changeable. Non-conformity to spatial practices can and does occur. To change space in this sense, however, one must challenge the power relations that define that space in the first place.

Chapter three addressed geography from the point of view of ancient geographers. The central concept of ancient geography is the *oikoumenē*, or the inhabited world. This space is primarily defined in social terms in Greek and Roman geographic literature, and it is distinguished clearly from those areas of the world which are not inhabited. Greek and Roman geography can be divided into two major types: scientific and human. Human geography is by far the more prevalent in most forms of literature, ranging from historiography, novels, drama, comedy, epic, and even the geography itself. This type of geography focused upon descriptions of the peoples who populate the various areas of the earth. Not surprisingly, the people at the center of the earth (that is the Greeks and Romans) were considered by Greek and Roman authors the most fit because of their geographical position for ruling the other peoples of the earth. Stereotypical

---

1. Tilley, *Phenomenology of Landscape*, 10–11.

ways of describing the types of people outside of these regions developed. In general, those who lived furthest from the temperate zone occupied by the Greeks and Romans were described in the most fabulous and grotesque terms. Peoples were judged not only by their physical distance from Greece or Rome, but also by their cultural difference in terms of spatial practice. Those who cultivated the soil, like the Greeks and Romans, were presented in far more human terms, while those who lived in areas where such cultivation was impossible were considered savages and uncivilized. People of certain places were thought to be all of one type. Ancient Greeks, Romans, and Israelites all accepted the idea that the environment determined not only one's physical appearance, but also one's character.

For the Greeks and Romans, spatial practice, though it varied some between these two civilizations and regionally within these civilizations, is marked in geographic texts by tilling the soil. Insofar as cultures adopted spatial practices that were like those of Greece and Rome, they were considered "normal." When Greeks, and especially Romans, encountered civilizations that did not operate with similar spatial practices, they marginalized these cultures in their geographic literature. Roman military policy regarding many of these places was to make them "wearers of the toga," that is, to adopt the spatial practice of the Romans themselves. The basic elements of territoriality appear time and again in the Greek and Roman geographical material. Locating Greece and Rome at the center of the earth, for example, gives Greeks and Romans the opportunity to define others by physical as well as cultural distance from their homelands. Sometimes, however, the socially produced spaces of the Greeks and Romans could be challenged, and this happened most often in textual worlds offered as alternatives to actual spatial practices.

Texts create spaces of their own in which exists the opportunity to challenge the social relationships inherent in spatial practices and representations of spaces within various social configurations. These spaces of texts are labeled by Lefebvre "representational spaces." Texts create imaginary worlds in which the "way things are done here" is not necessarily replicated. Different classifications for spaces might be found in texts. The different classifications challenge the communication and control of spaces which those in power offer.

Chapter four examined architectural and topographic places within the Greek and Roman *oikoumenē*. Two major social configurations, the city and village, were analyzed in order to show that the city was a place largely for elites and leached the resources from the villages around them. Cities, moreover, functioned as administrative centers in which certain types of spatial practices were conceived that were then imposed on the surrounding spaces. Villages, in turn, were home to peasants and produced much of what was consumed in the cities. The literary traditions of travel in the ancient world, both land and sea travel, demonstrated a remarkable portrait of lurking danger and overwhelming difficulties. While travel had expanded greatly by the Roman period, the literary imagination never relinquished its idea of travel as a terrifying and frequently deadly activity.

Chapter four also showed that the geographic stereotypes concerning people outside of the central geographic zone are frequently reapplied to those who live in the "uncivilized" borderlands within the *oikoumenē* such as mountains, border regions, and wilderness areas. These people are all marked by an inability to cultivate soil which makes them enemies of those people who live in fertile plains. The spatial practice of the "ideal" Greek or Roman, a tiller of the soil, is jeopardized by those who adopt different spatial practices, particularly when they encroach upon these "ideal" settlements. These borderlands spaces, however, sometimes provided refuge for those who encountered difficulty with the settlements of villages and towns, and they served as areas for the formation of new groups and new spatial practices. The formation of a new people in the wilderness is a frequent theme in early Jewish literature and an important component of the Gospel of Mark.

Finally, the role of people as geographic centers was explored. Such people included emperors, philosophers and teachers, among others. Emperors were considered geographic centers because when they left Rome, the center of the empire traveled with them. Embassies were not sent to Rome, but rather to the emperor wherever he happened to be. Teachers also were geographic centers since students might be sent to them from very long distances. Philosophers more frequently became geographic centers in the same manner as Apollonius of Tyana. They traveled abroad in order to see the great sites of the world, encounter the world's wisdom, and learn the rites of the gods. Upon returning from such wide travel, they were frequently considered the foremost experts on wisdom and were able to entertain and inform disciples and delegations on all matters of the *oikoumenē*.

The Gospel of Mark presents Jesus challenging the spatial practice of the synagogue and temple, which manifests itself in the purity rules incumbent upon the Jews of Judea and Galilee. Jesus rejects many of these purity rules (according to Mark). In doing so, he challenges the spatial power of those in charge of the synagogue and temple. In response, these leaders frequently spy on Jesus, hoping either to mitigate his effectiveness with the crowd through accusing him of demon possession or to remove him from the scene by arresting and killing him. Not only are they unable to restrain Jesus outside the physical spaces of the temple and synagogue, they are unable to control these physical spaces themselves when Jesus enters them. He has voice and they are unable to silence him. Further, he "cleanses" each of these institutions upon entering them, suggesting that, for Mark, they are both defiled and in need of purification. Ultimately, the temple as the center of this spatial complex, will be destroyed.

Jesus offers an alternative spatial practice, one that is centered on himself. The kingdom of God exists spatially in the area around Jesus in which the new community "gathers." People come to him, send embassies to him, and follow him throughout the Gospel. The role of the scribes in teaching and interpreting the law belong to Jesus in the Gospel, and they, too, have to come to Jesus in order to ask questions about the law's interpretation. Jesus sends out disciples to preach, heal, and exorcise in order to expand the space of the kingdom. This space will only be fully realized when the Son of man returns and gathers his elect. Mark rejects the current social configuration of space and establishes a new one in which proximity to Jesus is the key element.

Much more work could be done on the spatiality of early Jewish and early Jesus movement literature. The present study addresses only the Gospel of Mark, but work on the space of Acts has increased substantially in the last several years. Josephus' geography is now beginning to receive more attention as well.[2] James Scott's studies on the mental maps of early Judeans and followers of Jesus are an important contribution to this work. More work is needed on the role of travel in ancient literature, particularly in novels and biographies. Much of the work that has been done is not informed by modern critical theories of space, and further consultation of such work would enrich many of the studies which have been done.

Several questions remain concerning the Gospel of Mark. The present study makes no attempt to address either the date or place of Mark's composition. Mark's spatial presentation is not sufficient to answer this

---

2. See Shahar, *Josephus Geographicus*.

Conclusion

question. In detailing the ancient geographic traditions, however, it is impossible to rule out that Mark was familiar with the geography of ancient Palestine, since, as has been shown, cartographic exactness is not a mark of ancient geography generally. Perhaps one means of addressing the question of the place of Mark's composition would be to compare the spatial presentation of early Jewish texts from the Diaspora with those from Palestine to see whether any patterns might emerge for fruitful comparison with Mark's Gospel.

In sum, what may be said of the Gospel of Mark's presentation of space is that it locates a new spatial practice centered around the exorcising, healing, and teaching Jesus. The cosmic perspective of Jesus' teaching concerning the return of the Son of man enables Mark's readers to understand that the spatial practice of the temple/synagogue is coming to an end. In any case, it is occupied by unclean spirits. Jesus' new gathering, however, because of the power of the Holy Spirit, allows for the creation of pure spaces through exorcism. It is not Galilee and Jerusalem that are the primary points of opposition in the Gospel. Jesus' new gathering is not located specifically in the household. It is created in the spaces of the borderlands, areas that ancient geographers well knew were places for the formation of new movements. For the early Jews, these wilderness areas had always been the spaces for the formation of new spatial practices, especially in the Exodus and the return from exile. Jesus' new spatial practice, ultimately, will be fully consummated, according to Mark, when the Son of man returns, after the centers of civilization, that is, the temple and the city of Jerusalem have been destroyed.

Bibliography

Abegg, Martin, Jr. "Exile in the Dead Sea Scrolls." In *Exile: Old Testament, Jewish, and Christian Conceptions*, edited by James M. Scott, 111–25. JSJSup 56. Leiden: Brill, 1997.
Achtemeier, Paul J. "Towards the Isolation of the Pre-Markan Miracle Catenae." *JBL* 89 (1970) 265–91.
―――. "The Origin and Function of the Pre-Markan Miracle Catenae." *JBL* 91 (1972) 198–221.
Algra, Keimpe. *Concepts of Space in Greek Thought*. Philosophia Antiqua 65. Leiden: Brill, 1995.
Alvarez, Robert R., Jr. "The Mexican-US Border: The Making of an Anthropology of Borderlands." *ARA* 24 (1995) 447–70.
Anderson, Graham. *Philostratus: Biography and Belles Lettres in the Third Century A. D.* London: Croom Helm, 1986.
Antonaccion, Carla M. "Architecture and Behavior: Building Gender into Greek Houses." *CW* 93 (1999–2000) 517–32.
Appleton, Jay. "The Integrity of the Landscape Movement." In *Understanding Ordinary Landscapes*, edited by Paul Groth and Todd W. Bressi, 189–99. New Haven: Yale University Press, 1997.
Augé, Marc. *Non-Places: Introduction to an Anthropology of Supermodernity*. London: Verso, 1995.
Aujac, Germaine. *Strabon et la science de son temps*. Paris: Les Belles Lettres, 1966.
Aune, David E. "Jesus and the Romans in Galilee: Jews and Gentiles in the Decapolis." In *Ancient and Modern Perspectives on the Bible and Culture: Essays in Honor of Hans Dieter Betz*, edited by Adela Yarbro Collins, 230–51. Scholars Press Homage Series 22. Atlanta: Scholars, 1998.
―――. *Revelation*. 3 vols. Word Biblical Commentary 52 A-C. Nashville: Nelson, 1997–1998.
―――, and Eric Stewart. "From the Idealized Past to the Imaginary Future: Eschatological Restoration in Jewish Apocalyptic Literature." In *Restoration: Old Testament, Jewish, and Christian Perspectives*, edited by James M. Scott, 147–77. JSJSup 72. Leiden: Brill, 2001.
Avalos, Hector. *Health Care and the Rise of Christianity*. Peabody: Hendrickson, 1999.

Bekker-Nielsen, Tonnes. "Terra Incognita: the Subjective Geography of the Roman Empire." In *Studies in Ancient History and Numismatics Presented to Rudi Thomsen*, 148–61. Aarhus: Aarhus University Press, 1988.

Berggren, J. Lennart, and Alexander Jones. *Ptolemy's Geography: An Annotated Translation of the Theoretical Chapters*. Princeton: Princeton University Press, 2000.

Blenkinsopp, Joseph. "Temple and Society in Achaemenid Judah." In *Second Temple Studies: 1. The Persian Period*, edited by Philip R. Davies, 22–53. JSOTSup 117. Sheffield: Sheffield Academic, 1991.

———. "The Bible, Archaeology and Politics; or the Empty Land Revisited." *JSNT* 27 (2002) 169–87.

Bochum, Yves Lafond. "Gallia." In *Der Neue Pauly*, edited by Hubert Cancik and Helmuth Schneider, 4:763–67. Stuttgart: Metzler, 1996.

Bonz, Marianne Palmer. "Beneath the Gaze of the Gods: The Pergamon Evidence for a Developing Theology of Empire." In *Pergamon: Citadel of the Gods*, edited by Helmut Koester, 251–75. Cambridge: Harvard University Press, 1998.

Brodersen, Kai. "The Presentation of Geographical Knowledge for Travel and Transport in the Roman World: *Itineraria non tantum adnotata sed etima picta*." In *Travel and Geography in the Roman Empire*, edited by Colin Adams and Ray Laurence, 7–21. London: Routledge, 2001.

Brunt, P. A., and J. M. Moore, editors. *Res Gestae Divi Augusti: The Achievements of the Divine Augustus*. Oxford: Oxford University Press, 1991.

Burke, Peter. *History and Social Theory*. Ithaca, NY: Cornell University Press, 1992.

Burkert, Walter. "The Meaning and Function the Temple in Classical Greece." In *Temple in Society*, edited by Michael V. Fox, 27–47. Winona Lake, IN: Eisenbrauns, 1988.

Burnbury, E. H. *A History of Geography Among the Greeks and Romans from the Earliest Ages till the Fall of the Roman Empire*. 2 vols. New York: Dover, 1959.

Buxton, Richard. "Imaginary Greek Mountains." *JHS* 93 (1992) 1–15.

Campbell, Brian. "Surveyors in Ancient Rome." *JRS* 86 (1996) 74–99.

———. *The Writings of the Roman Land Surveyors*. Journal of Roman Studies Monographs 9. London: Society for the Promotion of Roman Studies, 2000.

Campbell, Jonathan G. "Essene-Qumran Origins in the Exile: A Scriptural Basis?" *Journal of Jewish Studies* 46 (1995) 143–56.

Caneday, A. B. "Mark's Provocative Use of Scripture in Narration: 'He was with the Wild Animals and Angels Ministered to Him.'" *Bulletin of Biblical Research* 9 (1999) 9–16.

Carney, T. F. *The Shape of the Past: Models and Antiquity*. Lawrence, KS: Coronado, 1975.

Carroll, Robert P. "The Myth of the Empty Land." *Semeia* 59 (1992) 79–93.

———. "Deportation and Diasporic Discourses in the Prophetic Literature." In *Exile: Old Testament, Jewish, and Christian Conceptions*, edited by James M. Scott, 173–218. JSJSup 56. Leiden: Brill, 1997.

Casey, Edward S. *Getting Back Into Place: Toward a Renewed Understanding of Place-World*. Studies in Continental Thought. Bloomington: Indiana University Press, 1993.

———. *The Fate of Place: A Philosophical History*. Berkeley: University of California Press, 1997.

Casson, Lionel. *Travel in the Ancient World*. London: Allen & Unwin, 1974.

———. *Ships and Seafaring in Ancient Times*. Austin: University of Texas Press, 1994.

———. *Ships and Seamanship in the Ancient World*. Baltimore: Johns Hopkins University Press, 1995.

Chapman, Dean W. "Locating the Gospel of Mark: A Model of Agrarian Biography." *BTB* 25 (1995) 24–36.
Chester, Andrew. "The Sibyl and the Temple." In *Templum Amicitiae: Essays on the Second Temple Presented to Ernst Bammel*, edited by William Horbury, 37–69. JSNTSup 48. Sheffield: JSOT Press, 1990.
Chilton, Bruce. "Salvific Exile in the Isaiah Targum." In *Exile: Old Testament, Jewish, and Christian Conceptions*, edited by James M. Scott, 239–47. JSJSup 56. Leiden: Brill, 1997.
Christensen, Kathleen. "Geography as a Human Science: A Philosophic Critique of the Positivist-Humanist Split." In *A Search for Common Ground*, edited by P. R. Gould and G. Olson, 37–57. London: Pion, 1982.
Clarke, Katherine. *Between Geography and History: Hellenistic Constructions of the Roman World*. Oxford Classical Monographs. Oxford: Clarendon, 1999.
Cole, Susan Guettel. "Landscapes of Artemis." *CW* 93 (1999–2000) 471–81.
Collins, Adela Yarbro. "Rulers, Divine Men, and Walking on the Water (Mark 6:45–52)." In *Religious Propaganda and Missionary Competition in the New Testament World: Essays Honoring Dieter Georgi*, edited by Lukas Bormann, Kelly Del Tradici, and Angela Standhartinger, 207–27. NovTSup 74. Leiden: Brill, 1994.
Cook, John Granger. "In Defense of Ambiguity: Is There a Hidden Demon in Mark 1:29–31?" *NTS* 43 (1997) 184–208.
Cuomo, Serafina. "Divide and Rule: Frontinus and Roman Land-Surveying." *Studies in the History and Philosophy of Science* 31 (2000) 189–202.
Davies, W. D. *The Gospel and the Land: Early Christianity and Jewish Territorial Doctrine*. Berkeley: University of California Press, 1974.
Dilke, O. A. W. *Greek and Roman Maps*. Ithaca, NY: Cornell University Press, 1985.
Diller, Aubrey. "Agathemerus, *Sketch of Geography*." *Greek, Roman & Byzantine Studies* 16 (1975) 59–76.
Donahue, John R. *Are You the Christ? The Trial Narrative in the Gospel of Mark*. Society of Biblical Literature Dissertation Series. 10. Missoula: Scholars Press, 1973.
―――, and Daniel J. Harrington, SJ. *The Gospel of Mark*. Sacra Pagina. 2. Collegeville, MN: Liturgical, 2002.
Dougherty, Carol. *Poetics of Colonization: From City to Text in Ancient Greece*. New York: Oxford University Press, 1993.
Downing, F. Gerald. "Common Strands in Pagan, Jewish and Christian Eschatologies in the First Century." *Theologische Zeitschrift* 51 (1995) 196–211.
―――. "Cosmic Eschatology in the First Century: 'Pagan,' Jewish and Christian." *L'Antiquité Classique* 64 (1995) 99–109.
Eade, John, and Michael J. Sallnow, editors. *Contesting the Sacred: The Anthropology of Christian Pilgrimage*. London: Routledge, 1990.
Eck, Werner. *The Age of Augustus*. Oxford: Blackwell, 2003.
Elliott, John H. *A Home for the Homeless: A Social-Scientific Criticism of 1 Peter, Its Situation and Strategy*. Rev. ed. 1990. Reprinted, Eugene, OR: Wipf & Stock, 2005.
―――. "Jesus the Israelite Was Neither a 'Jew' nor a 'Christian': On Correcting Misleading Nomenclature." *Journal for the Study of the Historical Jesus* 5.2 (2007) 119–54.
―――. *What is Social-Scientific Criticism?* Guides to Biblical Scholarship. Minneapolis: Fortress, 1993.
Elsner, John. "Hagiographic Geography: Travel and Allegory in the *Life of Apollonius of Tyana*." *JHS* 117 (1997) 22–37.

Elsner, Jas. "Structuring 'Greece': Pausanias' Periegesis as a Literary Construct." In *Pausanias: Travel and Memory in Roman Greece*, edited Susan E. Alcock, John F. Cherry, and Jas Elsner, 3–20. Oxford: Oxford University Press, 2001.
Esler, Philip F. "Models in New Testament Interpretation: A Reply to David Horrell." *JSNT* 78 (2000) 107–13.
Evans, Craig A. *To See and Not Perceive: Isaiah 6.9–10 in Early Jewish and Christian Literature*. JSOTSup 64. Sheffield: Sheffield Academic, 1989.
———. "Aspects of Exile in the Proclamation of Jesus and the Gospels." In *Exile: Old Testament, Jewish, and Christian Conceptions*, edited by James M. Scott, 299–328. JSJSup 56. Leiden: Brill, 1997.
Evans, Rhiannon. "Ethnography's Freak Show: The Grotesques at the Edges of the Roman Earth." *Ramus* 28 (1999) 54–73.
Evans, Rhiannon Menai. "Forma Orbis: Geography, Ethnography and Shaping the Roman Empire." Ph. D. dissertation, University of Southern California, 1999.
Fantuzzi, Marco. "'Homeric' Formularity in the *Argonautica* of Apollonius." In *A Companion to Apollonius Rhodius*, edited by Theodore D. Papanghelis and Antonios Rengakos, 171–92. Mnemosyne Supplements 217. Leiden: Brill, 2002.
Foster, John. *The Nature of Perception*. Oxford: Oxford University Press, 2000.
Foucault, Michel. *Power/Knowledge: Selected Interviews & Other Writings 1972–1977*. Edited and translated by Colin Gordon. New York: Pantheon, 1980.
———. "Of Other Space." *Diacritics* 16 (1986) 22–27.
Fraser, P. M. *Ptolemaic Alexandria*. 3 vols. Oxford: Clarendon, 1972.
Freyne, Seán. *Galilee, Jesus and the Gospels: Literary Approaches and Historical Investigations*. Philadelphia: Fortress, 1988.
———. *Galilee and Gospel: Collected Essays*. WUNT 125. Tübingen: Mohr/Siebeck, 2000.
———. "The Geography of Restoration: Galilee—Jerusalem Relations in Early Jewish and Christian Experience." *NTS* 47 (2001) 289–311.
Friesen, Steven J. *Twice Neokoros: Ephesus, Asia, and the Cult of the Flavian Imperial Family*. Religions in the Graeco-Roman World 116. Leiden: Brill, 1993.
Gee, Emma. *Ovid, Aratus and Augustus: Astronomy in Ovid's Fasti*. Cambridge Classical Studies. Cambridge: Cambridge University Press, 2000.
Geertz, Clifford. *The Interpretation of Cultures*. New York: Basic Books, 1973.
Giddens, Anthony. *Giddens Reader*. Stanford: Stanford University Press, 1993.
Glasson, T. Francis. *Greek Influence in Jewish Eschatology with Special References to the Apocalypses and Pseudepigraphs*. London: SPCK, 1961.
Goehring, James E. *Ascetics, Society, and the Desert: Studies in Early Egyptian Monasticism*. SAC. Harrisburg, PA: Trinity, 1999.
Gooch, Paul W. *Reflections on Jesus and Socrates: Word and Silence*. New Haven: Yale University Press, 1996.
Gould, Peter, and Rodney White. *Mental Maps*. Pelican Geography and Environmental Studies. Harmondsworth: Penquin, 1974.
Gruen, Erich S. *Diaspora: Jews Amidst Greeks and Romans*. Cambridge: Harvard University Press, 2002.
Gurevich, A. J. *Categories of Medieval Culture*. Translated by G. L. Campbell. London: Routledge & Kegan Paul, 1985.

Hanson, K. C. "Jesus and the Social Bandits." In *The Social Setting of Jesus and the Gospels*, edited by Wolfgang Stegemann, Bruce J. Malina, and Gerd Theissen, 283–300. Minneapolis: Fortress, 2002.

———. "Transformed on the Mountain: Ritual Analysis and the Gospel of Matthew." *Semeia* 67 (1995) 147–70.

———, and Douglas E. Oakman. *Palestine in the Time of Jesus: Social Structures and Social Conflicts*. 2nd ed. Minneapolis: Fortress, 2008.

Harley, J. B. "Maps, Knowledge, and Power." In *The Iconography of Landscape: Essays on Symbolic Representation, Design and Use of Past Environments*, edited by Denis E. Cosgrove and Stephen Daniels, 277–312. Cambridge Studies in Historical Geography 9. Cambridge: Cambridge University Press, 1988.

———, and David Woodward. *Cartography in Prehistoric, Ancient, and Medieval Europe and the Mediterranean*. History of Cartography 1. Chicago: University of Chicago Press, 1987.

Harris, R. Cole. "Power, Modernity, and Historical Geography." *Annals of the Association of American Geographers* 81 (1991) 671–83.

Hartog, François. *Memories of Odysseus: Frontier Tales from Ancient Greece*. Chicago: University of Chicago Press, 2001.

Harvey, David. *The Condition of Postmodernity: An Enquiry into the Origins of Cultural Change*. Oxford: Basil Blackwell, 1989.

Hedrick, Charles W. "What is a Gospel? Geography, Time, and Narrative Structure." *Perspectives in Religious Studies* 10 (1983) 255–68.

Herodotus. *The Histories*. Translated by Robin Waterfield. Oxford: Oxford University Press, 1998.

Hicks, D. R. "The KLIMATA in Greek Geography." *CQ* 5 (1955) 248–55.

———. "Strabo and the KLIMATA in Greek Geography." *CQ* 6 (1956) 243–57.

Himmelfarb, Martha. *Tours of Hell: An Apocalyptic Form in Jewish and Christian Literature*. Philadelphia: Fortress, 1985.

Hjelm, Ingrid. "Cult Centralization as a Device of Control?" *Scandinavian Journal of the Old Testament* 13 (1999) 289–309.

Holladay, Carl R. *Fragments from Hellenistic Jewish Authors: Vol. 1: Historians*. Texts and Translations 20. Chico, CA: Scholars, 1983.

Hollenbach, Paul W. "Jesus, Demoniacs, and Public Authorities: A Socio-Historical Study." *JAAR* 54 (1981) 567–88.

Homer. *The Odyssey*. Translated by Rodney Merrill. Ann Arbor: University of Michigan Press, 2002.

Horrell, David G. "Models and Methods in Social-Scientific Interpretation: A Response to Philip Esler." *JSNT* 78 (2000) 83–105.

Horsley, Richard A. *Galilee: History, Politics, People*. Valley Forge, PA: Trinity, 1995.

———, and John S. Hanson. *Bandits, Prophets, and Messiahs: Popular Movements at the Time of Jesus*. San Francisco: HarperSanFrancisco, 1985.

Isaac, Benjamin. "The Meaning of the Terms Limes and Limitanei." *JRS* 78 (1988) 125–47.

Jacob, Christian, and Anne Mullen-Hohl. "The Greek Traveler's Area of Knowledge: Myths and Other Discourses in Pausanias' Description of Greece." *Yale French Studies* 59 (1980) 65–85.

Jaeger, Mary. *Livy's Written Rome*. Ann Arbor: University of Michigan Press, 1997.

Japhet, Sarah. *I & II Chronicles*. Old Testament Library. Louisville: Westminster John Knox, 1993.
Johnston, R. J. *A Question of Place: Exploring the Practice of Human Geography*. Oxford: Blackwell, 1991.
Kant, Immanuel. *Critique of Pure Reason*. Translated by Norman Kemp Smith. New York: St. Martin's, 1965.
Kee, Howard Clark. "Defining the First-Century Synagogue: Problems and Progress." In *Evolution of the Synagogue: Problems and Progress*, edited by Howard Clark Kee and Lynn H. Cohick, 7–26. Harrisburg, PA: Trinity, 1999.
Kelber, Werner H. *The Kingdom in Mark: A New Place and a New Time*. Philadelphia: Fortress, 1974.
Knibb, Michael A. "The Exile in the Literature of the Intertestamental Period." *Heythrop Journal* (1976) 253–72.
Knibb, Michael A. "Exile in the Damascus Document." *JSNT* 25 (1983) 99–117.
Kotansky, Roy D. "Jesus and Heracles in Cádiz (τὰ Γάδειρα): Death, Myth, and Monsters at the "Straits of Gibraltar" (Mark 4:35–5:43)." In *Ancient and Modern Perspectives on the Bible and Culture: Essays in Honor of Hans Dieter Betz*, edited by Adela Yarbro Collins, 160–229. Scholars Press Homage Series 22. Atlanta: Scholars, 1998.
Kraus, Christina Shuttlewort. "'No Second Troy': Topoi and Refoundation in Livy, Book V." *Transactions of the American Philological Association* 124 (1994) 267–89.
Krause, Deborah. "Simon Peter's Mother-in-Law—Disciple or Domestic Servant? Biblical Hermeneutics and the Interpretation of Mark 1:29–31." In *A Feminist Companion to Mark*, edited by Amy-Jill Levine with Marianne Blickenstaff, 37–53. Feminist Companion to the New Testament and Early Christian Writings 2. Sheffield: Sheffield Academic, 2001.
Ladouceur, David. "Hellenistic Preconceptions of Shipwreck and Pollution as a Context for Acts 27–28." *Harvard Theological Review* 73 (1980) 435–49.
Langdon, Merle K. "Mountains in Greek Religion." *CW* 93 (1999–2000) 461–70.
Launderville, Dale. *Piety and Politics: The Dynamics of Royal Authority in Homeric Greece, Biblical Israel, and Old Babylonian Mesopatamia*. Grand Rapids: Eerdmans, 2003.
Laurence, Ray. "Space and Text." In *Domestic Space in the Roman World: Pompeii and Beyond*, edited by Ray Laurence and Andrew Wallace-Hadrill, 7–14. Journal of Roman Archaeology Supplementary Series 22. Portsmouth, RI: Journal of Roman Archaeology, 1997.
———. "Afterword: Travel and Empire." In *Travel and Geography in the Roman Empire*, edited by Colin Adams and Ray Laurence, 167–76. London: Routledge, 2001.
Lavik, Marta Høyland. "The 'African' Texts of the Old Testament and Their African Interpretations." In *Interpreting the Old Testament in Africa: Papers from the International Symposium on Africa and the Old Testament in Nairobi*, edited by Mary Getui, Knut Holter, and Victor Zinkuratire, 43–53. Bible and Theology in Africa 2. New York: Lang, 2001.
Lawrence, Denise L., and Setha M. Low. "The Built Environment and Spatial Form." *ARA* 19 (1990) 453–505.
Lefebvre, Henri. *The Production of Space*. Translated by Donald Nicholson-Smith. Oxford: Blackwell, 1991.
Levine, Lee I. *Ancient Synagogues Revealed*. Jerusalem: Israel Exploration Society, 1981.
Leyerle, Blake. "Landscape as Cartography in Early Christian Pilgrimage Narratives." *JAAR* 64 (1996) 119–41.

Lightfoot, Kent G., and Antoinette Martinez. "Frontiers and Boundaries in Archaeological Perspective." *ARA* 24 (1995) 471–92.
Lightfoot, Robert H. *History and Interpretation in the Gospels*. The Bampton Lectures. New York: Harper, 1934.
———. *Locality and Doctrine in the Gospels*. New York: Harper, 1938.
Lloyd, G. E. R. "Greek Cosmologies." In *Ancient Cosmologies*. Edited by Carmen Blacker and Michael Loewe, 198–224. London: Allen & Unwin, 1975.
Longenecker, Bruce W. "The Wilderness and Revolutionary Ferment in First-Century Palestine: A Response to D. R. Schwartz and J. Marcus." *JSJ* 29 (1998) 322–36.
Loymeyer, Ernst. *Galiläa und Jerusalem*. Forschungen zur Religion und Literatur des Alten und Neuen Testaments 34. Göttingen: Vandenhoeck & Ruprecht, 1936.
MacDonald, Dennis R. *The Acts of Andrew and the Acts of Andrew and Matthias in the City of the Cannibals*. Texts and Translations 33. Atlanta: Scholars, 1990.
———. "The Shipwrecks of Odysseus and Paul." *NTS* 45 (1999) 88–107.
———. *The Homeric Epics and the Gospel of Mark*. New Haven: Yale University Press, 2000.
———, editor. *Mimesis and Intertextuality*. SAC. Harrisburg, PA: Trinity, 2001.
———. *Does the New Testament Imitate Homer? Four Cases from the Acts of Apostles*. New Haven: Yale University Press, 2003.
Mack, Burton L. *A Myth of Innocence: Mark and Christian Origins*. Philadelphia: Fortress, 1988.
MacKay, Heather. "Ancient Synagogues: The Continuing Dialectic Between Two Major Views." *Currents in Research: Biblical Studies* 6 (1998) 103–42.
MacMullen, Ramsay. *Roman Social Relations 50 B. C. to A. D. 284*. New Haven: Yale University Press, 1974.
Malbon, Elizabeth Struthers. "Galilee and Jerusalem: History and Literature in Marcan Interpretation." *CBQ* 44 (1982) 242–55.
———. *Narrative Space and Mythic Meaning in Mark*. Biblical Seminar 13. Sheffield: JSOT Press, 1991.
———. *In the Company of Jesus: Characters in Mark's Gospel*. Louisville: Westminster John Knox, 2000.
Malina, Bruce J. *Christian Origins and Cultural Anthropology: Practical Models for Biblical Interpretation*. Atlanta: John Knox, 1986.
———. "Interpretation: Reading, Abduction, Metaphor." In *The Bible and the Politics of Exegesis: Essays in Honor of Norman K. Gottwald on His Sixty-Fifth Birthday*, edited by David Jobbing, Peggy L. Day, and Gerald T. Sheppard, 253–66. Cleveland: Pilgrim, 1991.
———. "Reading Theory Perspective: Reading Luke-Acts." In *The Social World of Luke-Acts: Models for Interpretation*, edited by Jerome H. Neyrey, 3–23. Peabody, MA: Hendrickson, 1991.
———. "Apocalyptic and Territoriality." In *Early Christianity in Context: Monuments and Documents. Essays in Honour of Emmanuele Testa*, edited by F. Manns and E. Alliata, 369–80. Studium Biblicum Franciscanum Collectio Maior 38. Jerusalem: Franciscan Publishing, 1993.
———. *The New Jerusalem in the Revelation of John: The City as Symbol of Life with God*. Collegeville, MN: Liturgical, 1996.
———. *The New Testament World: Insights from Cultural Anthropology*. 3rd ed. Louisville: Westminster John Knox, 2001.

———. "Exegetical Eschatology, the Peasant Present and the Final Discourse Genre: The Case of Mark 13." *BTB* 32 (2002) 49–59.
———, and Jerome H. Neyrey. *Portraits of Paul: An Archaeology of an Ancient Personality*. Louisville: Westminster John Knox, 1996.
Marcus, Joel. *The Way of the Lord: Christological Exegesis of the Old Testament in the Gospel of Mark*. Louisville: Westminster John Knox, 1992.
Marrou, Henri I. *A History of Education in Antiquity*. Translated by George Lamb. New York: Sheed & Ward, 1956.
Mauser, Ulrich W. *Christ in the Wilderness: The Wilderness Theme in the Second Gospel and its Basis in Biblical Tradition*. Studies in Biblical Theology 1/39. Naperville, IL: Allenson, 1963.
Meijer, Fik. *A History of Seafaring in the Classical World*. New York: St. Martin's, 1986.
Millar, Fergus. *The Emperor in the Roman World (31 BC–AD 337)*. Ithaca, NY: Cornell University Press, 1977.
Moloney, Francis J. *The Gospel of Mark: A Commentary*. Peabody, MA: Hendrickson, 2002.
Moors, Steven. "The Decapolis: City Territories, Villages, and *Bouletai*." In *Essays on Ancient History in Honour of H. W. Pleket*, edited by Willem Jongman and Marc Kleijwegt, 157–203. Mnemosyne Supplements 233. Leiden: Brill, 2002.
Moxnes, Halvor. "Placing Jesus of Nazareth: Toward a Theory of Place in the Study of the Historical Jesus." In *Text and Artifact in the Religions of Mediterranean Antiquity: Essays in Honour of Peter Richardson*, edited by Stephen G. Wilson and Michel Desjardins, 158–75. Studies in Christianity and Judaism 9. Waterloo: Wilfrid Laurier University Press, 2000.
———. "The Construction of Galilee as a Place for the Historical Jesus—Part I." *BTB* 31 (2001) 26–37.
———. "The Construction of Galilee as a Place for the Historical Jesus—Part II." *BTB* 31 (2001) 64–77.
———. "Kingdom Takes Place: Transformations of Place and Power in the Kingdom of God in the Gospel of Luke." In *Social Scientific Models for Interpreting the Bible: Essays by the Context Group in Honor of Bruce J. Malina*, edited by John J. Pilch, 176–209. Biblical Interpretation Series 53. Leiden: Brill, 2001.
———. *Putting Jesus in His Place: A Radical Vision of Household and Kingdom*. Louisville: Westminster John Knox, 2003.
Moynihan, R. "Geographical Mythology and Roman Imperial Ideology." In *The Age of Augustus*, edited by Rolf Winkes, 149–62. Archaeologica Transatlantica 5. Providence: Brown University Press, 1985.
Mussies, Gerard. "Jesus and 'Sidon' in Matthew 15/Mark 7." *Bijdragen* 58 (1997) 264–78.
Myers, Ched. *Binding the Strong Man: A Political Reading of Mark's Story of Jesus*. Maryknoll: Orbis, 1988.
Nevett, Lisa. "Continuity and Change in Greek Households Under Roman Rule: The Role of Women in the Domestic Context." In *Greek Romans and Roman Greeks*. Edited by Erik Nis Ostenfeld, 81–97. Aarhus Studies in Mediterranean Antiquity 3. Aarhus: Aarhus University Press, 2002.
Newman, David. "Boundaries." In *A Companion to Political Geography*, edited by John Agnew, Katharyne Mitchell, and Gerard Toal, 123–37. Blackwell Companions to Geography 3. Malden, MA: Blackwell, 2003.

Neyrey, Jerome H. *Honor and Shame in the Gospel of Matthew.* Louisville: Westminster John Knox, 1998.

———. "Space and Places, Whence and Whither, Homes and Rooms: 'Territoriality' in the Fourth Gospel." *BTB* 32 (2002) 60–74.

———. "'Teaching You in Public and from House to House' (Acts 20.20): Unpacking a Cultural Stereotype." *JSNT* 26 (2003) 69–102.

Nickelsburg, George W. E. "Enoch, Levi, and Peter: Recipients of Revelation in Upper Galilee." *CBQ* 100 (1981) 575–600.

Oakman, Douglas E. "Was Jesus a Peasant? Implications for Reading the Samaritan Story (Luke 10:30–35)." *BTB* 22 (1992) 117–25. Reprinted in *Jesus and the Peasants*, 164–80. Matrix 4. Eugene, OR: Cascade Books, 2008.

Oden, Robert A. Jr. "Cosmogony, Cosmology." In *The Anchor Bible Dictionary*, edited by David Noel Freedman, 1:1162–71. New York: Doubleday, 1992.

Osborne, Robin. *Classical Landscape with Figures: The Ancient Greek City and Its Countryside.* Dobbs Ferry, NY: Sheridan, 1987.

Paassen, Christiaan van. *The Classical Tradition of Geography.* Groningen: Wolters, 1957.

Painter, John. *Mark's Gospel: Worlds in Conflict.* New Testament Readings. London: Routledge, 1997.

———. "When is a House Not a Home? Disciples and Family in Mark 3.31–35." *NTS* 45 (1999) 498–513.

Pearson, Lionel. *The Lost Histories of Alexander the Great.* New York: American Philological Association, 1960.

Pedersen, Johannes. *Israel: Its Life and Culture.* 2 vols. 1926–40. Reprinted, USF Studies in the History of Judaism 28–29. Atlanta: Scholars, 1991.

Pezzoli-Olgiati, Daria. "Images of Cities in Ancient Religions: Some Methodological Considerations." In *SBL Seminar Papers, 2000*, 80–102. Society of Biblical Literature Papers 39. Atlanta: Scholars, 2000.

Pilch, John J. "Sickness and Healing in Luke-Acts." In *The Social World of Luke-Acts: Models for Interpretation*, edited by Jerome H. Neyrey, 181–209. Peabody, MA: Hendrickson, 1991.

———. "'Beat His Ribs while He is Young' (Sirach 30:12): A Window onto the Mediterranean World." *BTB* 23 (1993) 101–13.

———. *Healing in the New Testament: Insights from Medical and Cultural Anthropology.* Minneapolis: Fortress, 2000.

Pomeroy, Sarah B. *Families in Classical and Hellenistic Greece.* Oxford: Clarendon, 1996.

Porton, Gary G. "The Idea of Exile in Early Rabbinic Midrash." In *Exile: Old Testament, Jewish, and Christian Conceptions*, edited by James M. Scott, 249–64. JSJSup 56. Leiden: Brill, 1997.

Pothecary, Sarah. "Strabo and the Inhabited World." Ph. D. dissertation, University of Toronto, 1995.

Pred, Allan Richard. *Making Histories and Constructing Human Geographies.* Boulder, CO: Westview, 1990.

Rengakos, Antonios. "Apollonius Rhodius as a Homeric Scholar." In *A Companion to Apollonius Rhodius*, edited by Theodore D. Papanghelis and Antonios Rengakos, 193–216. Mnemosyne Supplements 217. Leiden: Brill, 2002.

Rhoads, David, Joanna Dewey, and Donald Michie. *Mark as Story: An Introduction to the Narrative of a Gospel.* 2nd ed. Minneapolis: Fortress, 1999.

Rich, John, and Andrew Wallace-Hadrill, editors. *City and Country in the Ancient World*. London: Routledge, 1991.

Richardson, Peter. "Early Synagogues as Collegia in the Diaspora and Palestine." In *Voluntary Associations in the Graeco-Roman World*, edited by John S. Kloppenborg and Stephen G. Wilson, 90–109. London: Routledge, 1996.

Riches, John K. *Conflicting Mythologies: Identity Formation in the Gospels of Mark and Matthew*. Studies of the New Testament and Its World. Edinburgh: T. & T. Clark, 2000.

Riggsby, Andrew M. "'Public' and 'Private' in Roman Culture: The Case of the *Cubiculum*." *Journal of Roman Archaeology* 10 (1997) 36–56.

Rihll, T. E. "Teaching and Learning in Classical Athens." *Greece & Rome* 50 (2003) 168–90.

Robbins, Vernon K. "By Land and By Sea: The We-Passages and Ancient Sea Voyages." In *Perspectives on Luke-Acts*, edited by Charles H. Talbert, 215–42. Edinburgh: T. & T. Clark, 1978.

Rogerson, John W. "Frontiers and Borders in the Old Testament." In *In Search of True Wisdom: Essays in Old Testament Interpretation in Honour of Ronald E. Clements*, edited by Edward Ball, 116–26. JSOTSup 300. Sheffield: Sheffield Academic, 1999.

Rohrbaugh, Richard L. "Models and Muddles: Discussions of the Social Facets Seminar." *Forum* 3 (1987) 23–33.

———. "The City in the Second Testament." *BTB* 21 (1991) 67–75.

———. "The Preindustrial City." In *Social Sciences and New Testament Interpretation*, edited by Richard L. Rohrbaugh, 107–205. Peabody, MA: Hendrickson, 1996.

———. *The New Testament in Cross-Cultural Perspective*. Matrix. Eugene, OR: Cascade Books, 2007.

Romm, James S. *The Edges of the Earth in Ancient Thought: Geography, Exploration, and Fiction*. Princeton: Princeton University Press, 1992.

Runesson, Anders. *The Origins of the Synagogue: A Socio-Historical Study*. Stockholm: Almqvist & Wiksell, 2001.

Russell, D. A., and N. G. Wilson, editors and translators. *Menander Rhetor*. Oxford: Clarendon, 1981.

Sack, Robert David. *Human Territoriality: Its Theory and History*. Cambridge Studies in Historical Geography 7. Cambridge: Cambridge University Press, 1986.

———. *Place, Modernity, and the Consumer's World: A Relational Framework for Geographic Analysis*. Baltimore: Johns Hopkins University Press, 1992.

Sambursky, Shmuel. *The Concept of Place in Late Neoplatonism*. Jerusalem: Israel Academy of Sciences and Humanities, 1982.

Sanders, E. P. *Jesus and Judaism*. Minneapolis: Fortress, 1985.

Sargent, Frederick II. *Hippocratic Heritage: A History of Ideas about Weather and Human Health*. New York: Pergamon, 1982.

Schimdt, Francis. *How the Temple Thinks: Identity and Social Cohesion in Ancient Judaism*. Biblical Seminar 78. Sheffield: Sheffield Academic, 2001.

Schmidt, Tassalio. "Oikumene." In *Der Neue Pauly*, edited by Hubert Cancik and Helmuth Schneider, 8:1137–40. Stuttgart: Metzler, 2000.

Schwartz, Daniel R. "On Religion and State in Judea in the Second Temple Period." In *Studies in the Jewish Background of Christianity*, 29–43. WUNT 60. Tübingen: Mohr/Siebeck, 1992.

Scott, James M. "Paul's "*Imago Mundi*" and Scripture." In *Evangelium, Schriftauslegung, Kirche: Festschrift für Peter Stuhlmacher zum 65. Geburtstag*, edited by Jostein Ådna, Scott J. Hafemann, and Otfried Hofius, 366–81. Göttingen: Vandenhoeck & Ruprecht, 1997.

———. "Exile and the Self-Understanding of Diaspora Jews in the Greco-Roman Period." In *Exile: Old Testament, Jewish, and Christian Conceptions*, edited by James M. Scott, 173–218. JSJSup 56. Leiden: Brill, 1997.

Sherwin-White, A. N. *Racial Prejudice in Imperial Rome*. Cambridge: Cambridge University Press, 1967.

Shields, Rob. *Places on the Margin: Alternative Geographies of Modernity*. International Library of Sociology. London: Routledge, 1991.

Sjoberg, Gideon. *The Preindustrial City*. New York: Free Press, 1960.

Smith, Jonathan Z. "Towards Interpreting Demonic Powers in Hellenistic Antiquity." In *Aufstieg und Niedergang der römischen Welt*, II.16.1:425–39. Berlin: de Gruyter, 1978.

———. *Map Is Not Territory: Studies in the History of Religions*. Studies in Judaism in Late Antiquity 23. Chicago: University of Chicago Press, 1978.

———. *To Take Place: Toward Theory in Ritual*. Chicago Studies in the History of Judaism. Chicago: University of Chicago Press, 1987.

Soll, Will. "Misfortune and Exile in Tobit: The Juncture of a Fairy Tale Source and Deuteronomic Theology." *CBQ* 51 (1989) 203–31.

Solmsen, Friedrich. "The World of the Dead in Book 6 of the *Aeneid*." *Classical Philology* 67 (1972) 31–41.

Sterling, Gregory E. *Historiography and Self-Definition: Josephos, Luke-Acts and Apologetic Historiography*. Supplements to Novum Testamentum 64. Leiden: Brill, 1992.

Stewart, Eric C. "The City in Mark—Reflections on a Spatial Theme." In *In Other Words: Essays on Social Science Methods and the New Testament in Honor of Jerome H. Neyrey*, edited by Anselm C. Hagedorn, Zeba A. Crook, and Eric Stewart, 202–20. Social World of Biblical Antiquity 2/1. Sheffield: Sheffield Phoenix, 2007.

Sundwall, Gavin A. "Ammianus Geographicus." *American Journal of Philology* 117 (1996) 619–43.

Talmon, Shemaryahu. "Wilderness." In *Interpreter's Dictionary of the Bible Supplementary Volume*, edited by Keith Crim, 946–49. Nashville: Abingdon, 1976.

Theissen, Gerd. *The Gospels in Context: Social and Political History in they Synoptic Tradition*. Translated by Linda M. Maloney. Minneapolis: Fortress, 1991.

Tilley, Christopher. *A Phenomenology of Landscape: Places, Paths and Monuments*. Explorations in Anthropology. Oxford: Berg, 1994.

Trainor, Michael F. *The Quest for Home: The Household in Mark's Community*. Collegeville, MN: Liturgical, 2001.

Van Eck, Ernest. *Galilee and Jerusalem in Mark's Story of Jesus: A Narratological and Social Scientific Reading*. Hervormde teologiese studies Supplementum 7. Pretoria: University of Pretoria, 1995.

Van Iersel, Bas. *Reading Mark*. Translated by W. H. Bisscheroux. Collegeville, MN: Liturgical, 1988.

VanderKam, James C. "Putting them in Their Place: Geography as an Evaluative Tool." In *Pursuing the Text: Studies in Honor of Ben Zion Wachholder on the Occasion of His Seventieth Birthday*, edited by John C. Reeves and John Kampen, 46–69. JSOTSup 184. Sheffield: Sheffield Academic, 1994.

VanderKam, James C. *The Dead Sea Scrolls Today*. Grand Rapids: Eerdmans, 1994.

———. "Exile in Jewish Apocalyptic Literature." In *Exile: Old Testament, Jewish, and Christian Conceptions*, edited by James M. Scott, 89–109. JSJSup 56. Leiden: Brill, 1997.

———. "The Judean Desert and the Community of the Dead Sea Scrolls." In *Antikes Judentum und Frühes Christentum: Festschrift für Hartmut Stegemann zum 65. Geburtstag*, edited by Bernd Kollman, Wolfgang Reinbold, and Annette Steudel, 159–71. Beihefte zur Zeitschrift für die neutestamentliche Wissenschaft 97. Berlin: de Gruyter, 1999.

———. "Identity and History of the Community." In *The Dead Sea Scrolls after Fifty Years: A Comprehensive Assessment*, edited by Peter W. Flint and James C. VanderKam, 2:487–533. 2 vols. Leiden: Brill, 1999.

Vasaly, Ann. *Representations: Images of the World in Ciceronian Oratory*. Berkeley: University of California Press, 1993.

Waetjen, Herman C. *A Reordering of Power: A Socio-Political Reading of Mark's Gospel*. Minneapolis: Fortress, 1989.

Weinfeld, Moshe. *The Promise of the Land: The Inheritance of the Land of Canaan by the Israelites*. Taubman Lectures in Jewish Studies 3. Berkeley: University of California Press, 1993.

Weitzman, Steven. "Allusion, Artifice, and Exile in the Hymn of Tobit." *JBL* 115 (1996) 49–61.

———. "The Samson Story as Border Fiction." *Biblical Interpretation* 10 (2002) 158–174.

Werlen, Benno. *Society, Action and Space: An Alternative Human Geography*. London: Routlege, 1993.

Westermann, Claus. *Genesis 1–11*. Translated by John J. Scullion. Continental Commentaries. Minneapolis: Augsburg, 1984.

Williams, Mary Francis. *Landscape in the Argonautica of Apollonius Rhodius*. Studien zur klassischen Philologie 63. Frankfurt: Lang, 1991.

Wright, M. R. *Cosmology in Antiquity*. London: Routledge, 1995.

Wright, N. T. *The New Testament and the People of God*. Christian Origins and the Question of God 1. Minneapolis: Fortress, 1992.

———. *Jesus and the Victory of God*. Christian Origins and the Question of God 2. Minneapolis: Fortress, 1996.

Zeitlin, Froma I. "Visions and Revisions of Homer." In *Being Greek under Roman Rule: Cultural Identity, the Second Sophistic and the Development of Empire*, edited by S. Goldhill, 195–266. Cambridge: Cambridge University Press, 2001.

www.ingramcontent.com/pod-product-compliance
Lightning Source LLC
Chambersburg PA
CBHW032056230426
43662CB00035B/561